EARTHQUAKES AND
GEOLOGICAL DISCOVERY

According to ancient Japanese folklore, a great catfish
(*namazu*) lying beneath the ground caused earthquakes
by thrashing its body. In this woodblock print, c. 1855,
the god-superior from the Kashima shrine tells the
lesser god, or daimyojin, to drive down the pivot stone
hard on the Edo (Tokyo) earthquake namazu to warn
other catfish. Each of the onlooking namazu is a
historical earthquake.

EARTHQUAKES AND GEOLOGICAL DISCOVERY

Bruce A. Bolt

51392

**SCIENTIFIC
AMERICAN
LIBRARY**

A division of HPHLP
New York

Library of Congress Cataloging-in-Publication Data

Bolt, Bruce A., 1930–
    Earthquakes and geological discovery / Bruce A. Bolt.
        p.   cm.
    Includes bibliographical references and index.
    ISBN 0-7167-5040-6: $32.95
        1. Seismology.   2. Earthquakes.   3. Earthquake prediction.
    I. Title.
    QE534.2.B65   1993
    551.2'2—dc20   93-12636
                                                                        CIP

ISSN 1040-3213

PRINTED IN THE UNITED STATES OF AMERICA

Scientific American Library
A division of HPHLP
New York

Distributed by W. H. Freeman and Company
41 Madison Avenue, New York, NY 10010
20 Beaumont Street, Oxford OXI 2NQ, England

1 2 3 4 5 6 7 8 9 0   KP   9 9 8 7 6 5 4 3

This book is number 46 of a series.

CONTENTS

PREFACE

When the Earthquake Strikes, Flee to the Bamboo Forest.
—Japanese proverb

As an educator in seismology (the science of earthquakes) for over thirty years, I have had the opportunity to reach many audiences. One of my hopes has been that people will come to understand that earthquakes are dangerous chiefly because we do not take adequate precautions against their effects. Indeed, the evidence is clear that, with serious preparation, seismic risk to both life and property can be made acceptably small, even in the largest earthquakes. This message is being spread more vigorously than ever during the last decade of the twentieth century, a period designated The International Decade of Natural Disaster Reduction by the United Nations.

Another aspect of seismology, however, goes well beyond the treatment of earthquake dangers and has contributed crucially to some of the most basic discoveries in all of geology. During this century, for example, earthquake measurements have provided fundamental information on global deformations such as the building of mountain ranges and the movement of the continents. Recordings of earthquakes have also exposed the mysteries of the deep interior of the Earth, especially the structure of its rocks and their elastic properties. Seismological observations have even provided clues to the chemical constitution and dynamic evolution of the Earth's whole interior. Modern technology, particularly high-speed computers, is now supplying this seismological information at a greater and greater pace and in finer detail.

This book is designed for the reader who would like to know how earthquake recordings, which appear on visual displays as wiggly lines, can provide answers to basic questions about the Earth's character far from the places where the recordings are made. Although it is not possible here to give complete coverage of all important geological work in which earthquakes now play a central role, the earthquake case histories and geophysical studies discussed give a realistic flavor of the broad scientific accomplishments of seismology and should satisfy the curious reader. I hope that some of the excitement of the process of geological discovery is also conveyed. The creative spirit of scientific inquiry is perhaps nowhere better exemplified than in the search for physical knowledge of our own planet.

As a quantitative observational science, seismology started in a small way about the end of the last century and has now grown into a major enterprise with applications to geology and geophysics; to seismic exploration in the oil industry; to seismic hazard assessment by geotechnical companies and government laboratories; and to the planning of land use, including the siting of critical structures such as nuclear power plants, large dams, and bridges. The simple mechanical seismographs of the last century have given way to the delicate and sensitive digital recording instruments used today.

I have been fortunate to know a number of the scientific pioneers of earthquake studies, including Professor Hugo Benioff, Professor K. E. Bullen, Professor Perry Byerly, Professor Maurice Ewing, Professor Beno Gutenberg, Sir Harold Jeffreys, Dr. Inge Lehmann, and Professor Charles Richter, all now deceased. I was introduced to seismology in 1949 when Bullen, then Professor of Applied Mathematics at the University of Sydney, Australia, suggested for my Ph.D. thesis that I examine the inferential basis for a transition shell that, it had been hypothesized, surrounds the inner core of the Earth. This mathematical application of earthquake measurements to remote geological sensing evolved into more immediately practical pursuits after I came to the University of California at Berkeley in 1963 as Professor of Seismology. My engineering and geology colleagues expected me to answer questions, not on properties near the center of the Earth, but on the vagaries of earthquake occurrence in California and other seismic regions. They seemed surprised when I had to tell them that their seemingly simple questions did not have reliable answers. Some still do not. Fortunately, the last three decades have seen much progress in the geological basis for the prediction of strong ground motion, and this knowledge has been applied to the design of earthquake-resistant structures and land-use zoning.

I have had help from many people in writing this book. I owe a great debt to friends in the earthquake profession in California with whom I continue to work as a consultant on practical aspects of earthquake risk. A number of colleagues and students read or commented on portions of the draft, and I am grateful to them. In particular, I thank N. A. Abrahamson, A. Becker, P. Dehlinger, J. Dewey, N. Gregor, J. Litehiser, A. Lomax, T. Tanimoto, B. Tucker, Y. B. Tsai, and A. Udias for valuable help with the book's content.

Many colleagues suggested and supplied fine illustrations; unfortunately, limited space dictated a winnowing from among those available. My wife, Beverley Bolt, helped in crucial ways: spotting errors and compiling the index. Claire Johnson, of the Earthquake Engineering Research Center at the University of California at Berkeley, applied her word processing skills under the considerable pressure of deadlines. I also thank the Scientific American Library staff at W. H. Freeman and Company. The editor, Susan Moran, delved deeply into the subject matter with me and made many improvements. It was a pleasure to share the search for enlightening color photographs with Travis Amos, who made some delightful artistic discoveries.

Bruce A. Bolt
Professor of Seismology
March 1993

1

THE ORIGINS
OF SEISMOLOGY

IN THE LAST five hundred years, more than 300 million people have died from earthquakes, and many millions more have seen their food sources and local economies destroyed. The hazard earthquakes present to a growing world population has often been the first concern motivating the scientists and engineers who study them. Yet earthquakes have proved to be not only a source of destruction but a source of geological knowledge. The analysis of seismic waves has provided geologists with detailed and often unique information about the Earth. The discovery of earthquake properties has gone hand in hand with our exploration of the constitution and restless reworking of our planet.

Seismology, the scientific study of earthquakes, is a young subject compared with chemistry, physics, or geology; yet in only one hundred

An artist's conception of the City Hall in the aftermath of the 1906 earthquake and fire in San Francisco.

years it has made remarkable strides in explaining the causes of earthquakes, the nature of seismic waves, the considerable variation in their intensity, and the remarkable patterns of earthquake activity around the globe. Although seismology has been recognized as a separate field of study only in the last century, people have been speculating about the causes of earthquakes for thousands of years. As early superstitions gave way to more scientific attempts to analyze these natural events, the inexorable succession of large earthquakes stimulated ever more sophisticated thinking about the origins of the shakings, until early in this century scientists reached the modern understanding of the immediate source of powerful ground motions.

THE EARLIEST RECORDS

The Earth has suffered earthquakes throughout geological time, and written accounts date back several millennia. In China, scholars have culled the ancient dynastic and literary works, temple records, and other sources for evidence of earthquakes from long ago. The oldest have been traced back to 1831 B.C. in Shandong province (the record states merely, "shaking of Taishan mountain"), but the record is fairly complete only from 780 B.C., the period of the Zhou Dynasty in northern China.

These historical reports are so detailed that from them modern studies have been able to establish the distribution of damage and, hence, the size of the earthquakes. For example, the San-ho earthquake of September 2, 1679, the greatest known near Beijing, was mentioned in the records of 121 cities. When modern researchers compared the descriptions of building damage, ground cracks, and other geological features near the source, together with reports of shaking from distant places, with earthquakes of recent times, they concluded that its size was similar to that of the San Francisco earthquake of 1906.

Despite their careful documentation of earthquakes, Chinese scholars were unable to achieve any real insight into the causes of catastrophic ground shaking. The prevailing thinking linked earthquakes with other natural afflictions such as floods, droughts, and pestilence and sought the origins of all these disasters in supernatural intervention.

The religious interpretation of earthquakes was shared by peoples in seismic regions throughout the ancient world. Many allusions to ancient earthquakes are found in the Bible and other religious writings of the time. Some notable events, such as the falling of the walls of Jericho and the parting of the Red Sea, have been explained as the effects of earthquakes by those who are not prepared to allow for miraculous intervention. The Book of Zechariah even has a remarkably modern description of a section of slipping rock at an earthquake source:

> The Mount of Olives shall cleave in the midst thereof towards the East and towards the West and there shall be a very great valley; and half of the mountain shall remove towards the North and half of it towards the South.

It was not until the twentieth century that the physical connection between rock slip and earthquakes, suggested by this passage, was understood. But the first steps toward a more physical understanding of the origins of earthquakes had been taken long ago by the ancient Greeks.

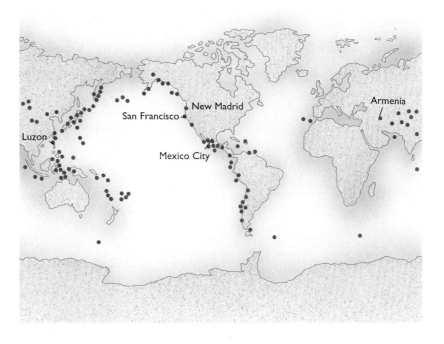

The epicenters of large-magnitude earthquakes that occurred from 1897 through 1992.

EARLY GREEK IDEAS

Seismic activity is high in parts of the Mediterranean Sea and surrounding countries, and it is there that natural explanations for earthquakes were first attempted. As Greek science dawned, its practitioners began to consider physical causes for earthquakes in place of the divine causes suggested by folklore and myth. One of the earliest Greek writers on scientific subjects (about 580 B.C.) was Thales, known for his discussions of magnetism. Thales was much impressed by the destructive power of the sea, clearly in evidence from his island home of Miletes. He believed that the globe of the Earth floated on the oceans and that movements of the water produced the seismic shaking. In contrast,

Anaximenes, who died about 526 B.C., thought that the rocks of the Earth were the cause of the shaking. As masses of rock fell in the Earth's interior, they would strike other rocks, producing reverberations. Another school, typified by the ideas of Anaxagoras (428 B.C.), saw fire as the cause of at least some earthquakes.

None of these seminal Greek commentaries, however, contained a general, rational theory of earthquake genesis. The first such account was developed by the Greek philosopher Aristotle (384–322 B.C.). The crucial importance of Aristotle's writings was that he did not seek an explanation in religion or astrology, such as that earthquakes are caused by the conjunction of planets or comets, but instead drew on the pragmatic background of his times. He discussed the

3

An early view of the Earth's interior, from about 1678. The writer Athanasius Kircher conceived the Earth as a ball of solid material fissured by tubes of magma, which connected pockets of eruptive gases to volcanic vents on the surface.

generation of earthquakes by drawing analogies first with frequently observed atmospheric events, such as thunder and lightning, and second with subterranean events associated with rising vapors from the Earth and volcanic activity. Like many of his contemporaries, Aristotle was convinced that there existed "a central fire" inside the Earth, although Greek thinkers differed as to its cause. Aristotle's theory held that caverns underground would produce fire in the same way as storm clouds produce lightning. This fire would rise rapidly and, if obstructed, would burst violently through the surrounding rocks, causing vibrations and noise. A later modification of this theory held that subterranean fires would burn away the supports of the outer parts of the Earth. The ensuing collapse of the cavern

roofs would create the shocks experienced as earthquakes. Aristotle's linking of subterranean and atmospheric events and his view that dry and smoky vapors cause earthquakes under the Earth, although incorrect, were widely accepted until the eighteenth century.

In an important step toward a physical explanation of the ground shaking, Aristotle also classified what he regarded as different types of earthquakes in terms of whether they shook structures and people in mainly vertical or diagonal directions and whether they were associated with the escape of vapors. According to Aristotle in his *Meteorologica,* in which he explained a wide variety of natural phenomena, "Places whose subsoil is poor are shaken more because of the large amount of wind they absorb."

4

In his *Quaestiones naturales,* Seneca (4 B.C. to A.D. 65) presented his theory of the cause of earthquakes and contrasted it with the theories of his predecessors. His work was inspired in part by the major earthquake that shook Compaigne, Italy, in A.D. 63. Seneca conjectured that the shaking was the result of air finding its way into underground passages. As this air became compressed, it produced violent storms, which created widespread devastation when they broke to the surface.

All the Greek explanations lacked a theoretical conception of the mechanical forces needed to produce the energy in earthquakes. The strength of Greek science was the curiosity of its practitioners, which led them to classify and speculate. Its weakness was its lack of experimentation and instrumentation for making quantitative observations of natural phenomena.

MODERN ENLIGHTENMENT

Many records of building damage in medieval times have come to us through artists' impressions on woodblock prints and through descriptions from diaries, letters, and travel logs. But as the centuries passed, the relationship between geological movements and earthquakes became understood only slowly. Geology remained throttled by the deep deficiency in the understanding of physical principles. A new era dawned in the eighteenth century under the powerful influence of Sir Isaac Newton's writings on waves and mechanics. Newton's *Principia mathematica* at last provided a formulation capable of unifying all terrestrial motions, including earthquakes. His laws of motion provided the physical theory needed to explain earthquake waves, and his law of gravitation provided the basis for understand-

A woodcut by Herman Gall depicts a comet seen at Constantinople in 1556, said to be the wondrous sign portending two earthquakes.

ing the geological forces that shape the Earth. This sudden advance is illustrated by his incisive proposition on Earth tides: "The flux and reflux of the sea arise from the [gravitational] actions of the Sun and Moon."

Nevertheless, the ancient attribution of earthquakes to supernatural causes died hard. Even in A.D. 1750, a writer in the Philosophical Transactions of the Royal Society of London apologized "to those who are apt to be offended at any attempts to give a natural account of earthquakes."

By the middle of the eighteenth century, scientists and engineers under the influence of Newtonian mechanics began to publish memoirs that associated earthquakes with waves traveling through rocks in the Earth. These memoirs gave a great deal of attention to the geological effects of earthquakes, including landslides, ground movements, changes of sea level, and damage to buildings. For example, some observers noted, as the Greeks had, that structures on soft ground were usually more damaged by earthquakes than those on hard ground. Interested persons began to keep and regularly publish lists of earthquakes, so that in 1850 K. E. A. Von Hoff was able to publish an earthquake list for the whole world.

Even as the age of reason spread across Europe and scientific inquiry grew apace, earthquakes were still usually ascribed to either supernatural causes or causes hypothesized by the Greek scholars of long ago. The attachment to the ancient theories can be illustrated by the reactions of men of letters in 1750 to "the year of the earthquakes," when London was jolted several times by seismic shocks. On February 8, people were sent into the streets by a foreshock that rattled windows and shook furniture. A

month later, a more powerful tremor knocked down chimneys, collapsed buildings, and rang church bells. These earthquakes stimulated the writing of more than fifty papers for presentation to the Royal Society of London.

One of these papers, entitled "Some Considerations on the Causes of Earthquakes," was authored by the Reverend Stephen Hales, who was active in church affairs and was associated with the trustees for establishing the colony of Georgia in America. In 1727, he had published *Vegetable Staticks,* the most original work in science to be published in Europe since Isaac Newton's *Optics* and a foundation stone of the model of the flow of sap in plants. Hales was a bold and happy experimenter, and his lively accounts pay all due tribute to Newton. He described the earthquake of March 6, 1750, in personal terms:

I'd been then awakened there on the ground floor in London, and very sensibly felt the bed heave and consequently the Earth must heave too. There was an obscure rushing noise in the house which ended in a loud explosion up in the air like that of a small cannon. The whole duration from the beginning of the earthquake to the end was 3–4 seconds.

Yet Hales's view of the cause of the London earthquakes was similar to the views expressed by the classical philosophers many centuries before:

We find in the late earthquakes in London, that before they happen there is usually a calm air with a black sulfurous cloud which cloud would probably be dispersed like a fog if there were a wind; which dispersion would prevent the earthquake which is probably caused by the explosive lightning of this sulfurous cloud; being both near the Earth and coming at a time when sulfurous vapors are rising from the Earth in greater quantity than usual which is often occasioned by a long period of hot and dry weather. Ascending sulfurous vapors in the Earth may probably take fire, and thereby cause Earth lightning which is first kindled at the surface and not at great depths as has been thought whose explosion is the immediate cause of an earthquake.

The scientific study of earthquakes received a critical stimulus in 1755, when a disastrous earthquake struck the Iberian peninsula on November 1. This earthquake was observed over many parts of Europe by people attending religious services who noticed the swinging of church chandeliers. It was felt strongly over Portugal and Spain and less intensely in many other European countries. Lisbon was overwhelmed, and some 60,000 of its residents were killed, many by a series of ocean waves that reached 30 or 40 ft above high tide level and swamped large parts of the city. Modern studies have determined that the site of origin of the great Lisbon earthquake was several hundred kilometers south-southwest of Portugal along a massive geological structure called the East Atlantic rise.

Survivors left accounts of the earthquake's effects in Lisbon. First, the city was said to have shuddered violently, and its tall spires were described as "waving like a corn field in a breeze." Then a second, stronger shaking arrived, sending the facades of the many grand buildings cascading down into the street and leaving a wasteland of broken stones—graves for those who were caught by the falling debris.

In some places lay coaches with their masters, horses and riders almost crushed to pieces; here mothers with infants in their arms; there ladies richly dressed, gentlemen and mechanics; some had their backs or thighs broken, others vast stones on their breasts; some lay almost buried in the rubbish.

A contemporary fanciful print portraying the destruction of Lisbon by the earthquake and tsunami of 1755.

Water rushed up the river Tagus and surged into the city several times, drowning untold masses of people and devastating the lower parts of the city. Subsequently, fires broke out in churches and private homes. The many fires gradually merged into a single holocaust that raged for three days, destroying the treasures of Lisbon.

The destruction of this rich capital, a repository of Christian art and civilization, struck at the heart of the faith and optimism of the century. Many influential writers took up the question of the place of such calamities in the natural world. In his novel *Candide,* Voltaire had his hero comment on observing the Lisbon earthquake, "If this is the best of all possible worlds, whatever must the others be like?"

The philosopher Jean-Jacques Rousseau endeavored to find a beneficial aspect to earthquakes. He suggested that if people would return to nature and live in open spaces, earthquakes would not harm them.

The Lisbon earthquake was a major source of inspiration for one of the first modern "fathers of seismology," the British engineer John Michell (c. 1724–1793). In a penetrating memoir on earthquakes written in 1760, Michell, while holding to erroneous ideas concerning the cause of earthquakes, discussed earthquake motions in terms of Newtonian mechanics. He believed that "earthquakes were waves set up by shifting masses of rock miles below the surface." Indeed, he classified earthquake motions into two types: a "tremulous" vibration followed shortly by "wavelike undulation" of the Earth's surface. This description is close to what actually happens, as we shall see in Chapter 2.

Michell concluded that the speed of earthquake waves could actually be measured from their arrival times at two different points. After reviewing the reports of witnesses, he calculated that the waves in the Lisbon earthquake had a speed of about 500 m/s. Michell's effort was the first, even if incorrect, attempt at such a calculation.

As European settlement spread in the New World, the global distribution of earthquakes was confirmed, and it became clear that such ground tremors occur at rather widely distributed locations quite remote from volcanoes. Observers should have realized that Aristotle's theory of earthquake origin, which depended on volcanoes, was not tenable. Yet the theory held on.

European settlers in the New World suffered their first significant earthquake on February 5, 1663. The earthquake occurred so early in colonial history that the accounts are not definite. Many of them are quite lurid, telling of mountains thrown down and of forests sliding into the St. Lawrence River. The best reports come from French priests, especially from one who had passed through the region of greatest geological change several years before.

There seems to be little doubt that the event so reported was a severe earthquake in the vicinity of Three Rivers (Trois-Rivières), Quebec, where large rock slides modified the river into a series of waterfalls. There were landslides along the St. Lawrence River, and in places the water remained muddied for months.

The earthquake was felt sharply in New England. In Massachusetts Bay, houses were shaken, objects fell from shelves, and chimneys were thrown down. If an earthquake of equal size had occurred in later years, no doubt property damage would have been extensive.

As the North American settlements matured and educational institutions were founded, enough earthquakes continued to occur to stimulate local scientific speculations on their nature and causes. One of the speculators was Benjamin Franklin, who had left his publishing business in 1748 to devote more time to science. Perhaps inspired by the proof of the existence of electricity in storms given by his famous kite experiment, Franklin judged that electricity played a key role in causing earthquakes. In this, he agreed with Aristotle's theory of two thousand years before.

On November 18, 1755, a sequence of earthquakes shook the area east of Cape Ann, Massachusetts. Accounts describe the main shaking as coming with a roaring sound and resembling a long rolling sea, so that it was necessary to hold onto something to prevent being thrown to the ground. The duration was reported to be as long as 3 minutes. The earthquakes were felt from Chesapeake Bay to Annapolis River, Nova Scotia; sailors on a ship at sea 200 miles east of Cape Ann thought it had grounded when it was hit by an earthquake wave.

In Boston, walls and chimneys fell, and the ground surface seemed to undulate "like swirls on the ocean." Stone fences were knocked down and large buildings were damaged. As was typical of the time, the earthquakes provoked sermons calling the events a sign of God's displeasure with human wickedness.

By contrast, the Professor of Mathematics and Natural Philosophy at Harvard College, John Winthrop IV, took a rational view and made a modest niche in the history of seismology by his study of this earthquake. On feeling the shaking, he consulted his watch and judged the duration to be 3 minutes. Winthrop endeavored to determine the velocities of motions in the earthquake by calculating the time it took

for bricks to fall from his chimney—a difficult task! But he clearly described the motions he felt in the earthquake and its aftershocks "as one small wave of Earth rolling along."

ROBERT MALLET AND THE GREAT ITALIAN EARTHQUAKE OF 1857

The firm foundations of modern seismology were laid by the field studies of Robert Mallet. The earthquake of December 15, 1857, near Naples in southern Italy provided Mallet with the opportunity to study seismic effects extensively. During his three-month visit to the damaged area, Mallet established much of the basis of observational field seismology, set forth in a major report entitled *The First Principles of Observational Seismology*. Its flavor is given by this quotation:

> When the observer first enters upon one of those earthquake shaken towns, he finds himself in the midst of utter confusion. He wanders over masses of dislocated stone and mortar . . . houses seem to have been precipitated to the ground in every direction. There seems to be no governing law. It was only by gaining some commanding point, whence some general view over the whole field of ruin can be had and then by patient examination, house by house and street by street, analyzing each detail, that at length we perceive once and for all that this apparent confusion is but superficial.

Mallet did much to further the interactions between engineering, geology, and mechanics that began to grow in the middle part of the

The Irish engineer Robert Mallet (1810–1881) in 1854, one of the founders of seismology.

was an Irish engineer, noted for his brilliant mechanical designs of railroad stations, bridges, and other major structures. His lifelong enthusiasm for the study of earthquakes arose from his attempt to solve an engineering problem related to the twisting of stone pillars in earthquakes that had shaken Italy before 1830.

Mallet assembled a comprehensive library of books, newspaper clippings, and journals on earthquakes and produced one of the first modern catalogues of earthquakes, with over 6800 listings giving locations and effects. From his catalogues were created some of the first reliable maps setting forth the zones of predicted earthquake effects.

Mallet is also notable for being the first to work with artificial earthquakes. He exploded charges of gunpowder underground, then recorded the waves by watching the surface of a container of mercury placed at a distance from the charge. A stopwatch gave him the elapsed time between the explosion and the ripples on the mercury surface. From these observations, he deduced that earthquake waves travel at different speeds through different materials. For the first time it was clearly understood that seismic waves are affected by the physical properties of the different types of rocks through which they pass. He calculated that the speed through sandy soil was 280 m/s, and through granite 600 m/s (in fact too small a value).

Believing that earthquakes, such as the Neapolitan earthquake, were produced from volcanic sources, he drew attention to the nearness of volcanoes to the stricken area. From this notion of a possible explosive source, now known to be wrong, Mallet inferred correctly that the seismic waves would start at a point, the focus or hypocenter. Further, he suggested that seismic

last century. His goal was to take earthquake studies from a stage of mystery by applying physical and engineering principles to the search for the real geological nature of earthquakes. Not only did he contribute significantly to this end, but by the conclusion of his seminal work, he had coined much of the basic vocabulary describing earthquakes that we shall use in this book.

Robert Mallet was ideally suited to be the first of a new breed of earthquake scholars. He

waves in the rock resembled sound waves traveling in the air (at least half the full story, as we shall see in Chapter 2). He then concluded that, if this were true, the first motion of the ground would show a regular direction away from the initiation point. It would follow that objects thrown down from a height or overturned would indicate a direction away from or toward the focus and that the direction of cracks in buildings would show the direction of travel of the wave front. By projecting these directions back to an intersection point, Mallet tried to calculate the position of the hypocenter.

We now know that, given the presence of waves of different types in earthquakes, Mallet's methods of tracing back to the source the directions taken by falling objects and cracks in buildings are impractical (cracking in buildings is mainly a function of the construction type). Nevertheless, in inventing and applying these methods to place the depth of the source of the Neapolitan earthquakes at about $6\frac{1}{2}$ miles, Mallet was the first to estimate from direct observations the location of the origin of an earthquake's motion. It was not until more than fifty years later, with the coming of modern seismographs, that focal depths could be estimated with any precision. Even now, there are difficulties in many cases.

TWO KEY EARTHQUAKES

Mallet's work on earthquakes coincided with the marked growth of vigorous geological endeavors generally. Many countries began to establish special organizations mandated to undertake studies of the Earth through the mapping of geological structures, fossil classification, and mineral analysis. Two that have contributed much to earthquake knowledge are the U.S. Geological Survey (established in 1879) and the Geological Survey of India (established in 1857). Among their many seismological accomplishments, each has produced outstanding reports on great earthquakes in its region.

An early such U.S. Geological Survey study was the work of an experienced geologist, M. L. Fuller, who in 1912 published the evidence on three extraordinary shocks that had occurred along the Mississippi River one hundred years before, in 1811 and the beginning of 1812. On December 16, 1811, a series of earthquakes began that shook the New Madrid region of southern Missouri for a year. The first big earthquake came on December 16, the second on January 23, and the sharpest shock on February 7, 1812. Between December 16 and March 16, more than 1870 of these shocks, of which 8 were severe, were felt in Louisville 200 miles away. Such a sequence is unusual; normally the principal shock (perhaps preceded by smaller foreshocks) is followed by a long series of smaller aftershocks that become progressively less frequent with time.

The reported damage covered a tract of 30,000 to 50,000 square miles bordering the Mississippi River southward from New Madrid. The damaged area included parts of western Tennessee and northeastern Arkansas. In Kentucky, the naturalist John Audubon reported that "the ground rose and fell in successive furrows like the waters of a lake. The earth waved like a field of corn before a breeze." The largest earthquake awakened President Madison in the White House, rang church bells in Boston, and tumbled chimneys in Cincinnati.

The formation of Reelfoot Lake in the great earthquakes of New Madrid, Missouri, from the Report of the Geological Survey in Kentucky, 1854–1855.

A very conspicuous feature was the formation of "sunken country": an area about 240 km long and 60 km broad sank 1 to 3 m. River water from the Mississippi rushed into the sunken region, forming new lakes, swamps, and bayous. Reelfoot Lake in Tennessee was formed at this time and at 8 miles in length and 2 miles in breadth is still substantial today. Observers reported that waves many feet in amplitude broke up the soil and left parallel fissures. Sand was ejected from cracks in the ground, forming fissures and craters. Vapors and dust filled the air and darkened the sky. There was a great destruction of timber; many trees were broken, many drowned because of the subsidence of the land, and many died from damage to their roots.

At the time of the earthquake, and even at the publication of Fuller's study in 1912, it was a geological puzzle why such immense earthquake energy was released in the continental hinterland, a region that in the short run is relatively aseismic compared to the continental periphery. We now understand the broad geological reasons for such spectacular events, and we can even estimate the average time (some thousands of years) expected between them (see Chapter 5). Nevertheless, from time to time, unfounded forecasts have been made of the imminent repetition of the 1811–1812 New Madrid earthquakes. The most recent prophecy, in 1989, was widely covered by newspapers and television reporters. Despite careful statements by well-informed seismologists in the region, this prediction by a single nonspecialist led to the closing of schools and other facilities near the presumed epicenter. The day and hour forecast came and went without even a mild ground tremor.

In 1899 the Geological Survey of India published a report describing one of the most violent earthquakes for which we have detailed records, the shock that struck the province of Assam in northeast India on June 12, 1897. The celebrated report of this earthquake was written largely by the head of the Indian Geological Survey, R. D. Oldham, who later became famous for his demonstration that the Earth's interior contains a large central liquid core (see Chapter 6). Oldham's report was a milestone in the study of earthquakes because of the great care with which it described the intensity of the shaking over a wide area, its inference of the ground velocity in the shaking, and its use of data from instrumental recordings of ground motion. Oldham marshaled clear evidence for the hypothesis that widespread warping and faulting of rocks produced the earthquake.

The Assam earthquake was felt over an area of $1\frac{3}{4}$ million square miles, and it almost completely devastated an area of 9000 square miles. Fewer than 1000 people died because the area was not densely inhabited and contained few large structures. Although the number of deaths was relatively small, the evidence is quite clear that there was very strong shaking lasting probably a little less than 1 minute. People reported being thrown to the ground, and powerful vertical accelerations of the Earth threw boulders straight up, leaving cavities in the ground with almost unbroken sides. Sandy soils behaved like a liquid, according to reports of houses sinking until only their roofs were visible.

Oldham also related that people in heavily shaken areas saw visible waves moving across the ground, and he estimated the waves to have been a foot high. Oldham reported:

In the western portion of the southern spur, and all around the civil surgeons' quarters to the distance of a mile down the Mankachar Road where the soil is sandy and the surface fairly level, the ground looks as if a steam plow had passed over it, tearing up the turf and throwing clods in every direction, some uphill and some down, and in many cases, turning the sods completely over so that only the roots of grass are visible.

Deadly landslides stripped hillsides bare of trees over distances of more than 20 miles. The lurching of the loose alluvial ground created many large fissures, and water and sand were ejected like fountains throughout the cultivated areas to an extent that hindered farmers in later cultivation. A special feature was the spreading of large faults in various directions: the maximum relative ground displacement was reported to be 35 ft vertically along the Chedrang fault, with the east side being elevated with respect to the west.

In fact, in its conclusions the Assam earthquake report turned away from Oldham's initial, and probably correct, hypothesis that the cause of the earthquake was deep-seated thrusting toward the Himalaya Range along a structural fault under the Assam hills. Such a hypothesis also would have explained the extreme deformation of rock structures during the thrust. Because the terrain is of difficult access, geological mapping was limited at the time and insufficient field evidence was obtained to confirm the hypothesis. Soon, however, a major earthquake occurred in the Western Hemisphere, where field access was easy and a base of geological measurements was already in place.

THE 1906 SAN FRANCISCO EARTHQUAKE CONTRIBUTION

The turning point in our understanding of the causes of earthquakes came from studies of the earthquake that shook central California on April 18, 1906. Because there are no active volcanoes in this area, geologists were not tempted to turn to the old Greek notions of underground explosions or volcanic stimulus. In addition, the source of the 1906 earthquake lay beneath a readily traversed area of land that surveyors had already covered with survey markers showing the distances and relative heights between points. These so-called geodetic measurements allowed the well-trained geologists already on hand to map the ground deformation.

To study the earthquake, the State Earthquake Investigation Commission was set up under the chairmanship of Professor Andrew Lawson of the University of California. The scientists assembled by Lawson compared the geodetic measurements made before and after the earthquake and studied the ground displacements observed following the tremor. Their subsequent report contained the fundamental theory that has dominated seismology to this day. (We will discuss this theory in detail in Chapter 4.) The report concluded that the severe ground shaking had been generated by sudden slip on what Lawson called the San Andreas fault, a fracture zone in the bedrock that was later mapped as stretching from the Mexican border to well north of San Francisco. Rocks on the fault had broken, and the block of rocks on the west side of the fracture had slid several feet northward past the other side. The fault had slipped over a section extending for more than 400 km, from San Juan Bautista, south of San Francisco Bay, to a spot about 250 km north of San Francisco. The line of this immense rupture passed just west of the Golden Gate Strait.

The size of the earthquake can be grasped partly by considering the area over which it was felt, some 180,000 sq km. Fortunately, the number of deaths in the earthquake was not high, although the exact figure is not fixed even now. Early reports placed the number of people killed at about 700, but more recent estimates have suggested that up to three or four times as many died.

Future earthquakes of similar size will strike metropolitan areas of California, so it is of the greatest importance to consider what happened in 1906. San Francisco then was a city of about 400,000 people. Built in a series of frenzied bursts, it contained both old and new structures, which had been erected with no systematic regard to earthquake hazards. The numerous wooden structures, many of them jerry-built, were mixed in with unreinforced and partially reinforced brick buildings. Well-built wooden and masonry structures were relatively unaffected when situated on firm foundations and solid ground. Unfortunately, many buildings stood in the wharf area at the foot of Market Street, on marshland that had been reclaimed by dumping refuse on the mud flats of San Francisco Bay. These suffered severe damage. By contrast, the high-rise steel-frame buildings that already dotted the downtown were not structurally damaged by the shaking. The 19-story Spreckles building and the new 16-story Chronicle building both survived intact.

The National Board of Fire Underwriters had published a report in 1905 stating that fire in San Francisco was inevitable:

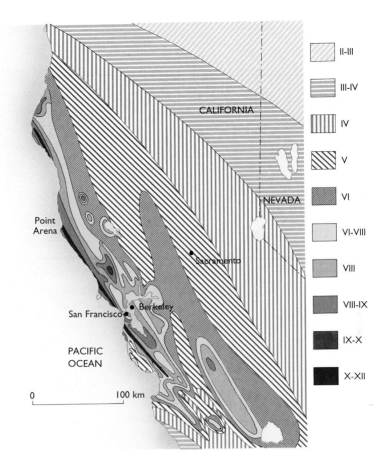

CALIFORNIA

NEVADA

Point
Arena

Sacramento

San Francisco • Berkeley

PACIFIC
OCEAN

0   100 km

II-III

III-IV

IV

V

VI

VI-VIII

VIII

VIII-IX

IX-X

X-XII

Contours separate areas of equal intensity of shaking in the 1906 San Francisco earthquake, as rated on the modified Mercalli scale (see the appendix). The thin dark brown line of heaviest intensity corresponds to the ruptured segment of the San Andreas fault.

In view of the exceptionally large areas, great heights, numerous unprotected openings, highly combustible nature of the buildings, almost total lack of sprinklers . . . and comparatively narrow streets, the potential hazard is very severe. . . . In fact, San Francisco has violated all underwriting traditions and precedent by not burning up.

The board's fears were realized when the widespread fires that followed the earthquake in San Francisco developed into a conflagration that burned a large part of the city in the next few days.

Eyewitness accounts obtained immediately following the disaster were recorded in the Report of the State Earthquake Investigation Commission. For example, Professor Alexander McAdie, who was in charge of the weather bureau in San Francisco, said, "My custom is to sleep with my watch open, my notebook open at the date, pencil ready with also a hand torch. They are laid out in regular order—torch, watch, book, and pencil." He continued, "I entered severe shaking lasting 40 seconds. After waking I remembered getting the minute hand positioned previous to the most violent portion of the shock." The astronomer Professor

Top: The view down Sacramento Street, San Francisco, on Wednesday, April 18, after the earthquake but before the fire had spread. *Bottom:* The view up nearby Market Street after the fire.

Leuschner of the University of California stated afterward that, across the bay in the city of Berkeley, "the earthquake consisted of two main portions; the first part was 40 seconds based on counting seconds while carrying my small children out of the house." The interested reader will find in the commission's report one of the most fascinating accounts ever written of the effects of earthquakes and will also learn a great deal about what to expect when similar large earthquakes occur.

The geologists and engineers of the investigation commission made a substantial effort to gather systematically all possible information of relevance to understanding both the nature of earthquake motions and the reasons for structural damage. Of special interest was the finding that the damage was not uniformly spread out from the source of the waves along the San Andreas fault. There were concentrations of destruction in a number of cities, such as Santa Rosa to the north and San Jose to the south, that had been built in alluvial valleys or basins, where the soft soil amplified the shaking. In most parts of the Great Valley of California, the strength of the shaking was lower, but there were notable exceptions. For example, moderate amounts of damage were reported within the city of Los Banos.

In Berkeley, a large majority of the brick chimneys were broken or overthrown, and the upper walls of several brick buildings were thrown down or damaged by cracks. Some areas of the city seemed immune to the destruction that was so marked in neighboring areas in the form of toppled chimneys. The buildings on the campus of the University of California, for example, sustained no serious damage, and there not a single chimney was down although some were cracked. The low intensity of the earthquake on the Berkeley campus sharply contrasted with its intensity on the campus of Stanford University in the south bay, which was notable for the collapse of its unreinforced masonry structures. This campus is considerably closer to the San Andreas fault than is Berkeley, but differences in construction and building type undoubtedly played a very large part in determining the degree of damage.

In Sacramento, the state capital, the ground shaking was not extreme. Mr. Jones, a resident, was reported as saying, "I was awakened by the earthquake, arose and, with my wife, verified the phenomena." At considerable distances from the center of the seismic disturbance, information was obtained bearing on the crucial question of the distance damaging waves can travel. From the city of Santa Barbara, 400 km south, Mr.

After the 1906 earthquake, unreinforced stone masonry collapsed at Stanford University, about 5 miles from the ruptured San Andreas fault.

Dodge reported, "I was aroused from a half-sleeping condition by a singular rustling noise in the house. None of us recognized it as an earthquake at the time. My bed was not perceptibly shaken." Mr. J. D. Hooker, also of Santa Barbara, observed a slight shock and then a heavier one, "then a smart shock which caused windows and doors to rattle. The window curtains swung in and out." In Chapter 7, we shall address the underlying geological reasons for the variation in the strength of shaking, and in Chapter 9 its implications for achieving earthquake-resistant buildings.

One of the important lessons from the 1906 earthquake was that, although it occurred at a time when no specific building codes had been adopted addressing resistance to ground shaking, most structures survived the earthquake. Much of the damage in San Francisco resulted from the fire. Engineers thus learned which types of building design would best provide safe construction in earthquake country.

There were other positive and fundamental results. One was the careful mapping of the intensity of the shaking in the affected region, which today provides the basic guide to shaking hazards in the San Francisco Bay Area. Not the least of the earthquake's beneficial consequences was the creation of the Seismological Society of America to achieve the following objectives:

1. To promote research in seismology, the scientific investigation of earthquakes and related phenomena,
2. To promote public safety by all practical means,
3. To enlist the interest of engineers, architects, contractors, insurance men, and property owners, in the obligation to protect the community against disasters due to earthquakes and earthquake fires, by showing it is reasonably practical and economical to build for security,
4. To inform the public by appropriate publications, lectures, and other means to an understanding of the fact that earthquakes are dangerous chiefly because we do not take adequate precautions against their effects, whereas it is possible to ensure ourselves against damage by proper studies of their geographic distribution, historical sequence, activities, and effects on buildings.

These noble aims remain in place, and the Seismological Society of America still flourishes along with similarly dedicated groups in engineering, architecture, and public policy. After almost ninety years, these wise objectives, which are now mirrored in the efforts of many other organizations around the world, remain the centerpiece of our efforts to reduce the threat of earthquakes to humankind.

THE JAPANESE EARTHQUAKE OF 1923

By the 1920s scientists were looking for patterns in seismic events that might point to the location of future earthquakes. Japan, where seismology had already developed and records were being kept by trained scientists, was the first country for which estimates of earthquake potential were made. Professor Fusakichi Omori (1868–1923), the director of the Seismological

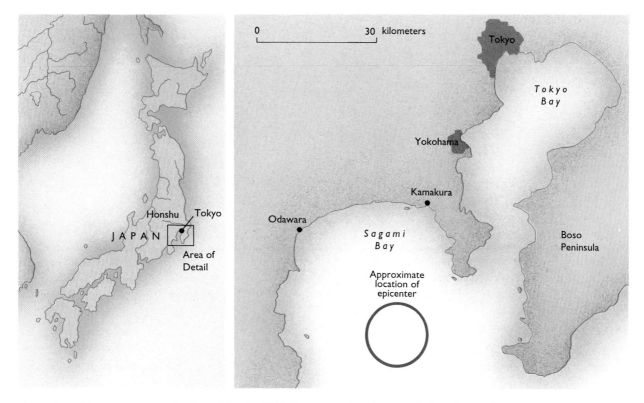

The region of Japan most strongly affected by the 1923 Kwanto earthquake, named after the province.

Institute of Japan, had been studying the apparent distribution of large earthquakes in the main Japanese island of Honshu and in 1922 had written:

> At present, the immediate vicinity of Tokyo remains seismically quiet, while the mountainous regions surrounding Tokyo at a mean distance of 60 km are causing the frequent occurrence of earthquakes, which though often sharply felt in the city are harmless, as the districts in question do not belong to a great destructive seismic zone. In the course of time, however, the active seismic districts will become gradually quiet while Tokyo Bay may as a compensation recommence its seismic activity and may result in a production of a strong earthquake. Such an earthquake with its origin some distance from Tokyo would be of the nature of a semi-destructive local disturbance.

This remarkable prediction was incorrect only in underestimating the strength of the earthquake that was shortly to devastate the very area suggested by Omori.

About a year after Omori's statement, one of the most disastrous earthquakes in living memory occurred at the head of Sagami Bay, the basin leading into the bay on which stands the city of Tokyo. The earthquake, called the Kwanto earthquake after the province most affected, struck on September 1, 1923, at about noon, when the streets of Tokyo were filled with people. Professor Akitune Imamura of Tokyo University was sitting at the Seismological Institute on the grounds of the university when the shock began:

> At first, the movement was rather slow and feeble so that I did not take it to be the forerunner of so big a shock. As usual, I began to estimate the duration of the preliminary tremors. Soon the vibration became large and after 3 or 4 seconds from the commencement I felt the shock very strongly indeed. Seven or eight seconds passed and the house was shaking to an extraordinary extent, but I considered these movements not yet to be the principal portion. . . . The motion went on to increase its intensity very quickly, and after 4 or 5 seconds I felt it to have reached its strongest. During this epoch, the tiles were showering down from the roof making a loud noise, and I wondered whether the building could stand or not.

The shaking was much amplified by the soft soil of filled areas in the downtown part of the city; the upper town on firmer soil experienced much less ground motion. Over 50 percent of the brick buildings and 10 percent of the reinforced concrete buildings in the city were destroyed. On the other hand, the more than 16 high-rise steel-frame buildings were unharmed. Other buildings were damaged to various degrees, including the famous Imperial Hotel built by the American architect Frank Lloyd Wright.

Although the shock was centered 57 miles away from Tokyo and 40 miles from Yokohama, it was in those cities that the disaster was most spectacular. After the violent shaking, innumer-

WRIGHT'S IMPERIAL HOTEL

Wright had designed his Imperial Hotel of 250 rooms as a showplace for foreigners. While residing in Tokyo during the construction of his ornate edifice, he felt many earthquakes and noted that "the terror of the tremblor never left me while I planned the building." He knew that the site of his hotel would be exceptionally dangerous in an earthquake because the 8 ft of top soil overlying 60 ft of soft mud would not offer firm support. To meet the threat, he introduced a number of innovations, including shallow foundations on broad footings supported by small groups of short concrete pilings placed every 2 ft along the foundation wall. Wright believed that his plan would let the hotel float on the underlying mud "as a battleship floats on salt water." Rather than unreinforced brick walls, the Imperial Hotel had double-course walls composed of two outer layers of brick bonded in the middle with a core of steel reinforcing bars set in poured concrete. Wright designed the first-floor walls to be especially rigid and thick; the walls of higher floors tapered upward and contained fewer windows. Instead of the roof tiles typical of Japanese buildings, which had "murdered countless thousands of Japanese in upheavals," Wright installed a light, hand-worked, green copper roof. Wright was also among the first to appreciate that mechanical systems in buildings, such as plumbing and wiring, could be a hazard in an earthquake. To lessen this danger, he ran the hotel's pipes and wires through trenches or hung them from the structure, so that "any disturbance might flex and rattle but not break the pipes or wiring." He also conceived the beautiful reflecting pool at the front of the hotel as a reservoir of water for fire fighting; its merit was proved when the Imperial Hotel was threatened by the fires that followed the 1923 Kwanto earthquake.

2

SEISMIC
WAVES

American scientist H. F. Reid in his studies of the 1906 San Francisco earthquake, has expanded and deepened. First and foremost, we now have a theory involving the deformation of the whole Earth that explains why great earthquakes occur in places such as Japan and California but not in the prairies of Canada or the fields of France. This geological theory also explains the creation of mountain ranges, volcanoes, and the deep trenches of the ocean floor, and it explains their pattern of occurrence on the Earth's surface. The formulation of this global connecting scheme has depended to a large extent on the evidence provided by the study of earthquakes themselves.

We shall see how earthquakes have also served as one of the key tools for probing the structure and dynamics of the Earth's interior; indeed, we can claim fairly that seismology is the most effective deep probe of the inner parts of our planet. Earthquake waves probing the Earth's interior have recently shown up variations in the rock density and rigidity deep below us as small as 10 percent. These new studies rely heavily on the method of tomography, better known from its role in medicine, which uses large-memory, high-speed computers to create images of remote regions.

To learn from earthquake waves, it is first necessary to understand the nature of the shaking in earthquakes. It turns out that the seismic waves that travel through the rocks of the Earth have certain complications not experienced in more usually encountered waves, such as sound waves, radio waves, or light waves. Nevertheless, they carry with them evidence of their geological sources and of the structural variations along their path. Seismologists are becoming more and more skillful in extracting this information from wave patterns recorded by special instruments, called seismographs, of continually increasing sensitivity.

In an observational program as remarkable as any in the history of the science, a far-flung network of seismographs was established at the turn of the century around the surface of the globe. Although most people are not aware of its consequences or even of its existence, this worldwide network of earthquake observatories has been strengthened more and more in the last few decades and now constitutes one of the great scientific accomplishments. From recordings of these observatories, scientists have been able to infer both the causes of specific earthquakes and the paths along which they propagate through the Earth, and they have learned to distinguish the seismic waves of natural earthquakes from those produced by underground nuclear explosions.

Earthquakes have enormous consequences as natural hazards that threaten our more and more heavily populated planet. In the hope of reducing the risk posed by these events, great attention has been given to predicting the intensities of earthquakes that will strike inhabited areas and shake critical structures. The assessment of the variation of ground shaking has become one of the most rewarding parts of seismology.

able fires broke out in Tokyo, and fanned by the high winds, firestorms enveloped the city in flames. Before nightfall, 1 million of Tokyo's $2\frac{1}{2}$ million inhabitants were homeless.

The death toll in Tokyo was about 68,000, of which many had died from the fires. Much of Yokohama also burned, resulting in a death toll of about 33,000. The 5500 houses in Odawara were practically razed, partly by fire. In the ancient city of Kamakura, 84 percent of the houses collapsed. A large water wave 35 ft high, called a tsunami, caused further destruction around Sagami Bay. The total dead throughout the area of severe shaking came to almost 100,000, and there were an equal number of injured.

Investigations of the 1923 earthquake by Japanese scientists and engineers, as well as by foreign specialists who visited the area subsequently, were of the greatest importance. At the time of the earthquake, Omori, who was appointed president of the Imperial Earthquake Investigation Committee, was visiting Australia. Acting at the Tokyo Observatory in his absence was Imamura, a seismologist of unusual insight. Shortly after his return to Tokyo on November 8, Omori died, so that the burden of directing the earthquake investigation fell on Imamura. The Earthquake Investigation Committee immediately acted to appoint subcommittees to deal with seismological, geological, and geodetic aspects of the devastating earthquake, as well as with architectural, civil, and engineering matters. The reports of the subcommittees and government departments were brought together in five large volumes, constituting a most valuable source of information on all aspects of a major earthquake.

These seminal memoirs were, unfortunately for Western readers, written in Japanese, and their impact on seismology and earthquake engineering was therefore considerably reduced. Subsequently, an English translation of some of the most valuable memoirs was published, and gradually most of the scientific facts became accessible to readers outside Japan.

Among the myriad observations of this earthquake recorded in these volumes, some of the most amazing were the extraordinary changes in depth in Sagami Bay. An area of 280 square miles was depressed, at one location by as much as 690 ft. Other areas were uplifted as much as 820 ft. Many faults were observed on the Boso Peninsula and on the west side of Sagami and Tokyo bays; these faults displayed up to 6 ft of mostly vertical displacement over many miles. The magnitude of the earthquake was estimated to be as large as that of the San Francisco earthquake of 1906. The shocking destruction and failure of buildings led to intensive studies on improved designs for earthquake-resistant structures.

Today the full weight of Japanese seismological knowledge is brought to bear on the possibility of another great earthquake on the west coast of Honshu, where the shaking would again affect the densely populated metropolitan areas around Tokyo and southward to Osaka. There is, indeed, cause for concern: most of Japan is subject to strong earthquakes.

PRESENT-DAY SEISMOLOGY

In the years since World War II, there has been a remarkable advance in our knowledge of almost every aspect of earthquakes. Our understanding of earthquake genesis, so well founded by the

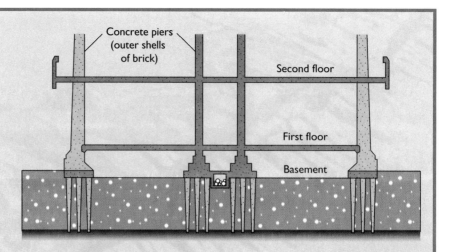

Concrete piers
(outer shells
of brick)

Second floor

First floor

Basement

A structural section of the Imperial Hotel, showing the floor slabs balanced over central columns supported by foundation piles to prevent collapse.

The Imperial Hotel still stood after its battering in the 1923 earthquake, which shattered 5000 other buildings, but the damage and cracking within the building were considerable. It is now known that large structures built on soft soil should be supported by deep pilings rather than the short, stubby ones used by Wright. The use of these short pilings allowed the Imperial Hotel to sink slowly into the mud and the top soils to amplify the seismic motion. Nevertheless, many of the measures taken by Wright were well conceived and are now adopted as a matter of course in earthquake country.

A sketch of an early design for Tokyo's 250-room Imperial Hotel. Commissioned in 1915, it was designed by the American architect Frank Lloyd Wright to resist earthquakes, like "a superdreadnought, floating on the mud as a battleship floats on salt water."

DURING THE LATE afternoon of Good Friday, 1964, a great earthquake struck the sparsely inhabited mountainous area of northern Prince William Sound in south-central Alaska. Waves from the earthquake source spread through the Earth, causing serious damage over more than 20,000 sq km. In the area of significant damage, or meizoseismal zone, the largest city affected was Anchorage, some 130 km from the earthquake's center.

In the Hillside Manor apartments, Mr. John R. Williams, a geologist, was sitting on a couch in his living room. He recalled:

> At first we noticed a rattling of the building. The initial shaking lasted perhaps five to ten seconds. The first shaking was followed without any noticeable quiet period by a strong rolling motion which

Water waves spread as circular ripples on a pond. In an analogous way, seismic waves travel outward in all directions from the source of an earthquake.

appeared to move from east to west. After a few seconds of the strong rolling motion, I took my son to the door leading to the hall, opened the door to prevent jamming, and stood in the doorway. I looked in the hallway and back in the apartment and noticed blocks working against one another in interior walls and saw some fall into the street and into the apartment and hall. I took my son and ran to a parked car. I looked at the building, which was swaying in an east-west direction. Blocks were toppling, ground heaving, trees and poles were swaying strongly. The Hillside apartment building was a total loss.

This graphic account describes the motion in an earthquake: the duration and amplitude of the waves, the pattern of wave arrival, and even the direction of the ground movements. The theory of seismic waves provides a complete understanding of such descriptions.

THE PRIMARY AND SECONDARY EARTHQUAKE WAVES

Wave motion is perhaps most familiar to us from our observations of waves on water. When a stone is thrown into a pool, the surface of the water is disturbed where the stone strikes, and ripples move outward from the place of disturbance. This wave train is produced by movements of the particles of water in the vicinity of the ripples. The water, however, does not actually flow in the direction in which the ripples travel: a cork on the surface will bob up and down but not move away from its original posi-

tion. The disturbance is passed on continuously by the brief, back-and-forth movements of water particles, which impart motion to particles farther ahead. In this way, the water waves carry energy from the broken surface where the stone lands to the edge of the pool where they break forcefully. Earthquake motions are quite analogous. The shaking we feel is the vibration of the elastic rocks by the energy in seismic waves.

If an elastic body, such as a rock, is struck a blow, two kinds of elastic waves are produced and travel out from the source. The first of these is exactly the same in its physical properties as a sound wave. Up to supersonic wave speeds, sound waves are transmitted by alternate compressions (pushes) and dilations (pulls) on the air. Because liquids and solid rock, like gases, can be compressed, the same type of wave travels through bodies of water such as oceans and lakes and through the solid Earth. In earthquakes, waves of this type are transmitted outward at an equal speed in all directions from the fault rupture, alternately compressing and dilating the rock through which they travel. The particles of rock move forward and backward in the direction of propagation of these waves—in other words, the particles move perpendicular to the wave front. The amount of displacement forward and backward is the wave amplitude. In seismology, this type of wave is called a *P* wave, for primary wave.

Unlike air, which can be compressed but not sheared, elastic materials allow a second type of wave to propagate that shears and twists the material. When produced by an earthquake, this secondary wave is called an *S* wave. The behavior of the rock in the passage of *S* waves is quite different from its behavior in the passage of *P* waves. Because *S* waves involve shearing rather

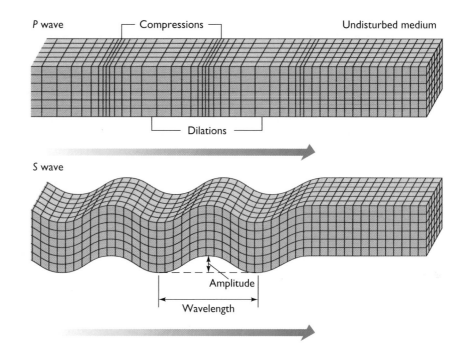

The forms of elastic rock motion during the passage of earthquake *P* (primary) and *S* (secondary) waves.

than compression, they move the particles of rock transverse to the direction of propagation. These rock motions may be in a vertical or a horizontal plane, and they are similar to the transverse motions in light waves. The presence of both *P* and *S* waves gives earthquakes an interesting combination of effects that is absent in either the physical behavior of light or the physical behavior of sound.

Because shearing motion is not possible in either liquids or gases, *S* waves do not travel through them. This sharp contrast in the properties of *P* and *S* waves can be used to detect the presence of liquid zones deep in the Earth (see Chapter 6).

Only *S* waves exhibit the phenomenon called polarization. The polarization of light is familiar to anyone who has worn polarized eyeglasses to cut down on scattered light. Only those light waves that are vibrating transversely in certain planes (up and down, horizontally, and so on) can pass through a polarized lens. The transmitted light waves are said to be plane-polarized. Sunlight coming through the atmosphere is not polarized, in the sense that there is no preferred transverse direction of vibration of the light waves. However, by interaction with reflecting surfaces such as the ocean surface, by refraction through crystals, or by passage through specially prepared plastic as in Polaroid eyeglasses, this unpolarized light can be made to be plane-polarized.

As *S* waves travel through the Earth, they encounter structural discontinuities that refract or reflect them and polarize their vibrations. When an S wave is polarized so that the particles of rock move only in a horizontal plane, it is denoted by the symbol SH. When the particles of rock all move in the vertical plane containing the direction of propagation, the S wave is called an SV wave.

Most rocks, if not forced to vibrate at too great an amplitude, behave in an elastic linear way; that is, the displacement due to the application of a force follows a linear curve. Such linear elastic behavior is said to obey Hooke's law, named after the British mathematician Robert Hooke (1635–1703), a contemporary of Newton. The linear relation is illustrated in the figure on this page by the extension of a weighted elastic spring. If the mass of the weight is doubled, then the extension of a linear spring is doubled. If the mass is returned to its original size, then the spring returns to its original position. Similarly during an earthquake, the rock will experience proportionally greater displacement in response to a larger force. In most cases, the displacement will remain within the linear elastic range, and the rock will return to its original position at the shaking's end. Important exceptions to this behavior sometimes occur in earthquakes, however. When energetic shaking occurs in soft soils, for example, the wave displacements do not always return the soil to its original position. In such cases, the seismic intensities become more difficult to predict. We will return to these crucial nonlinear effects later in the book.

The motion in a spiral spring offers an excellent illustration of the energy changes that take place in rocks when seismic waves pass through. The total energy at any time is the sum of the elastic energy due to spring compression or ex-

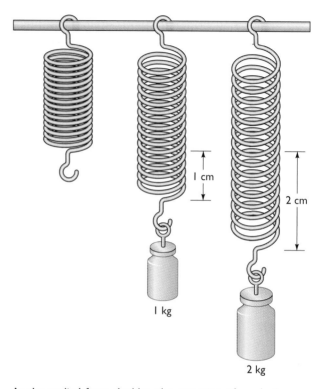

As the applied force doubles, the extension of an elastic spring also doubles.

tension and the kinetic energy due to the velocity of parts of the spring. For a perfectly elastic medium, the total energy is a constant. At positions of maximum wave amplitude, the energy is all elastic, while the energy is all kinetic when the spring is at an equilibrium position. We have assumed that there are no frictional or dissipative forces present, so that the springing back and forth, once started, will continue indefinitely with the same amplitude. This is, of course, an idealized situation. In an earthquake, friction between the moving rocks gradually dissipates some of the wave energy as heat. Thus, vibrating springs like the Earth eventually come to rest unless some extraneous source of energy is added. Measurement of the energy dissipation in earthquake waves gives important clues to the nonelastic properties of the Earth's interior. In addition to friction, however, there is still another explanation for the gradual weakening of an earthquake.

The sound carried by an expanding spherical surface of sound waves becomes weaker with distance. Similarly, as water waves spread outward in a pool, we observe a gradual decrease in their height, or amplitude. The amplitude diminishes because the initial energy is spread out over a wider and wider area, producing an attenuation called geometrical spreading. This type of spreading also attenuates seismic waves as they pass through the rocks of the Earth. Unless there are special circumstances, the farther earthquakes spread from their sources the more their intensity decreases.

PROPERTIES OF WAVES

The pure musical tone produced by striking a tuning fork is said to have a certain pure pitch or frequency. That frequency is the number of times that the sound waves compress and dilate in a second, or, for water waves and other types of vibration, the number of times the wave rises or falls in a second. Frequencies are given in hertz, abbreviated Hz, a unit of measurement named in honor of Heinrich Hertz, the German physicist who in 1887 first produced electromagnetic waves. One hertz is equal to one cycle of rise and fall per second. The time between the

crests is the wave period; it is equal to the reciprocal of the wave frequency.

Human beings can detect sounds having frequencies between 20 and 10,000 Hz. A seismic *P* wave can refract out of the rock surface into the atmosphere, and if the frequencies are in the audible range, the wave can be heard as a rumble as it travels by the ear. Most earthquake waves have frequencies lower than 20 Hz, however, and are thus usually felt by human beings rather than heard.

In the simplest case, a wave is a harmonic motion, a sine wave with a single amplitude at a single frequency, like the wave represented in the box on the next page. The waveforms that occur in earthquakes, however, are more complicated than such a simple wave. In the actual recording of an earthquake, like that shown on page 39, the waveforms consist of short wavelengths superimposed on longer ones. The quantitative model, described first by the French physicist Jean Baptiste Joseph Fourier in 1822, is that complex wave trains consist of a mix of harmonic waves, which can be expressed as the sum of sinusoidal components like those shown in the figure below. The higher harmonic waves

Complex waveform = Sinusoidal components

The addition of the three simple waveforms on the right produces the complex waveform on the left.

WAVE MOTION

Waves can be described by a few parameters. Consider the simple harmonic wave drawn as a solid line below with wave height y at a particular position x and time t. Suppose that the maximum amplitude of the wave is A and that the wavelength λ is the distance between the crests.

The time for a complete wave (say, crest to crest) to travel one wavelength is called the period T. Thus the wave velocity v is the wavelength divided by the period:

$$v = \frac{\lambda}{T}$$

The frequency of the wave, f, is the number of complete waves that pass every second, so that

$$f = \frac{1}{T}$$

The actual position of a wave depends on its position relative to the origin time and distance. Consider the light line in the figure. This wave is ahead of the first wave by a short distance. It is said to be *out of phase* by this shift.

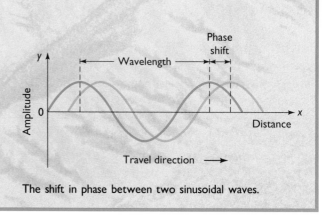

The shift in phase between two sinusoidal waves.

have frequencies that are multiples of the lowest or base frequency. The more realistic ground shaking can be analyzed using the methods of Fourier by computer examination of the individual component harmonic waves separately.

The wave train may also be shifted back or forward in time so that the peak no longer occurs at the same time or place as before. When such shifted waves are summed, the pattern of the complex waveform looks different, although its components are exactly the same in amplitude and frequency. This shift is measured in terms of an important quantity called the phase of the wave, which is the stage of the wave with re-

spect to its starting point. As we shall see, it has significant consequences in the effect of earthquakes on large engineered structures.

THE SPEED OF *P* AND *S* WAVES

At my home in Berkeley on October 27, 1989, when the Loma Prieta earthquake struck, I suddenly felt the house shaking and started counting seconds. Ten seconds later the shaking abruptly became much more alarming—the *S* waves had arrived. *P* waves always arrive from the earthquake source first because they travel faster along the same path than do S waves. Using this property of the waves, I could then calculate that the source of this earthquake was over 80 km away.

The actual velocities at which P and S waves travel depend on the densities and inherent elastic properties of the rocks. For linear elastic behavior when the direction of wave travel is not a factor, wave speed depends on the measures of only two elastic properties, called elastic moduli: the incompressibility (k) and the rigidity (μ) of the rock.

When a uniform pressure is applied to the surface of a cube of rock, its volume is reduced, and a measure of its change in volume per unit volume is called its incompressibility. This type of deformation occurs when P waves propagate through the Earth's interior; because it involves only volume changes, it applies quite as well to liquids as to solids. Usually, the greater the incompressibility, the greater the P-wave velocity.

A second type of deformation occurs when equal but opposite tangential pressures are applied to opposite faces of a cube of rock. The cube will deform by shearing out of its rectangular shape, without any change of volume. The same strain occurs when a cylindrical rock core is twisted by equal and opposite pressures applied at the opposite ends. The greater the resistance of the rock to the shearing or twisting pressures, the greater its rigidity. Because S waves propagate by shearing the rock, the rigidity modulus gives a measure of their speed. Usually, the greater the rigidity, the greater the S-wave velocity.

The simple formulas for the P and S wave velocities are given in the box on the next page. These expressions are consistent with important wave properties mentioned already: because liquid has zero rigidity, the velocity of shear waves in water is zero, and because the two elastic moduli are always positive, the P wave travels faster than the S wave.

Because of the great pressures inside the Earth, the rock density increases everywhere with depth. As a consequence, it would appear from the position of the density in the denominator of the ratio that P and S wave velocities would decrease with depth in the Earth. It turns out, however, that the incompressibility and rigidity increase more quickly than the rock density. (The rock rigidity drops to zero, of course, as the rock becomes molten.) Thus, as we shall discuss in detail in Chapter 6, P and S seismic velocities generally increase with depth in our planet.

Although the elastic moduli for a given rock type are constant, in some geological circumstances they may vary significantly in different directions through the rock. In this case, called anisotropy, P and S waves will have different speeds in different locations. Such anisotropic behavior provides information about geological conditions in the Earth and is the subject of wide investigation at the present time. In the discussion that follows, however, earthquake motions will be limited to isotropic conditions, by far the most dominant situation.

THE EFFECT OF GEOLOGICAL STRUCTURES ON EARTHQUAKE WAVES

When water waves encounter a boundary such as a steep shoreline, they are reflected back from the boundary; an outgoing train of waves devel-

ELASTIC MODULI AND WAVE SPEED

The elasticity of a homogeneous, isotropic solid can be defined by two constants, k and μ. Both constants may be expressed as force per unit area.

k is the modulus of incompressibility, or bulk modulus:

For granite, k is about 27×10^{10} dyne/cm^2.
For water, k is about 2.0×10^{10} dyne/cm^2.

μ is the modulus of rigidity:

For granite, μ is about 1.6×10^{10} dyne cm^2.
For water, $\mu = 0$.

Within the body of an elastic solid with density ρ, two elastic waves can propagate:

P waves   Velocity $\alpha = \sqrt{\left(k + \frac{4}{3}\mu\right)/\rho}$

For granite, $\alpha = 5.5$ km/s.
For water, $\alpha = 1.5$ km/s.

S waves   Velocity $\beta = \sqrt{\mu/\rho}$

For granite, $\beta = 3.0$ km/s.
For water, $\beta = 0$ km/s.

ops, which may be seen passing through the incoming train. When ocean waves roll obliquely onto a shallow beach, the waves in the shallower depths travel more slowly and lag behind the waves in the deeper water. As a consequence, the waves are bent toward the shallower water. The lines of waves thus turn more and more parallel to the beach before they break. Refraction is the term used to describe the change in the direction of a wave front due to shifts in speed produced by changing conditions of the propagation path. Reflection and refraction are also well-known properties of light passing through lenses and prisms.

Like sound, light, or water waves, seismic waves may also be reflected or refracted at a boundary, but unlike these other waves, seismic waves show a unique behavior when incident on a reflecting surface within the Earth. For exam-

Ocean waves running up to a sloping beach refract around to face parallel to the beach.

ple, a *P* wave hitting a boundary surface at an angle breaks up into both a reflected *P* wave and a refracted *P* wave. As well, however, it generates a reflected *S* wave and a refracted *S* wave. The reason is that at the point of incidence the rock at the boundary is being not only compressed but also sheared.

In other words, an incident *P* wave results in four transformed waves. This proliferation of wave types by conversion of one wave type to another also occurs when an *SV* wave hits an internal boundary obliquely; both reflected and refracted *P* and *SV* waves result. In this case, both the reflected and refracted *S* waves are always of *SV* type because of the way that the rock particles move transversely in a vertical plane as the incident *SV* wave approaches. By contrast, if the incident *S* wave is of the horizontally polarized *SH* type, so that the particles are moving backward and forward out of the plane but parallel to the surface of the boundary, there will be none of the compression or vertical displacements produced at this discontinuity needed to generate new *P* and *SV* waves, respectively. Therefore, there is only one reflected wave and one refracted wave, both of *SH* type. By physical reasoning, when a *P* wave strikes a reflecting boundary straight on, there is no component of shear at the surface, and so there is only a reflected *P* wave and no reflected *SV* or *SH* waves at all. The restrictions discussed above are vital in fully understanding the complication of ground shaking and in interpreting the pattern of earthquake waves in seismograms.

Many of the striking earthquake effects that we shall consider later in the book can be readily explained by the reflection and refraction of waves. Consider, for example, an *S* wave moving from a deep source upward to the ground sur-

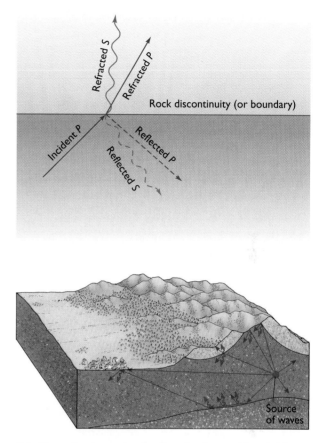

Top: The reflection and refraction of a *P* wave after it hits a boundary between two types of rock. *Bottom:* The transmission paths of seismic *P* and *S* waves being reflected and refracted in geological structures.

face. The wave will roughly double its amplitude and quadruple its energy right at the surface because there the incident and reflected wave trains add together. This prediction is in accord with the experiences of miners, who in many cases have not been aware that a strong earthquake has occurred. A dramatic case is the destructive earthquake at Tangshan, China, in 1976. Coal miners working underground felt moderate shaking and knew there were problems when the electricity supply failed. But when they reached the surface, to their horror they found the city devastated; the shaking ultimately resulted in the loss of more than 250,000 lives.

Wave amplification can also be blamed for the severe damage to structures built on soft deep soils, such as the sediments deposited along a river in an alluvial valley. When we vibrate two springs attached together, the weaker one will have the greater amplitudes. In the same way, when seismic S waves emerging from depth pass from the more rigid deeper rock to less rigid alluvium, the soft rock and soil will amplify the shaking by a factor of four or more depending on the wave frequency and the thick-

ness of the layer of alluvium. In the Loma Prieta earthquake that shook central California in 1989, buildings on the sand and artificial fill of San Francisco's Marina district were much more damaged than were similar houses on firm ground some distance away.

EARTHQUAKE RESONANCE IN THE EARTH

The reflection and refraction of earthquake waves may also trap the seismic energy in a geological structure such as an alluvial valley where softer rocks or soils exist near the surface. As will be discussed later, the trapping of energy explains the patterns of heavy damage in both the 1985 Mexico City earthquake and the 1989 Loma

A collapsed apartment building on the artificially filled ground in the Marina district of San Francisco after the 1989 Loma Prieta earthquake.

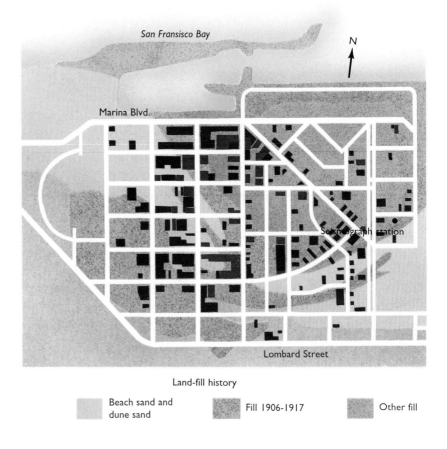

San Fransisco Bay

N

Marina Blvd.

Seismograph station

Lombard Street

Land-fill history

Beach sand and
dune sand

Fill 1906-1917

Other fill

In the 1989 Loma Prieta earthquake, the ground subsided by as much as 5 inches in the landfill of the Marina district. The buildings were most damaged where filled land overlapped old beach sands. Demolished or severely damaged buildings are shown in red. Less damaged but uninhabitable buildings are shown in dark brown. The solid circle indicates the site of an instrument for recording strong ground motion, used to compare the shaking on soft soil with that at a nearby rock site.

Prieta earthquake. The effect is similar to the trapping of sound waves in a room where the sound energy echoes back and forth from the walls. In an earthquake, seismic P and S waves approaching from a distance are refracted into the valley, where their speed decreases in the less rigid rocks. They propagate under the valley floor until, upon reaching the margins, part of the energy is refracted out into the rock of the surrounding hills and part is reflected back into the basin. In this way, waves begin traveling backward and forward, analogously to water waves in a pool. The various P and S waves interlace: the returning wave crests pass through arriving wave crests, causing changes in ampli-

tude. In such cases, the phase of each component wave is critical, since when crossing waves are in phase, the energy is reinforced. By means of this "positive interference," earthquake energy can be built up at selective wave frequencies. The consequences would be catastrophic if the growth were not mitigated by the geometrical spreading of the waves and by the friction of the vibrating rocks and soil, which transforms some of the wave energy into heat.

There is a useful alternative way to look at the behavior of seismic waves in an enclosed geological structure. Like the crisscrossing water waves seen in a pool, interfering seismic waves create standing waves: when perceptible, the in-

Fundamental mode · First mode · Second mode · Third mode

Modes of vibration of an elastic string.

terfering waves seem to be standing still and the ground surface seems to be vibrating purely up and down. In the same way, such standing waves are set up when the string of a musical instrument such as a harp is plucked. Typically in an earthquake, both P and S standing waves of many different frequencies and amplitudes are generated in a valley or similar structure. The soft soils can thus enhance shaking at many frequencies, producing, as in the musical analogy, significant overtones or higher modes of vibration. These overtones can sometimes be distinguished if sufficient instruments are present in the area to record the wave motion.

Sometimes earthquakes cause the whole Earth to ring like a bell. Since the eighteenth century mathematicians have analyzed the vibrations of an elastic sphere; in 1911 the English mathematician A. E. H. Love predicted that a steel sphere as large as the Earth would have a period of fundamental (gravest) vibration of about one hour and that there would be overtones of lesser periods. Nevertheless, for more than half a century after Love's prediction, it remained doubtful whether even high-magnitude earthquakes contain sufficient energy to vibrate the planet and produce this deep-toned seismic music of our terrestrial sphere. Imagine the excitement among seismologists when for the first time, after the massive Chilean earthquake of May 1960, the few very long period seismographs then in opera-

tion around the world clearly recorded extremely long period waves that lasted for many days! The longest period of vibration measured was 53 minutes, not very different from the 60 minutes predicted by Love. Analysis of these ground motion records gave the first unequivocal evidence that the theoretically predicted free vibrations of the Earth had, in fact, been generated.

After an earthquake source releases its energy, the resonant vibrations of the terrestrial globe continue in an unforced way at frequencies that depend only on the properties of the elastic globe itself. The exact mathematical analogy is again the plucked stringed instrument from which, as the Greeks recognized more than two thousand years ago, come musical harmonics that depend only on the length, density, and tautness of the plucked string. Such free oscillations are called eigenvibrations. So, too, the eigenvibrations of the plucked Earth depend on the geological structural dimensions, density, and elastic moduli throughout the interior.

There are two, and only two, separate types of eigenvibrations of an elastic sphere. One type, called T modes or torsional vibrations, involves only horizontal displacements of the Earth's rocks: the particles of rock vibrate back and forth on a spherical surface—on the outside of the Earth or on some interior "shell." In the second type, called S modes or spheroidal vibrations, the elements of the sphere have components of motion along the radius as well as the horizontal.

In recent years, measurements of these S and T eigenvibrations generated by large earthquakes have provided a totally new way of inferring the physical constitution of the Earth's interior, a subject we shall return to in Chapter 6.

EARTHQUAKE WAVES ALONG THE GROUND SURFACE

The rock motions that are produced when P and S waves arrive at the free surface of the Earth or at the boundaries of a layered geological structure generate other types of traveling seismic waves under certain conditions. The most impor-

tant of these waves are called Rayleigh waves and Love waves. Both types of wave propagate along the surface of the Earth; the rock motions decrease to zero with depth. The energy of these surface waves is trapped along and near the ground surface; otherwise such waves would reflect downward into the Earth and have only an ephemeral life at the surface. These waves are analogous to the sound waves that are trapped near the wall surface in "whispering galleries" such as the dome of St. Paul's Cathedral in London. Only when the ear is placed near the wall can a whisper from the opposite wall be heard.

Love waves are the simplest type of surface seismic wave. They are named after A. E. H. Love, who first described them in 1912. As illustrated on this page, this type of wave moves the rock just like an SH wave in which the mo-

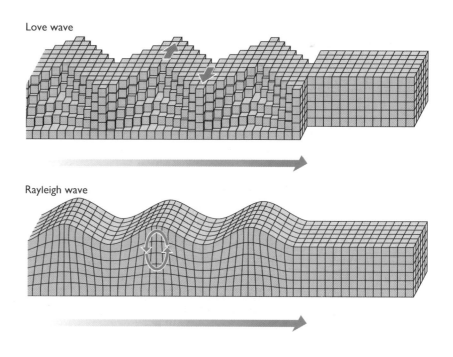

Love wave

Rayleigh wave

The forms of rock motion near the ground surface during the passage of Love and Rayleigh waves.

tion has no vertical displacement. Thus, the rock moves from side to side in a horizontal plane at right angles to the direction of travel. Although Love waves include no vertical ground motions, they can be some of the most destructive waves in an earthquake because they often have large amplitudes that produce horizontal shearing under the foundations of structures.

In contrast, Rayleigh surface waves have quite a different ground motion. First described by Lord Rayleigh in 1885, these are the earthquake waves that most closely resemble water waves. Rayleigh waves are formed by rock particles moving forward, up, backward, and down, transcribing elliptical orbits oriented in a vertical plane that contains the direction of wave propagation. The speeds of Love and Rayleigh waves are always less than those of P waves and equal to or less than those of S waves.

Because the types of ground motions involved are similar, traveling Rayleigh waves are the counterpart of the standing spheroidal S modes, and Love waves are the counterpart of T modes.

EARTHQUAKE WAVES IN SUCCESSION

Because of their differing speeds, the several seismic wave types arrive in a set sequence that explains what we feel when the ground starts shaking in an earthquake. Recording instruments actually allow us to see the pattern of ground motion, as shown on the next page.

The first waves to arrive at a given location from the earthquake's source are the "push and pull" P waves. They generally emerge at the surface at a steep angle, thus creating ground motion in the vertical direction. Vertical shaking is more easily withstood than horizontal shaking, and so P waves are usually not the most damaging waves. Sometime later, because the S waves travel about half as fast as the P waves, the relatively strong secondary tremors arrive. These consist of transverse SV and SH motions in two planes: one horizontal and the other vertical. These S motions last somewhat longer than the P wave trains. Earthquakes cause buildings to shake up and down through the action of P waves and sideways mainly through the action of S waves.

Just after the S waves, or coincident with them, the Love surface waves start arriving. The ground then begins to shake at right angles to the direction of travel of the waves. This property makes it difficult to tell the direction of the earthquake source from feeling the ground shaking, despite eyewitness claims to the contrary. Next, the Rayleigh waves travel across the Earth's surface, creating shaking in both the longitudinal and the vertical directions. These waves may last for many cycles, giving rise to the well-known descriptions of "rolling motion" in large earthquakes. Because they attenuate with distance at a lower rate than P or S waves, it is the surface waves that are felt or recorded with a long duration at great distances from the source. The earthquake records reproduced on the opposite page show the Love and Rayleigh waves lasting more than five times longer than the P and S waves.

This train of surface waves constitutes a substantial part of what is called the earthquake coda, by analogy with the final section of a musical composition. This dying end of an earthquake is in fact composed of a mixture of P, S,

There are dramatic differences between seismograms from a local microearthquake (magnitude 1.8) recorded in Japan (top three waveforms) and seismograms from a moderate earthquake (magnitude 5.1) in the Norwegian Sea recorded in Germany (bottom three waveforms), yet the order of wave arrivals is the same (although the microearthquake did not develop surface waves). Each earthquake is represented by three seismograms, each recording a different direction of shaking: east-west (E), north-south (N), and up-down (Z).

Love, and Rayleigh waves that have arrived along scattered paths through the complex rock structure. The continuing wave cycles in the coda may trigger the collapse of structures already weakened by the earlier-arriving and more energetic S waves.

The spreading out of surface waves into long codas is an example of wave dispersion. The effect is common in all types of wave propagation through media with varying physical properties or dimensions. Close scrutiny of water waves on a pool shows that the waves with short wave-

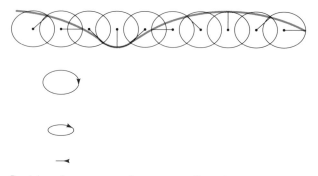

Particles of water or rock trace out ellipses in a water wave or a seismic surface wave. The ellipses become smaller with depth until the movement disappears. The seismic motion may be clockwise or anticlockwise.

lengths (ripples) pass ahead of the waves with longer wavelengths (swells). The speed of the crest is not constant but depends on the wavelengths of the waves. Thus, as time passes after a stone hits the water, the initial wave begins to sort itself out into a procession of crests and troughs as the shorter waves move farther and farther ahead of the longer ones. Surface earthquake waves behave in an analogous way.

Wave dispersion is possible in an earthquake because the wavelengths of the seismic waves vary considerably, from as large as several kilometers to tens of meters. The diagram on this page shows how the motion of the rock in a typical surface wave changes with depth from the ground surface down into the deeper rocks. As expected for surface waves, most wave energy is trapped near the surface: after a certain depth, depending on the wavelength, the rocks are not affected by the passage of the wave. It will be seen that the longer the wavelength, the deeper the wave motion will penetrate into the Earth.

Because, in general, the deeper the rocks in the Earth, the faster seismic waves travel in them, it follows that long-period (long-wavelength) surface waves generally travel faster than short-period (short-wavelength) ones. This speed differential allows surface waves to disperse into long trains. In contrast to water waves, however, the longer surface waves are the ones to arrive first.

We need to understand one other wave behavior to complete the full picture of the fascinating world of earthquake wave motion. This is the phenomenon of wave diffraction. When trains of water waves encounter an obstacle such as a vertical pipe jutting out of the water, most of the wave energy is reflected away, but some waves will run around the pipe into its shadow, and there is no completely quiet water behind the pipe. Indeed, the diffraction of waves of all types—whether water, sound, light, or earth-

Ocean waves being diffracted into the sheltered water behind a breakwater.

quake waves—causes them to deviate from straight paths and dimly illuminate the regions behind obstacles and barriers.

Both theory and observation agree that longer waves are diffracted more into the quiet zone than shorter ones; that is, like dispersion, diffraction is a function of the wavelength. The important point for geological interpretation is that in earthquakes, P and S waves and surface waves are not completely stopped by anomalous rock inclusions; some of the seismic energy is diffracted around geological structures and some is refracted through them.

As described in Chapter 6, a striking illustration is provided by the behavior of P and S waves in earthquakes that pass through the deep interior of the Earth. These waves are partly blocked by a massive liquid region toward the Earth's center. Nevertheless, some of the wave energy creeps around the surface of this great object to appear as weak waves on the other side of the globe.

3

THE INSTRUMENTAL
SURVEILLANCE
OF EARTHQUAKES

FROM EARLY TIMES, human curiosity about the world has stimulated attempts to make measurements of natural events. Insights into the attributes and even the causes of natural phenomena hinge on such quantitative representations. To understand rainfall, we must measure the air pressure with barometers; to understand the rhythm of the heart, we must record blood pressure. So it is with earthquakes. The ground shaking that inspires apprehension or even terror must be encapsulated in a wavy line traced on film or tabulated as a list of numbers in a computer memory.

Earthquake recorders are called seismographs or seismometers if they track the complete history of the shaking throughout the earthquake. Instruments that do not record the time of arrival of the earthquake waves are called seismoscopes. Seismographs are essential for accurately defining

The observation room in an earthquake observatory.
On the light screens are displayed
seismograms from many seismographic stations.

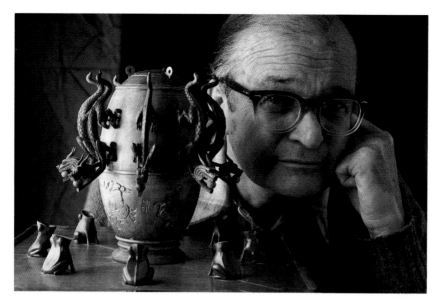

The author peers around a model of Chang Heng's seismoscope built at about one-fifth actual size.

the locations of remote earthquakes, measuring earthquake size, and determining the mechanism of the fault rupture. The design of such instruments is not entirely simple because of the great range of earthquake amplitudes and frequencies. Even today, seismographs that are really useful for recording earthquakes in any detail are very expensive.

CHANG HENG'S EARTHQUAKE WEATHERCOCK

The earliest known seismoscope was constructed by a Chinese scholar, Chang Heng, about the year A.D. 132. This instrument was an artistic device called an "earthquake weathercock"; it was designed to indicate both the occurrence of earthquake waves and their direction of approach. The descriptions that have come down to

us give a detailed account only of the outside of the instrument. It was a metal bowl, about 2 m in diameter; as the scaled-down model on this page shows, there were eight dragons attached to the outside of the vessel, facing in the principal directions of the compass. Below each dragon head rested a frog with its mouth open toward the dragon. The mouth of each dragon held a ball secured in place by a small lever connected to some interior mechanism, the details of which were unfortunately not described.

At the onset of earthquake shaking, one of the interior mechanisms (perhaps a pendulum) was supposed to move, releasing a ball into the open mouth of a frog. The direction faced by the dragon that had dropped the ball would be the direction from which the shaking came. It was claimed that the device did respond to at least one earthquake centered at a remote place. The story is that one day a ball fell even though local people felt no ground shaking. Chang Heng's reputation was much enhanced when a rider later came into the city and announced the occurrence of a distant earthquake.

We now know that Chang Heng's seismoscope would have been, at best, a poor earthquake recorder. Because of mechanical friction in the moving parts, the instrument would not have been much more sensitive to the tiny motions of the ground than were the local inhabitants themselves. Human beings and animals at rest are very sensitive to earthquake motions; indeed, they are able to feel accelerations of the ground down to one-thousandth of the acceleration of gravity. Moreover, even if earthquake motions had swung a pendulum inside the earthquake weathercock, the direction of the swing could not have indicated uniquely the direction toward the earthquake source. Because earthquakes consist of both P and S waves, the ground movement is both toward and away from the source of the waves, and, in the case of S waves, to and fro in a perpendicular direction as well. In fact, this ingenious device had little or no influence on the design of modern, scientific-

ally useful instruments. Even reference to it in China died out for centuries. Not until much later were instruments constructed that could measure faithfully the entire progress of the ground motion, not just its initiation.

THE COMING OF THE MODERN SEISMOGRAPH

The first accounts in Europe of devices for recording earthquakes come from the early part of the eighteenth century, when pendulums were employed to indicate ground motion. A series of earthquakes that struck Naples in 1731 were measured in this way by Nicholas Cirrillo. Progress was slow, however, and the early detectors could not record the time of the arrival of the waves or give a permanent record of the ground motion.

In the middle of the nineteenth century, the Italian Luigi Palmieri built a seismoscope in the volcano observatory on Mount Vesuvius that also recorded the time of earthquakes. With his *sismografo elettro-magnetico,* first used in 1856, Pal-

The electromagnetic seismograph constructed by the Italian geologist Luigi Palmieri in 1856. Note that the local time of an earthquake could be recorded.

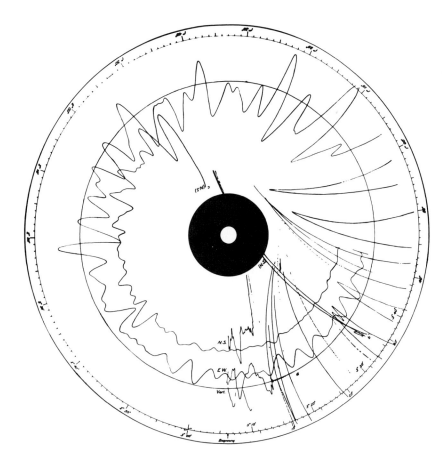

During the 1906 San Francisco earthquake, seismic waves in the north-south, east-west, and vertical directions of the ground were recorded on a rotating circular plate by the Ewing seismograph at Lick Observatory, University of California.

mieri detected the vertical motion of the ground by the movement of a mass on a spiral spring and the horizontal motion of the ground by the movement of mercury in U-tubes. Although Palmieri's instrument and others of the era were not seismographs in the modern sense, they did give the direction, intensity, and duration of the earthquake, and they were capable of responding to both horizontal and vertical motions.

A major step forward was taken in Japan in about 1892 when a visiting English professor of engineering, John Milne (1850–1913), aided by his colleagues at the Imperial University James Ewing and Thomas Gray, developed instruments that were able to record the ground shaking as a function of time. The instruments were sufficiently compact and simple in operation to be installed as practical working seismographs in many parts of the world. In fact, a Ewing seismograph was stationed in 1897 at the first earthquake observatory in North America, established and operated by the University of California at Lick Astronomical Observatory in that state.

Although modern seismographs are more sophisticated than those of Milne and his colleagues, the basic principle employed is the same. If we could float in the air quite unaffected by an earthquake, we could make a seismogram by reaching down with a pencil and allowing it to move across a sheet of paper fastened to the shaking ground. However, because gravity prevents levitation, seismographs are constructed by freely suspending a mass from a frame attached to the ground; the mass is therefore reasonably independent of the frame's motion. When the frame is shaken by earthquake waves, the inertia of the mass causes it to lag behind the motion of the frame. In the classical instrument used before the coming of digital displays, this relative motion was recorded by pen and ink on paper wrapped around a rotating drum, or by a light spot on film, producing the familiar record known as a seismogram.

During an earthquake, the ground moves simultaneously in three dimensions: for example, up-down, east-west, and north-south. A single seismograph records only one of these three components of motion. Milne realized that he could reconstruct the complete record of the ground motion by combining the records from three separate seismographs, one for each component of the motion. Vertical motion can be recorded by attaching the mass to a spring hanging from the frame; the bobbing mass will inscribe a record. For measurements of the sideways motion of the ground, the mass is usually attached to a horizontal pendulum, which swings like a door on its hinges. In most recordings, the relative motion between the mass and the frame is not the true motion of the ground. The actual motion must be calculated by taking into account the physics of the pendulum's motion.

Seismographs often must record waves with amplitudes as small as 10^{-9} m, the size of a molecule of gas. These relative motions were once magnified by mechanical means—for example, by connecting a series of jointed levers or by swinging a spot of light. Projecting the light spot onto a surface from a distance amplified its motion. In modern seismographs, the relative motion between the pendulum and frame produces an electric signal that is magnified electronically thousands and even hundreds of thousands of times before it is used to drive an electric stylus writing on sensitive paper. The electric signal from a seismograph pendulum can also be recorded onto magnetic tape or stored as a series of numbers in a computer.

John Milne surmised in 1883 that "it is not unlikely that every large earthquake might with proper appliances be recorded at any point of the globe." Milne's prediction was fulfilled in 1889 when the German physicist E. Von Rebeur Paschwitz "was struck by the coincidence in time" between the arrival of singular waves registered by delicate horizontal pendulums at Potsdam and Wilhemshaven in Germany and the time of a damaging earthquake that was reported to have shaken Tokyo at 2 hours, 7 minutes Greenwich mean time on April 18. He concluded that "the disturbances that were noted in Germany were really due to the earthquake in Tokyo." The significance of this identification—an early example of what is now called "remote sensing"—was that earthquakes in inhabited and uninhabited parts of the world alike could be monitored uniformly. Thus patterns of geological activity could be mapped without bias. With this unrestricted global surveillance, a new era in the study of earthquakes and in geology itself had begun.

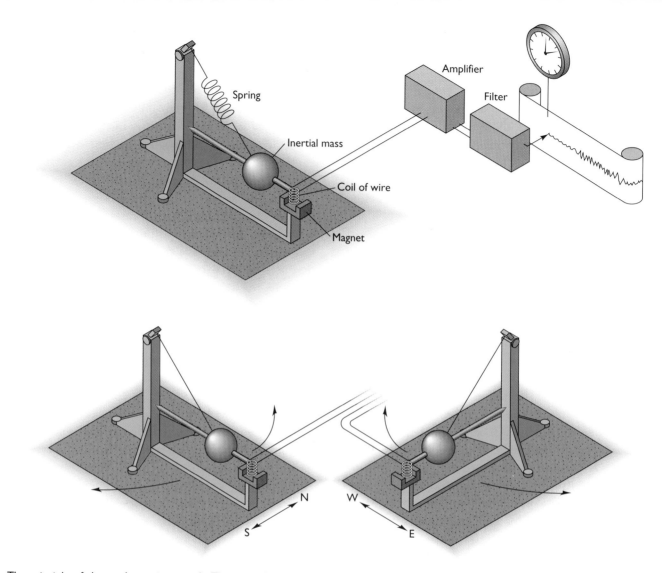

The principle of the modern seismograph. The vertical component of seismic wave motion is recorded by a pendulum attached to a spring, whereas two horizontal components of seismic wave motion at right angles are recorded by pendulums hinged to swing like a gate.

THE EARTHQUAKE OBSERVATORY

Milne, on his return to Britain in 1895, established what was to become a famous center for earthquake research at Shide on the Isle of Wight. Within a few years he had organized the first global network of seismographic stations, comprising 10 stations in the British Isles and 30 overseas. With recordings collected at Shide, he began a systematic analysis of earthquake patterns.

The number of seismographic stations grew steadily, and by 1957 about 600 were listed by the International Seismological Summary, an international organization operated in Britain as a successor to Milne's Shide observatory. For his contributions to earthquake observation, Milne has been called "the founder of modern seismology."

Modern seismographs record the ground motion uninterruptedly, and they contain clock devices that continuously provide the time. It is thus possible to measure, with high fidelity, the wavelengths and amplitudes of the waves. Just as modern astronomy depends on a variety of sophisticated optical and radio telescopes, a modern, well-equipped earthquake observatory has a wide variety of seismographs. Ideally, these instruments are able to record, over a very wide spectrum of frequencies, the vertical and two horizontal components of the earthquake motion that arrives at the recording station from remote sources.

Displacements of the rock in earthquakes vary in direction throughout the motion. From the three components of a seismograph, the complete wave motion as it evolves with time can be reconstructed. Nowadays this ever-changing pattern can be followed on a computer graphics screen as a sequence of elliptical orbits, which sometimes have mainly horizontal amplitudes and sometimes have predominantly vertical axes. These complete representations of the ground shaking enable the seismologist to identify seismic wave types as predominantly P, S, or surface waves and to compute the total energy in the shaking.

A pendulum swings and an elastic spring vibrates at a characteristic or "natural" rate, which depends on the pendulum's length and the spring's elasticity. Thus, the period of a single unforced oscillation remains constant, independent of the amplitude. As a consequence of this property, the sensitivity of a seismograph varies with the period of the ground motion in an earthquake (that is, with the frequency of ground motion, which is the reciprocal of the period). When the ground moves slowly back and forth at frequencies much smaller than the natural frequency of the pendulum, the displacement of the pendulum's mass relative to the frame closely follows the acceleration of the ground. Although the ground acceleration is useful information for structural engineers, seismologists often prefer their seismographs to measure ground displacement rather than acceleration. If the seismic wave frequencies approach the pendulum's natural frequency of vibration, the amplitude will be greatly magnified by the resonant vibrations of the pendulum. At frequencies well above the pendulum's natural frequency, the mass does not move much at all. In that case, the relative displacements between the pendulum and the frame can be amplified to give a true measure of the displacement of the seismic waves. Traditionally, observatories operate a number of seismographs designed with varied sensitivity to the frequencies in an earthquake, which range from 10^{-3} Hz to more than 10 Hz.

The modern seismograph has become more compact yet is able to record with high fidelity both high-frequency (low-period) and low-frequency (high-period) waves. Present-day electronic amplifiers, first introduced in the 1960s, are able to amplify satisfactorily the lower-frequency waves that would previously have been unacceptably contaminated with extraneous instrumental noise. The electric voltages produced by the responses of the inertial masses to the ground motion are nowadays passed through low-noise electronic circuits that act as filters. These filters are set to pass through only those waves in the frequency range of scientific interest. Even with the digital systems now in use, however, the very large dynamic range of earthquakes, not only in frequency but also in wave amplitude, requires several differently responding seismographs if the whole range of both quantities is to be spanned.

Seismographs are sensitive to ground shaking from any source. They will record the shaking that arises from great storms in the ocean and the crashing of ocean waves on a coastline, as well as the ground vibrations from road traffic and other works of man. These background noises are called microseisms. They create the wiggles that are traced on a seismogram even on quiet days. Wherever possible, the sites for seismographs are carefully selected so that the ground shaking from nonseismic sources will not mask the earthquake signals. One very quiet station that became famous in the United States was operated from 1964 to 1984 on hard rock in an abandoned mine shaft near the town of Jamestown in the western foothills of the Sierra Nevada, California. At this site, the average microseismic ground motion has an amplitude of only about 10^{-8} m (10 nanometers) because it is remote from the ocean waves along the coastline and from human activities. Placing the seismograph underground also significantly reduced the

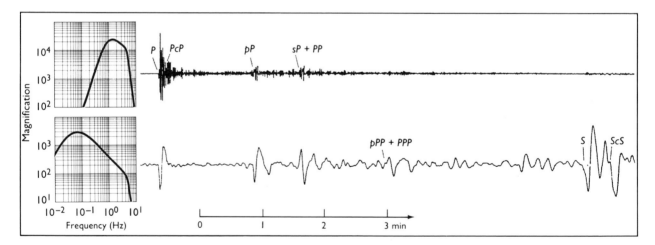

These computer simulations of the shaking from a deep-focus earthquake of magnitude 5.9 that struck the Sea of Japan on March 9, 1977, demonstrate the influence of electronic filters on the complexity of recorded waveforms. The displayed traces are vertical-component seismograms that would have been recorded at Erlangen, Germany, by a short-period seismograph (*top*) and a long-period seismograph (*bottom*). The filters used are given at the left.

noise from locally generated high-frequency surface waves that run through the surface soils. In the near absence of background noise, the Jamestown seismograph could record even the faint echo of an earthquake on the other side of the world, which would be carried by waves that had passed through the deep interior of the Earth. An example of its amazing detection feats is given in Chapter 6.

The activity at an earthquake observatory falls into a daily routine. The photographic paper film or magnetic tapes are changed each day so that the records of the previous day's earthquakes can be preserved and analyzed. A seismologist interprets the wave patterns by selecting the onsets of earthquake waves from the microseismic wiggles.

Seismologists require great skill in pattern recognition to pick out the P and S waves that have traveled along different paths inside the Earth. They look for the sudden increase in amplitude, often associated with a change in wave frequency, that signals the arrival of a particular earthquake wave. The analysts will then read the time of arrival of the first onset of this wave as closely as possible, to the nearest tenth of a second. Often the amplitude and period of the wave are also read.

In some of the more advanced observatories, the seismic signals are recorded by magnetic tape or in the memory of a high-speed computer as a regular series of discrete numbers. These digital series give an arithmetic sample of the continuous signal. The analyst can then scan the recorded ground motion on a graphics screen connected by a modem to the computer and make selections exactly as would be done with film records. Alternatively, the analyst may ask the computer to flag the arrivals of P and S waves

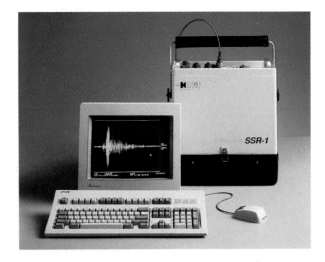

A modern field seismograph, fitted in a compact box (*rear*), feeds a digital readout to a computer, which transforms the numbers into the familiar waveform on its screen.

according to preprogrammed rules. In addition, the computer program can check the accompanying time code and print the arrival time and amplitude of each selected onset. In this way, much of the drudgery formerly performed by observatory seismologists has disappeared. For research into esoteric seismic waves, an experienced seismologist must still give the seismograms individual scrutiny.

After recording the arrival time of every main wave, the analyst identifies each selected wave according to its type and path and assigns to it a standard symbol. Thus, the first wave is simply a P and the first shear wave simply an S. Other onsets would be given notations such as PP, SS, PcP, and SKS (defined on page 130), which indicate the wave's approximate course and tell whether it was ever reflected from a surface during its travels. The entire process is very much like that carried out by a cryptologist trying to break a secret code.

The final step is to record the arrival times, amplitudes, periods, and identity of these onsets and transmit them to a catalogue or directly to regional or international seismological centers.

THE GLOBAL DISTRIBUTION OF EARTHQUAKES

The first glittering scientific reward from the far-flung network of seismographic observatories pioneered by John Milne was an unbiased picture of the distribution of the world's earthquakes. Through the end of the last century, seismologists had a very warped picture of the distribution of earthquakes because their knowledge was restricted mostly to earthquakes felt on conti-

nents. As the twentieth century advanced, the efforts by the global seismograph network to locate earthquakes gradually bore fruit: today we have unbiased maps, such as that on the facing page, showing the positions of thousands of earthquakes recorded between 1977 and 1986. It is worth emphasizing that this observational accomplishment has depended on the universal co-operation by seismologists of all nations—in war and in peace—in exchanging travel times of seismic waves. In 1990, there were about 3300 seismographic observatories participating in international data exchange.

Many seismographic stations of the first rank from around the world each day send readings of earthquakes or underground explosions by cable or airmail to the National Earthquake Information Center (NEIC) of the U.S. Geological Survey in Golden, Colorado. These readings are used by the NEIC to compute rapidly the locations and magnitudes of earthquakes around the world. Readings also go to the International

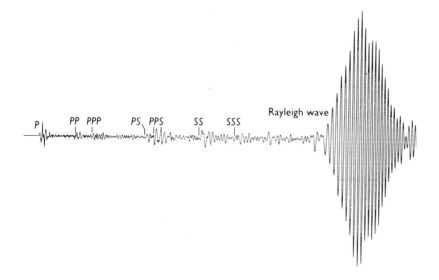

A recording made in Bayern, Germany, of the sizable Costa Rica earthquake of April 3, 1983, showing the vertical component of motion. The *PP*, *PPP*, *PS*, and *PPS* seismic waves are *P* waves that have been reflected once or twice from the Earth's surface, in two cases traveling the last leg as *S* waves. The *SS* and *SSS* are surface reflections of *S* waves. The record is dominated by a Rayleigh wave, developed along a mainly oceanic path.

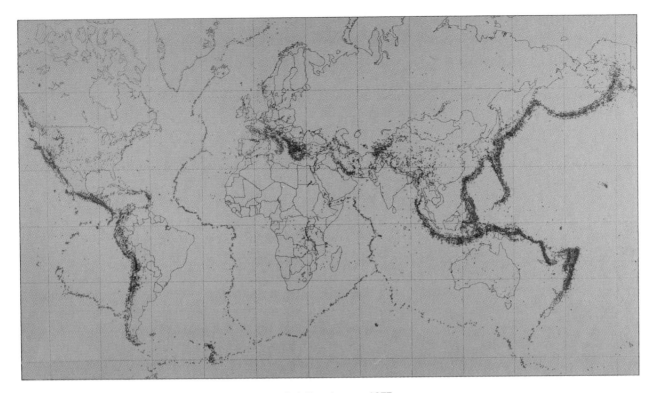

The global distribution of earthquake epicenters recorded from January 1977 through December 1986. The hypocenters are colored red, green, and blue to represent focal depths of 0 to 70 km, 70 to 300 km, and 300 km and below, respectively.

Seismological Center in England, which prints permanent records of the world's seismicity in the form of catalogues listing the locations of earthquakes. It is these catalogues that provide the elegant maps of earthquake distribution, such as that on this page. These maps in turn provide the basis for studies of the tectonic deformations of the Earth and for calculation of earthquake hazard in countries around the world.

Studies of the global earthquake distribution have provided crucial evidence on the present geodynamics and deformation of the whole Earth. They have thrown light on the long-standing puzzles of mountain building and volcanic belts, the spreading of the seafloor, and the stresses within the the continental rocks. Excellent treatments have been published over the years of the meaning of these intriguing global patterns of earthquake activity, with their concentrated belts separated by almost aseismic areas, and references are given at the end of the book. It is of interest first to examine the geographic patterns, searching anew for clues that led not so long ago to an overall geological explanation of the restless seismic nature of the Earth. In Chapter 5, we shall describe the current theory of Earth dynamics that gives an explanation of earthquakes.

Like volcanoes and high mountain ranges, earthquakes are not randomly scattered but are,

A SAMPLE CALCULATION OF THE LOCATION OF AN EPICENTER

An earthquake of magnitude 5.7 occurred near the town of Oroville in northeastern California on August 1, 1975. In this earthquake, P and S waves arrived at the stations Berkeley (BKS), Jamestown (JAS), and Mineral (MIN) at the following times (universal time):

	P			S		
	hr	min	s	hr	min	s
BKS	15	46	04.5	15	46	25.5
JAS	15	46	07.6	15	46	28.0
MIN	15	45	54.2	15	46	07.1

The following epicentral distances are estimated from the S minus P times above (from the left column of the box on page 58).

	S minus P (seconds)	Distance (kilometers)
BKS	21.0	190
JAS	20.4	188
MIN	12.9	105

With these distances as radii, one can draw three arcs of circles, as shown in the illustration. Note that these do not quite intersect at one point, but interpolation from the overlapping arcs yields an estimated epicenter of 39.5°N, 121.5°W, with an uncertainty of about 10 km from these readings.

for the most part, concentrated in narrow zones. Many earthquakes occur in remote regions along ridges in the centers of oceans and pose no hazard to humans. But the greatest seismic activity is concentrated along the Pacific margins of the continents and in southern Europe and Asia, which are densely inhabited. In contrast, the interiors of the oceans, away from the seismic ridges, are almost but not quite aseismic. The Antarctic has the quietest margins and almost no interior earthquakes. According to the most recent global list of earthquakes, each year there are between 18,000 and 22,000 shallow-focus earthquakes of magnitude 2.5 or greater.

In natural earthquakes, the depth of focus can range from a few kilometers down to depths of almost 700 km. Earthquakes having foci below 70 km are especially intriguing. These deep-focus earthquakes were discovered at the beginning of the century, and their existence was established by the Japanese seismologist Kiyoo Wadati in 1928.

The geographic spread of deep-focus earthquakes is quite restricted. Most lie along island arcs, such as the Aleutian arc; the Japanese arc; the Marianas; the Tonga-Kermadic-New Zealand arc; Indonesia; the New Hebrides chain; and the arcs of the Caribbean, Antilles, and the Aegean Sea. Deep-focus earthquakes also occur along continental margins where there are deep ocean trenches, such as under the South American Andes and under Central America. A few concentrations of deep-focus earthquakes are also generated under inland mountain chains like the

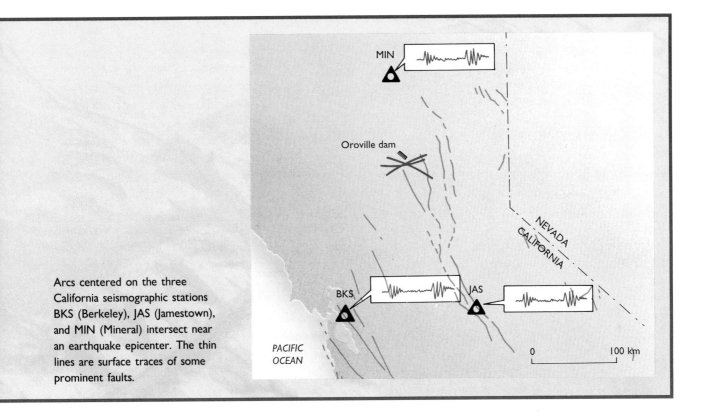

Arcs centered on the three California seismographic stations BKS (Berkeley), JAS (Jamestown), and MIN (Mineral) intersect near an earthquake epicenter. The thin lines are surface traces of some prominent faults.

Himalayas and the Carpathians, and a very few under Spain. It was not until the 1970s that their distribution and hence their geological meaning became clear, as we shall discuss in Chapter 5.

LOCATING EARTHQUAKES

Seismic waves first emanate from a point within the Earth identified in Chapter 1 as the earthquake focus or hypocenter, located directly below the point on the Earth's surface called the epicenter. The first task seismologists tackled after establishing observatories was developing a method to locate accurately the epicenter and, if possible, the hypocenter of each recorded earthquake.

In the simplest method, the location of the epicenter is found through a straightforward triangulation. From timing information gathered from previous studies of explosions or of earthquakes from other regions, curves are constructed showing the average time required for *P* or *S* waves to travel various distances from an epicenter. These seismic travel-time curves are the basic tools for determining the distance of any earthquake source from the seismograph that records it.

Consider three seismographic observatories, each of which records an earthquake and each of which lies in a different direction from the source of the waves. The observatory staffs at the three stations can read the time of arrival of the *P* waves and sometimes that of the *S* waves. Because a *P* wave travels about twice as fast as an *S* wave, the farther the two waves travel, the wider becomes the gap separating the wave fronts. Thus, if the arrival times of both the *P* and *S* waves are available, the interval between the two types of wave will give a direct measure of the distance to the focus. Three circles are then drawn, each centered on one of the stations, with radii equal to the computed distances. The three circles will intersect, at least approximately, at the required epicenter.

Even when the arrival time of only the *P* waves is known, the time of occurrence of the first radiation of the *P* waves, called the origin time of the earthquake, can be roughly estimated. The arrival times minus the origin time give the travel times of the *P* waves to the three stations. As in the first method for finding the epicenter, three circles are drawn centered on the three stations, but now the radii are proportional to the travel times of the *P* waves. After several adjustments of the origin time and location, the intersection of the three circles will define a small area within which lies the epicenter. Thus, from three measurements of *S* and *P* arrival times (or *P* arrival times alone), the latitude and longitude of the epicenter, as well as the origin time, can be determined.

Values of these three quantities must come from three earthquake observatories at three distances and directions from the epicenter. If the focal depth is also to be estimated, a fourth measurement is needed, either of the arrival time of a *P* or *S* wave at another seismographic station or of the arrival times of some additional *P* or *S* waves at the original three stations. If a seismographic station happens to be immediately above the focus of the earthquake, then the travel time of either the *P* or *S* wave upward from the focus to the station is a direct measure of the depth of the earthquake.

These days, computer programs apply sophisticated statistical methods to analyze readings of *P* waves and *S* waves from many stations and determine the location of an earthquake focus anywhere in the world. To ensure accuracy, the stations must be distributed reasonably uniformly around the earthquake focus, and there should be an even distribution of near and far stations. Foci can be located more precisely by calibrating the calculations against previous recordings from earthquakes in the same region with particularly well-known locations. In most regions of the world today, the accuracy of epicentral location is about 10 km and of focal depth about 20 km.

More precise locations and wave measurements of distant earthquakes can be obtained using linked seismographic stations. Such links may be either by electrical wire connections or, for arrays with large distances between seismographs, by having accurate clocks or radio receivers place universal time marks at intervals on each record. It is this common time-base that turns a group of recorders in a region into a seismic array. The great advantage for earthquake analysis is that seismic wave variations from neighboring stations across the array can be correlated with high precision. The gradients of such variations can be directly related by theoretical formula to the propagation paths of the waves.

One such large-aperture seismic array (LASA) was installed near Billings, Montana, in the mid-1960s by the U.S. Department of Defense. It was one of the largest of the arrays installed throughout the world to detect underground nuclear explosions with greater fidelity than is possible with single stations. LASA consisted of 525 linked seismometers grouped in 21 clusters spread over an area 200 km in diameter. After its uses were explored, it was closed in 1982. Similar arrays in, for example, Norway, Australia, and Alaska still monitor earthquakes from distant seismic sources. Seismic arrays that record earthquakes centered near them will be discussed in Chapter 7.

ASSESSING EARTHQUAKE SIZE

One of the first questions asked about an earthquake by both scientists and the public is its size. Thus seismologists have developed simple ways to identify earthquake size from the records of seismographs. The most common measure of size used at observatories is seismic magnitude. Astronomers have long graded the size of the stars according to the stellar magnitude scale, which is based on the relative brightness of stars as seen through a telescope. In 1935, Charles Richter developed at the California Institute of Technology an analogous measure for earthquakes, similar to one already being used by Kiyoo Wadati for assessing Japanese earthquakes. Richter proposed that earthquakes be graded according to the seismic wave amplitudes detected by a seismograph. Originally applicable only to earthquakes measured locally in southern California, this system of measurement has now been applied in studies of earthquakes throughout the world.

Because earthquakes vary in size over a huge range, it is convenient to compress the measured wave amplitude by using logarithms. To put the

Charles Richter (1900–1985), the inventor of the Richter magnitude scale.

definition precisely, the Richter magnitude, M_L, is the logarithm to base 10 of the maximum seismic wave amplitude. This amplitude is measured in thousandths of a millimeter as recorded on a special seismograph called the Wood-Anderson seismograph. Richter specified no particular wave type, so this maximum amplitude may be taken from whichever wave has the amplitude of greatest height. Because the amplitude generally decreases with distance, Richter selected the distance 100 km from the earthquake epicenter as a standard. According to the definition, if the Wood-Anderson seismograph gives a peak wave amplitude of, say, 1 cm (or 10^4 thousandths of a millimeter) for an earthquake 100 km away, the magnitude is 4.

The magnitude itself does not have any upper or lower limit (although earthquake size

A SAMPLE CALCULATION OF THE RICHTER MAGNITUDE (M_L)

Using specially prepared scales, the procedure for calculating the magnitude M_L of a local earthquake is straightforward:

1. Measure the distance to the focus using the time interval between the S and the P waves ($S - P = 24$ seconds).

2. Measure the height of the maximum wave motion on the seismogram (23 millimeters).

3. Place a straight edge between appropriate points on the distance (left) and amplitude (right) scales to obtain magnitude $M_L = 5.0$.

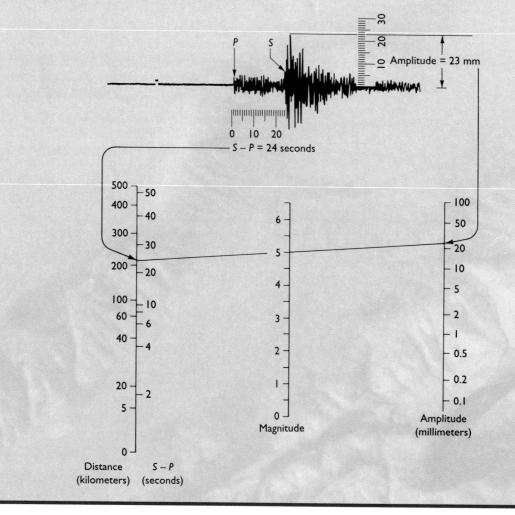

certainly has an upper limit). Only a few earthquakes recorded since the introduction of seismographs in this century have reached estimated magnitudes above 8.5. For example, the great Alaska earthquake of March 27, 1964, in Prince William Sound had a Richter magnitude of about 8.6. At the other extreme, slips on small faults may produce earthquakes of magnitude less than zero (that is, negative values). Very sensitive seismographs recording locally detect earthquakes of magnitude less than −2.0. Such earthquakes release about the same seismic energy as a brick dropped from a table to the ground.

The best practice at earthquake observatories in recent years has been to concentrate on three newer magnitude scales, denoted M_s, m_b, and M_w. The Richter magnitude M_L is still popular among the news media and general public. However, because the wave type used is not defined and because the Wood-Anderson instrument has only limited recording ability, M_L is not widely used in research. For shallow earthquakes with well-recorded surface waves, seismologists select the greatest amplitude of the surface waves with periods close to 20 seconds. The resulting calculated value is called the surface wave magnitude, M_s. Whereas the Richter magnitude was conceived to apply only to local earthquakes, an M_s magnitude may be assigned to earthquakes at great distances from the receiving station. M_s values give roughly a continuation of the local Richter magnitude for large-distance earthquakes and overall give a reasonable estimate of the potential damage from very large as well as moderate earthquakes. The 1906 San Francisco earthquake had an M_s magnitude of 8.25.

The M_s scale cannot be applied to deep earthquakes because they do not generate large surface waves. Thus, seismologists have developed a second magnitude scale, m_b, which determines the magnitude of the earthquake from the size of the P wave rather than the surface waves. All earthquakes start with a P onset that can be read unequivocally, and thus the use of the P wave gives the m_b scale the great advantage that it can provide a value for any earthquake, deep or shallow, even out to large distances.

Magnitude conveniently allows us to describe the approximate size or "strength" of an earthquake by just one number. Unfortunately, this parameter does not have a physical basis. It is often erroneously thought of as a measure of the energy of an earthquake. It does not directly measure the overall mechanical power of the seismic source, just as the strongest wind gust is not a reliable measure of the overall force of a wind storm.

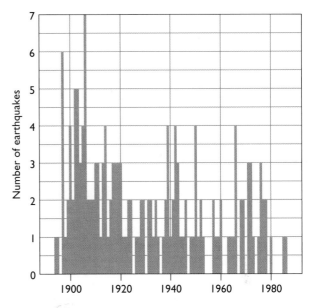

The variation in the number of earthquakes, magnitude 8 and higher, that have occurred around the world during this century.

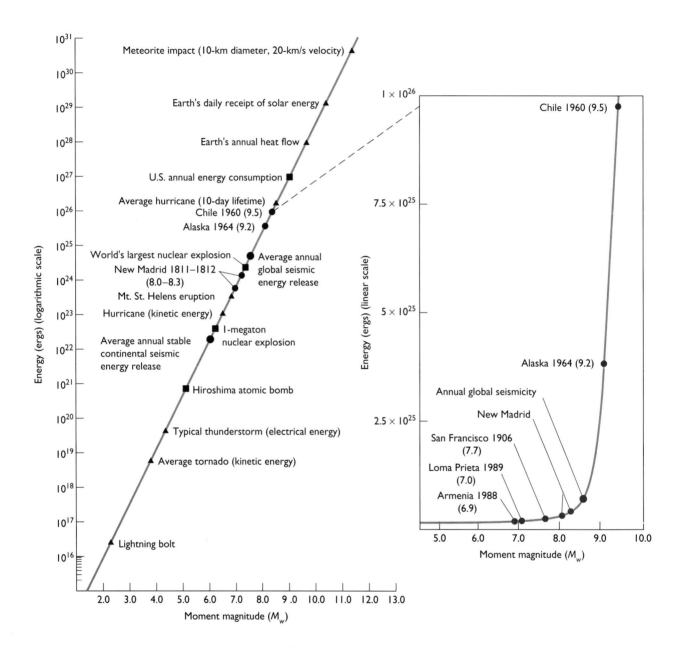

The amount of energy released in earthquakes compared with other phenomena.

In seeking a physically meaningful measure of earthquake size, seismologists have looked to the classical theory of mechanics, which describes the movements of bodies as resulting from the application of forces. One such measure, called the seismic moment, has been widely adopted. We shall describe it in detail in Chapter 4.

The advantage of this method of identifying earthquake size is that a measure of earthquake moment can be calculated either by analysis of seismograms or by field measurements of the dimensions of the fault rupture, including depth. The measurement may be calculated from seismograms recorded by any common modern seismograph, and it takes account of all wave types present in the earthquake. Because of its advantages, the moment magnitude of an earthquake, written M_w, is now widely computed.

The new scale gives more physically meaningful measurements, especially of the strongest earthquakes. For example, the 1989 Loma Prieta earthquake had a surface wave magnitude of 7.1 M_s and a moment magnitude of 6.9 M_w. Both the San Francisco earthquake of 1906 and the Chilean earthquake of 1960 had a surface wave measurement of 8.3, but on the moment magnitude scale, the magnitude of the San Francisco earthquake has been demoted to 7.9 and that of the Chilean earthquake advanced to 9.5.

OTHER MEASUREMENTS OF GROUND MOTION

We have mainly considered instruments based on simple pendulums that swing when the base of support is displaced in the earthquake. Other ingenious devices have been conceived over the years, some of which have become a part of modern practice.

As P waves pass through the rocks of the Earth, they alternately compress and dilate the rocks, producing fluctuations in volume and hence in density. This behavior of the rock suggests that if water were placed in a large hole underneath the ground where it could not escape, and a tube were to connect the hole to the ground surface, then the squeezing of the volume of trapped water (being largely incompressible) would force the level of the water in the small outlet tube to rise and fall. This change in level would give a measure of the compressional component of the P wave and the Rayleigh wave motion. The water level would not be affected by the shear S waves. Such devices, called dilatometers, were proposed early in the century.

In the 1950s and 1960s, attempts were made to use water trapped underground as a dilatometer. Floats were placed in wells, and the rise and fall of the float, much amplified by the great volume of water contained in the underground cavities, would be a measure of the wave motion in the earthquake. Although these efforts did not prove practical, satisfactory modern instrumental dilatometers are used nowadays for special purposes. In Japan, for example, dilatometers are operated not specifically to measure the seismic wave motion but to measure the slow compression of the rocks that might precede an earthquake.

The dilatometer is the simplest example of an instrument that measures the changes in ground deformation, rather than the inertial forces involved in seismic shaking. Another early device for measuring ground deformation, which

Hugo Benioff (1899–1968), designer of important modern earthquake recorders who also studied zones of deep earthquakes.

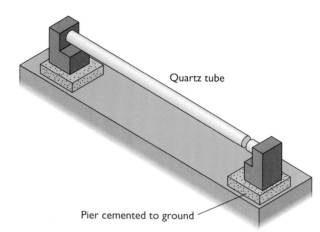

Quartz tube

Pier cemented to ground

The Benioff strain extensiometer. The distance between two piers attached to the ground varies as the ground changes in length as a result of either the buildup of elastic strain or the release of strain in an earthquake. These variations are measured by placing an electronic motion detector in the gap.

has had wider success, is the strainmeter. During his residence in Japan, John Milne devised one of the first of these devices, which measured the changes in the distance between two monuments fixed in the ground. The most versatile American maker of seismographs, Hugo Benioff, pioneered a more practical instrument, which recorded variations in the distance between piers set in the ground 20 m apart. The instrument measured the shifting length of the gap between one pier and a standard-length tube extending from the other pier. The tube was originally of steel, but the material was later replaced by quartz to reduce expansions caused by temperature variations. Such an instrument is called a strain extensiometer. Similar devices, involving wires stretched between points, have been used to measure the slow length changes of the ground due to the buildup of elastic strain in the deforming rocks. Such measurements are important to understanding earthquake genesis.

Finally, slow angular displacements of the ground, which take place over days or longer, can be measured either by recording the shift in position of a suspended long-period pendulum or by gauging the differential heights of fluid reservoirs connected by a tube.

On the whole, however, the recording of differential movements between a suspended mass and the moving ground has proved to be the most effective way of measuring seismic waves of various kinds, and devices exploiting this method remain, after about one hundred years of use, by far the most common instrumentation.

STRONG-MOTION ACCELEROMETERS

Seismographs using pendulums are most effective for recording small ground motions or for recording waves at considerable distances from the seismic source. Near the source of large earthquakes, the ground shaking is so severe that normal pendulum devices are overdriven by the severity of the motion. Sometimes the pendulums come off their pivot points or even break. Even when the instruments remain intact, the large excursion of the pendulum's swings greatly exceeds the length of swing that the instruments were designed to record. Moreover, very long period pendulums, which until quite recently consisted of meter-long booms, are unstable over hours and days. Deviations in their swings arise from the slow changes of temperature in the recording vaults, convection currents in the air, or slow tilting of the ground itself. To prevent these instabilities, operators must give these devices continued attention.

After the 1906 San Francisco earthquake, the State Earthquake Investigation Commission voiced the need for a device that could be left at unattended sites, in or near ordinary buildings, for months or years before a strong earthquake occurred. The instrument had to be rugged, it had to be very stable in operation, and it had to possess a reliable trigger that would set the instrument in rapid motion after the first strong shaking arrived.

After considerable trial and error, an instrument was created that has become universally adopted to record large earthquakes close by. This instrument, called an accelerometer, came into use in California about 1925. The first such instruments had pendulums with very short periods of natural oscillation; nowadays small inertial spring devices are used. Such short-period sensors are not nearly as sensitive to slow ground tilts and temperature changes as longer-period pendulums. In addition, the sensor's short period of natural oscillation meant that when ground motions of longer period shook the instrument, the amplitude of the signal produced was directly proportional to the acceleration of the ground rather than its displacement. These accelerometers could record the actual ground acceleration accurately over a wide range of wave frequencies. The very low sensitivity of the instrument also ensured that ground shaking up to accelerations exceeding that of gravity would stay on the scale.

The first generation of strong-motion accelerometers, which used optical recording systems, was soon seen by engineers to provide the long-desired reliable, quantitative knowledge of the ground motions experienced by structures, whether damaged or not in the strong shaking. In the last decade, the growth of digital technology has led to improved strong-motion accelerometers that are both simpler and more informative than their predecessors. The first major technical advance was to provide strong-motion accelerometers with absolute timing, as ordinary seismographs have. The correct Greenwich mean time is continuously supplied to the instruments by attaching them to very accurate crystal clocks, inexpensive radio time receivers, or, more recently, time services supplied by satellites. Second, the new instruments avoid a serious drawback of the first-generation instruments, which after being triggered lost the first few seconds of *P*-wave motion while the motors came up to

These instruments are now incorporated into personal computers. Digital strong-motion accelerometers have solid-state memories on computer chips so that ground motion signals can be recorded digitally and stored directly on floppy disks, optical disks, or magnetic tape. Now the operator of the instrument can take a laptop computer into the field after an earthquake, plug it in to the digital strong-motion recorder, transfer the digital recording into the portable instrument, and take the recording back to headquarters for processing. Sometimes the strong-motion instruments are actually connected by telephone line to the central observatory. In this way, the recording of strong motion can be viewed on a graphics screen or television set within a very short time of the actual high-intensity motion at the remote site. Such rapid availability of strong-motion data in earthquake country is now in demand by utility and transportation organizations, which use the data to judge quickly after an earthquake which critical structures such as dams, railroads, and road overpasses are most likely to have sustained damage.

Most observatories in earthquake country now have digital strong-motion accelerometers running alongside more traditional instruments. In the 1960s when I became the director of the University of California's seismographic network in northern California, I feared that, despite our claim to have some of the best seismographic instrumentation in the world, the severe ground motions of a great earthquake would send the recordings of all the sensitive seismographs at our observatories offscale. I would then face a curious and excited press corps eager to learn the strength of ground shaking, only to reply, "Our

The installation of seismographs on a California hillside.

speed. By contrast, the new generation of strong-motion accelerometers is designed to continuously place the ground motion even at quiet times in a memory lasting up to 10 seconds. Thus, when the device is triggered by a large-amplitude wave, a few seconds of motion *before* that first *P*-wave arrival can be saved.

instruments in the big shake could not provide any information!" For this reason, I began to install strong-motion accelerometers, previously used mainly for engineering studies, alongside the high-magnification seismographs traditionally operated for geophysical research. Fortunately, today the directors of observatories in earthquake country do not have my old worry. The new-generation seismographs with digital recording and wide frequency response are valuable instruments of research to all disciplines interested in earthquakes.

4

THE SOURCES OF EARTHQUAKES: NATURAL AND ARTIFICIAL

ONE OF THE great achievements of seismology has been to work out fully the mechanism by which earthquake waves are generated. As recently as the turn of the last century, a leading writer on earthquakes commented that "the causes of earthquakes are still hidden in obscurity, and probably will ever remain so, as these violent convulsions originate at depths far below the realms of human observations." Many of his contemporaries regarded volcanism as the general prime cause of large earthquakes, while others suspected the gravity differences that are associated with high mountain ranges.

After establishment of the seismographic networks at the beginning of the twentieth century, the global surveillance of earthquake activity made it clear that many large earthquakes occur far from volcanoes and moun-

A fresh scarp photographed after the 1988 Armenia earthquake.
The town of Spitak lies in the background.

tains. More and more, geologists made it their business to visit the sites of damaging earthquakes. They were struck by the occurrence of large surface ruptures, which could often be mapped into linear systems of abrupt topographic changes. It became clear early in the century that ordinary earthquakes are intimately connected with the broad deformation of the Earth's surface that creates mountains, rift valleys, mid-oceanic ridges, and ocean trenches. Geologists speculated that quick large-scale shifts of the surficial rocks were the cause of the intense ground shaking. Their speculations soon evolved into more confident statements that the mechanism for the generation of the great majority of earthquakes had been found.

Nowadays, shallow natural earthquakes are regarded as almost all having the same cause. These ground tremors ultimately stem from the large-scale deformation of the outer part of the Earth resulting from deep-seated global forces, called tectonic forces. The immediate cause of the radiation of seismic wave energy is the sudden slip along a geological fault.

GEOLOGICAL FAULTS

Rocks can be made to "break" and "fail" in a variety of ways when they are put under pressure in the laboratory. In some catastrophic failures, fractures form that divide the rock in sections, and the sides of the fractures, called failure surfaces, slip abruptly past each other as the rock breaks into pieces. If the sides of the broken pieces can be fitted together again, this type of failure is called brittle fracture. In other failures, the sides of the specimen do not suddenly slip but grind slowly, maintaining cohesion along an oblique failure surface. Such rock failure cannot release stored elastic energy quickly, as a brittle fracture does.

In nature, failure surfaces of large extent are classified as geological faults. Like the rock fractures seen in the laboratory, the sides of a fault may slide gradually and imperceptibly past each other, or they may rupture suddenly, releasing energy in an earthquake. In the latter case, the two sides of the fault slip in opposite directions, so that rocks once aligned across the fault are now displaced. Many faults are enormously long; some can be traced for thousands of kilometers on the land surface.

Faults can exhibit a very large range of properties. They can be clean fractures with only small displacements visible, or they can be diffuse shattered zones of rock, tens or hundreds of meters wide, the result of movements along the fault zone repeated time and time again. Once a fault is formed, it becomes a locus of continued displacement in response to continued stresses. This is evidenced by the crushed rock and clay materials that are found near the fault surface. Most bodies of rock on the surface contain an abundance of fractures across which rock displacement has taken place. The rock in a fault zone may become so finely crushed and sheared in the course of numerous earthquakes that it is altered to a plastic clay material, called fault gouge. This material has little strength, so elastic energy cannot be stored in it as it can in the brittle elastic rocks at greater depth.

Faults have been classified according to their geometry and direction of relative slip. As indicated in the illustration on page 70, the orientation of the fault in three dimensions is given by two angles. The first is the dip of the fault, which is the angle the fault surface makes with

Small, but clear, normal faults run through these rock strata near Kanab, Utah.

the horizontal plane. The second is the strike of the fault, which is the direction of the fault line exposed at the ground surface relative to the direction north.

Faults are classified in terms of the orientation of their movements along the dip and along the strike. A strike-slip fault, sometimes called a transcurrent fault, causes the two sides to shift horizontally relative to each other. The rock is displaced laterally parallel to the strike. If, when we stand on one side of such a fault, we see that the motion on the other side is from left to right, the fault is called a right-lateral strike-slip. Similarly, we can identify left-lateral strike-slip faulting.

The motion of a fault may be entirely vertical along the dip. In a dip-slip fault, one side shifts upward relative to the other. The motion is largely parallel to the dip of the fault, and

rocks are displaced vertically, sometimes creating a small visible rock wall called a scarp. This type of fault is in turn classified into two subtypes. A normal fault is a dip-slip fault in which the rock above the inclined fault surface moves downward relative to the rock below the fault. By contrast, a reverse fault is a dip-slip fault in which the rocks above the inclined fault surface move upward. Thrust faults are reverse faults where the dip angle is small. Rarely are faults purely strike-slip or dip-slip; usually they have both horizontal and vertical components of motion. Such a fault is termed an oblique fault.

Some fault fractures do not penetrate from the bedrock through the overburden of soil because the soil near the ground surface has absorbed the differential slip. In such cases, the slip can be detected only by digging trenches or cuts across the hidden fault scarp.

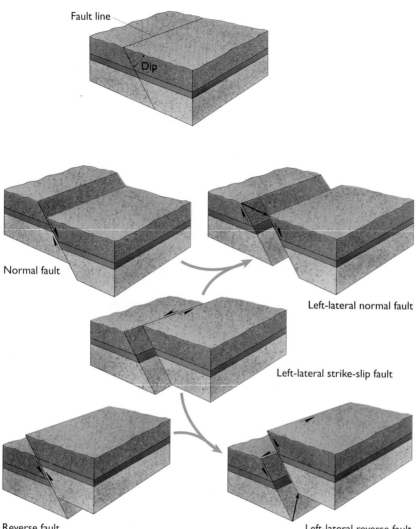

Fault line

Dip

Normal fault

Left-lateral normal fault

Left-lateral strike-slip fault

Reverse fault

Left-lateral reverse fault

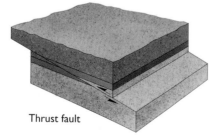

Thrust fault

The types of geological faults. Oblique faults (on the right) share characteristics both of faults having horizontal movement (strike-slip faults) and of faults having vertical movement (normal and reverse faults).

OTHER SOURCES OF SEISMIC VIBRATIONS

The majority of damaging earthquakes—such as the 1906 San Francisco earthquake, the 1988 Armenia earthquake, and the 1992 Landers earthquake in California—are produced when rocks break suddenly in a fault rupture. Although these so-called tectonic earthquakes are the type we normally associate with the word *earthquake,* strong ground motion may result from many other sources.

A second well-known type of earthquake accompanies volcanic eruptions. Many people, like the early Greek philosophers, thought that earthquakes are linked to volcanic activity, and it certainly is impressive that earthquakes and volcanoes occur together in many parts of the world. We now know that volcanic eruptions and earthquakes both result from tectonic forces in the rocks but need not occur together. Today, we define a volcanic earthquake as one that occurs in conjunction with volcanic activity.

The actual mechanism of seismic wave generation in the larger volcanic earthquakes is probably the same as that in tectonic earthquakes. Near an erupting volcano, elastic strains build up in the rocks in response to the accumulation and movement of magma. These strains lead to fault ruptures just like those of tectonic earthquakes in no way related to volcanoes. In addition, however, the rapid movement of erupting magma in the underground tubes of a volcano, as well as the explosive venting of superheated steam and gases, may excite vibrations in the surrounding rocks, known as volcanic tremors.

Another type of earthquake occurs when the roof of an underground cavern or mine collapses, producing a small "collapse" earthquake. An often-observed variation of this phenomenon is the so-called mine burst, produced when induced stress around the mine workings causes large masses of rock to fly off the mine face explosively, creating seismic waves.

A spectacular landslide on April 25, 1974, along the Mantaro River in Peru produced seismic waves equivalent to an earthquake of magnitude 4.5. A volume of rocks measuring some 1.6 cu km slid 7 km, killing about 450 people. This landslide was not triggered by a nearby tectonic earthquake but by normal instability of the mountainside. Part of the gravitational energy lost in the rapid downward movement of the soil and rock was converted to seismic waves, which were clearly recorded by seismographs hundreds of kilometers away. A seismograph 80 km away recorded ground motion for 3 minutes. This duration of shaking is compatible with the speed and extent of the slide, which traveled at about 140 km per hour over the observed slippage distance of 7 km.

Because earthquakes commonly generate landslides, sometimes of gigantic size, it can be difficult to separate cause and effect. Perhaps the greatest landslide in recent history occurred in 1911 at Usoy in the Pamir Mountains of Russia. Prince B. B. Galitzin, a pioneer of modern seismology, recorded earthquake waves on his seismograph near St. Petersburg that must have radiated from the landslide area over 3000 km away. He first thought that he had recorded a normal tectonic earthquake. It was not until 1915 that an expedition sent to investigate the Usoy landslide found that the slide involved 2.5 cu km of rock!

Rarely, very massive meteorites collide with the atmosphere or surface of our planet to produce an impact earthquake. A fascinating case is

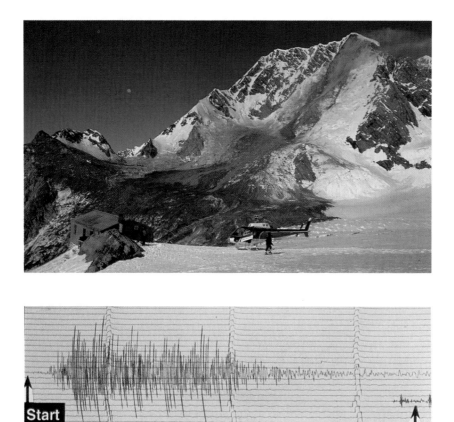

Top: The scene on Mt. Cook, New Zealand, after 14 million cubic meters of rock and snow hurled down the mountainside in an avalanche on December 15, 1991. *Bottom:* The seismic signature of the Mt. Cook avalanche recorded at a distance of 75 km. The wave crescendo equaled a tectonic earthquake of magnitude 3.9.

the Tunguska meteorite, which entered the Earth's atmosphere on June 30, 1908, in a remote region of Siberia. Under the stress and heat of its rapid deceleration in the atmosphere, the meteorite exploded less than 10 km above the Earth's surface, flattening a huge area of forest. Many seismographs in Russia and in Europe, as far away as 5000 km, recorded seismic waves. The readings were assumed at first to be the product of a great tectonic earthquake.

Several cases have been well documented of earthquakes set off after the injection of fluid into deep wells or the filling of large reservoirs. Although the mechanism is still thought to be the release of strain by fault fracture, these cases raise the question: To what extent does the pres-

ence of water in a well or reservoir trigger events that might otherwise have taken many years to occur?

A well-documented case history relates the experience at Lake Mead, which was filled in 1935 behind the Hoover Dam on the Colorado River. Before the lake's creation, there had been no historical record of earthquake activity in the area, but afterward small earthquakes became frequent. Moreover, local seismographic stations, established after the filling of the reservoir, showed that the number of shocks correlated rather closely with changes in reservoir loading.

The effect is most marked for large reservoirs exceeding 100 m in depth and 1 cu km in volume. The majority of such large reservoirs are, however, aseismic; of the 26 largest reservoirs in the world, only about 5 have undoubtedly induced earthquakes, including Kariba Dam in Zambia and the Aswan High Dam in Egypt. Perhaps the most viable explanation is that the rocks in the vicinity of the well or reservoir are already strained from tectonic forces, so existing faults are almost ready to slip. The head of water then adds a pressure pulse that increases the stresses in the rocks and triggers the slip.

Finally, human beings cause explosion earthquakes by detonation of chemicals and nuclear devices. In near-surface explosions, the compression of the rock in the fractured region produces seismic waves that travel outward in all directions. When the first compressive seismic wave reaches the surface, the ground arches outward; if the wave energy is sufficient, the soil and rock will be blasted away, as in a rock quarry, and fragments of rock will be thrown into the air.

Of course, people and animals sometimes produce earthquakes (usually small) in other ways, such as by mechanical bumping of the ground.

THE SLOW GROWTH OF ELASTIC ENERGY

Let us consider in more detail the cause of tectonic earthquakes. As time passes in seismically active regions, deep-seated forces underground steadily deform the rocks. A great deal of this deformation, at least at time scales of thousands of years, is in the form of elastic strain. The size and shape of a volume of rocks change, and if the forces are removed the rocks will spring back to their initial state, like a squeezed rubber ball.

Such elastic rock movements can be detected by careful systematic geodetic surveys, which allow the elastic and nonelastic (nonreversible) strains to be differentiated.

There are three major types of geodetic surveys useful for this purpose. In two, the degree of horizontal movement is determined. In the first type, small telescopes are used to measure angles between markers on the ground surface; this process is called triangulation. In the second, called trilateration, distances between markers on the surface are measured along extensive profiles. In a modern trilateration technique, light (sometimes a laser beam) is reflected from a mirror on a distant high point, using an instrument called a geodimeter, and the time it takes for the light to travel the two-way path is measured. Over long distances the speed of light varies with atmospheric conditions; thus, in a precise survey, small airplanes or helicopters fly along the lines of sight and measure the air temperatures and pressures so that corrections can be made. These surveys are found to be accurate to about 1.0 cm over a distance of 20 km.

The third type of survey determines the degree of vertical movement by establishing level lines across the countryside. Such leveling surveys simply measure differences in the elevation between vertical wooden rods placed at fixed bench marks at various points on the surface. Repetition of these surveys reveals any variations in these differences that occur between measurements. The bench marks are located on a national grid of fixed locations across the country. Wherever possible, level lines are extended to the continental edge, so that the mean sea level can be used as the reference point for determining the absolute change in land elevation. In recent years, geostationary satellites have also

At Parkfield, California, laser beams for taking geodetic measurements are directed at distant mirrors.

served as known reference points; distances are measured by the travel time of radio waves from transmitters at fixed points on the Earth's surface.

The various survey methods show that in seismically active areas such as California and Japan, the Earth's surface is moving horizontally and vertically in quite measurable amounts. They also show that in the stable areas of continents, such as the ancient rock masses of the Canadian and Australian shields, little change is taking place, at least during the recent past.

Perhaps the most important geodetic measurements of regional deformation related to earthquakes have come from California. There they began as early as 1850 and were crucial in developing the modern theory of earthquake genesis following the 1906 San Francisco earthquake. In recent decades, improved measurements have been made along the San Andreas fault system with an eye to earthquake prediction. Using optical and laser-beam geodimeters,

surveyors measure the distance between bench marks on the tops of mountains on each side of the San Andreas fault system. Trends in the strain are spectacularly clear: measurements show right-lateral deformation along the fault, whereas survey lines that do not lie across the major fault zone show very little change in length.

THE ELASTIC REBOUND THEORY

In scientific discovery it is often not the first description of an event or hypothesis that is remembered, but the one that convinces the scientific community that something new has indeed been found. Thus, the now generally accepted physical theory of earthquake generation by a fault rupture mechanism is held to have been first established by the convincing studies of the 1906 San Francisco earthquake. Before

1906, two sets of triangulation measurements had been taken across the region traversed by the San Andreas fault, one set for 1851–1865 and the other for 1874–1892. The American engineer H. F. Reid noticed that distant points on opposite sides of the fault had moved 3.2 m over the fifty-year period before 1906, with the western side moving north-northeast. When these measurements were compared with a third set taken just after the earthquake, it was found that significant horizontal shearing, displacing the rock parallel to the ruptured San Andreas fault, had occurred both before and after the earthquake.

Since this work of Reid, the seismological theory is that a natural earthquake is caused by sudden slip taking place successively along a geological fault in the upper part of the Earth. According to this view, called the elastic rebound theory, strain *slowly* builds up in the rocks over hundreds and even thousands of years. Finally, at the weakest part of the strained volume of rock, usually on a pre-existing fault, *sudden* slip occurs as the two opposing faces of the fault move in opposite directions. This slip spreads out along the fault face at a velocity that is less than that of seismic shear waves in the surrounding rocks. Stored elastic strain energy is released by the slip as the two sides of the fault rebound to a more or less unstrained position. It follows that, at least in most cases, the longer and wider the area of dislocation, the more energy will be released and the larger the tectonic earthquake will be.

Forces like those that produced the 1906 earthquake are drawn in the diagram on page 76. Imagine this illustration to be a bird's-eye view of a fence running at right angles across the San Andreas fault. The fence runs straight for

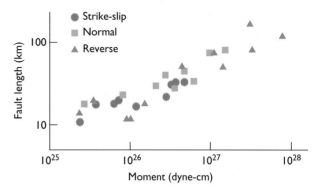

This plot of large intraplate earthquakes illustrates that the seismic moment increases with the length of the fault rupture.

many meters on each side of the fault line. Tectonic forces, shown as yellow arrows, are working to strain the elastic rocks. As they slowly do their work, the line bends, the left side shifting in relation to the right. The rock displacements amount to a few meters in the course of fifty years or so. Such straining cannot continue indefinitely; sooner or later the weakest rocks, or those at the point of greatest strain, break. This fracture is followed by a springing back, or rebounding, on each side of the fracture. Thus, in the figure, the rocks on both sides of the fault at D rebound to the points D_1 and D_2. The photograph shows the offset of a fence across the fault displacement after the 1906 earthquake rupture.

This elastic rebound has been confirmed over the years since 1906 to be the immediate cause of tectonic earthquakes. Like a watch spring that is wound tighter and tighter, the more that rocks are elastically strained, the more energy they store. When a fault ruptures, the elastic energy stored in the rocks is released quickly,

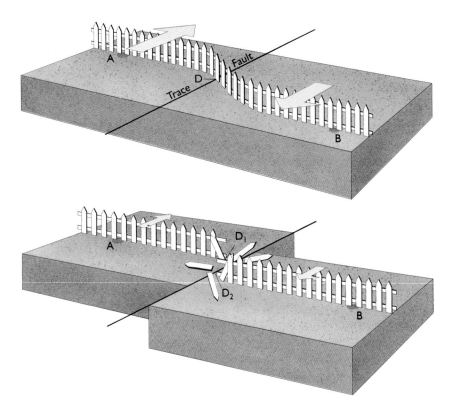

An aerial view of a fence crossing a fault trace shows the displacement that occurs as a result of elastic rebound. *Top:* In response to the action of tectonic forces, points A and B move in opposite directions, bending the fence across the fault. *Bottom:* Rupture occurs at D, and strained rocks on each side of the fault spring back to D_1 and D_2.

This fence running across the San Andreas fault in Marin County was offset 8.5 ft in the 1906 San Francisco earthquake as the land on the far side of the fault moved to the right.

partly as heat and partly as elastic waves. These waves constitute the earthquake.

Straining of rocks in the vertical direction is also common. In such cases, the elastic rebound occurs along dipping fault surfaces, causing vertical disruption in level lines at the surface and creating fault scarps. The fault scarps produced by large earthquake sources amount to many meters in height, sometimes extending along the strike of the rupture fault for tens or hundreds of kilometers.

Experiments performed in rock mechanics laboratories have elucidated the changes that occur in the rocks of the Earth as they are being strained in a pre-earthquake phase. In these experiments, samples of water-saturated rock are squeezed at high temperatures in hydraulic jacks. Such research indicates that the slow straining of the crust under the local tectonic forces produces a concentration of microcracks throughout the rock in the neighborhood of a tectonic fault. Slowly, water diffuses into and fills the cracks and pores of the rocks. During this period, the volume of the highly stressed region along the fault increases; initially this process of dilation further weakens the fault zone. At the same time, the presence of water in the cracks reduces the restraining forces and lowers the friction across the contiguous faces of the fault, allowing a segment to unlock so that a major crack extends by slip along the fault surface. In this way, the elastic rebound of the strained fault begins and spreads.

Earthquake foreshocks and aftershocks can also be understood by studying the process of crack development in the vicinity of the principal slip. A foreshock is caused by an incipient rupture in the strained and cracked material along the fault. The crack does not progress, however, because the physical conditions are not yet optimum. The restricted slip in foreshocks slightly alters the pattern of forces, the movement of water, and the distribution of microcracks. Eventually, a more extended rupture commences, producing the principal earthquake. The flinging of the rocks along the major rupture, together with the heavy shaking and the local generation of heat, leads to physical conditions along the fault zone very different from those before the main shock. The result is that additional small ruptures occur, producing aftershocks. Gradually, the strain energy in the region decreases, like a clock running down, until, perhaps after many months, stability returns.

THE LARGEST U.S. EARTHQUAKE IN FORTY YEARS

We tend to think that because a strong earthquake eases the strain on a fault, it will be followed by quiescence in a region once the aftershocks have ended. But a major fault is usually only one in a complex network of faults threading through a region. The cataclysmic release of strain on one fault may increase pressure on neighboring faults. The largest earthquake to strike the continental United States in recent years illustrates the unpredictable effects of a large earthquake on the seismicity of a region and hence on the immediate seismic hazard.

At 4:58 A.M. on Sunday, June 28, 1992, a strong shock struck near the town of Landers in the remote Mojave Desert of California. The surface wave magnitude of this, the principal earthquake, was 7.5 and the moment magnitude 7.3. A large series of major faults were found after-

77

ward to have rebounded, thus creating strong shaking over much of southern California and milder shaking as far away as Denver, Colorado.

Near the epicenter between the towns of Landers and Yucca Valley, approximately 30 km northeast of the San Andreas fault zone, inhabitants of this lightly populated area reported shaking at high intensity. Mr. Jerry Gobrogge described the motion that cost him the side wall of his bowling alley in Yucca Valley: "It was terrible, it was just terrible, it never quit, it just kept on shaking and it hasn't stopped." This earthquake, officially named the Landers earthquake, was the strongest since the often-cited seismic event in Kern County, California, in 1952. Yet because of its location in the desert, it resulted in only one death and 25 serious injuries. Over 77 homes were destroyed and 4300 damaged. The property losses were estimated at about $50 million.

Hundreds of seismologists and geologists who came gathering information in the ensuing days saw dramatic evidence of the fault rupture.

Spectacular right-lateral surface offsets traced the rupture of a series of strike-slip faults arranged "en-echelon," laid end to end with each fault somewhat to the right or left of the fault in front like a series of steps. This series of major faults had already been mapped on the California State geological map, but because they are separated at their ends by up to 10 km, they are thought to be separate faults rather than segments of one continuous deeper fracture. These separate faults are known to have slipped more than 12,000 years ago but are not believed to have been active since. In this light, an earthquake of magnitude 7.5 involving 80 km of fault dislocation overall was unexpected.

The surface slip measured along the fault ranged from an average of about 2 m near Landers, as shown in the photograph on the next page, to as much as 5.5 m along the northwestern part of the rupture. Also surprising were the substantial, 1-m-high scarps that appeared at bends in the fault segments along a limited part of the main rupture.

A pair of satellite images of an area 2.56 km across along the Emerson fault in the Mojave Desert, one of several faults that broke during the Landers earthquake. The image at left was taken on July 27, 1991, 11 months before the earthquake. In the image at right, taken just 27 days after the earthquake, ground cracks created by fault breakage during the earthquake are clearly evident, trending from upper left toward lower right. Motion across the fault at this site was about 4 m.

The fresh face of the Emerson fault scarp, showing slip lines (called slickensides), after the 1992 Landers earthquake.

A most unusual seismic chain reaction followed the main Landers earthquake. Although the main shock was succeeded by a large sequence of aftershocks along the slipped faults, as is the rule following large, shallow earthquakes, seismic activity within a much wider area increased dramatically and abruptly in the ensuing days. Three hours after the main shock, the ground again shuddered in a strong second earthquake ($M_s = 6.5$) centered near Big Bear Lake. This shock was generated by slip on a separate fault about 45 km from the first fault source. Computer models were used to calculate the changes in stress along the regional fault systems. The results indicated that slip on the faults that produced the Landers earthquake increased stress on the fault that produced the Big Bear earthquake. The computations also suggested that the Landers earthquake may have heightened the stress on the southern San Andreas fault, increasing the tendency for strike-slip shearing, while at the same time lowering the pressures that pin the sides of the San Andreas together, like an invisible row of staples. Both

these consequences may have increased the chance of a major future earthquake in the region.

In the 24 hours immediately following the Landers main shock, 11 separate earthquakes with magnitudes greater than 3.4 were located by seismographic networks within 600 km of its epicenter. Given the normal rate of earthquake occurrence in this region of California and Nevada, the odds of this conjunction of events taking place by chance alone is one in 100 billion. Indeed, this chance simultaneity would be one of the most improbable events in geological history! We must assume that the Landers earthquake caused this surge of earthquakes, either by directly increasing the elastic strain in the rocks or by the passage of seismic waves through each separate fault changing stresses on them.

Most difficult to understand were significant increases in the rate of small earthquakes occurring along the east side of the Sierra Nevada, from south of the Owens Valley north to the Long Valley Caldera, a distance of 400 km from Landers. Background seismicity also appeared to increase significantly as far north as Mono Basin,

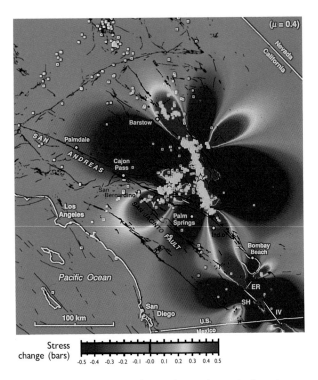

(μ = 0.4)

Barstow
Palmdale
SAN ANDREAS
Cajon Pass
San Bernardino
Los Angeles
SAN JACINTO FAULT
Palm Springs
Indio
Bombay Beach
Pacific Ocean
ER
SH
San Diego
IV
U.S.
Mexico
Nevada
California
100 km

Stress change (bars)
-0.5 -0.4 -0.3 -0.2 -0.1 -0.0 0.1 0.2 0.3 0.4 0.5

This map of southern California shows the region's main faults and the epicenters of earthquakes that occurred within 25 days of the Landers main shock. The colors show changes in stress caused by regional earthquakes from 1979 to 1992. Stress has increased on the San Andreas fault to the east of Cajon Pass and decreased to the west.

ments of the ground at stations at the north end of the fault were very much more energetic than those recorded adjacent to the fault in the south. A listener experiences this same effect when the sound level increases as a loudspeaker is moving closer. The technical term *directivity focusing* describes the concentration of energy in one direction caused by the movement of the source of the waves. This effect must be kept in mind when assessing predictions of strong ground motion in the vicinity of active faults. Because of it, motions can be either greater or less than the average values, depending on the direction of the rupture.

SEISMIC MOMENT

The mechanical model of a fault surface suddenly slipping in response to tectonic stresses has led to a most useful measure of overall earthquake size. This measure, mentioned in Chapter 3, is called the seismic moment; it was first proposed by the American seismologist K. Aki in 1966. It is now favored by seismologists because it is related directly to the physics of the fault rupture processes. Indeed, it can be used to infer geological properties along active fault zones.

The underlying mechanical concept of moment can be described by a simple experiment. Place both hands on opposite edges of a heavy table and push on one and pull on the other in a horizontal direction. The more widely separated the hands, the easier it is to rotate the table. In other words, the effort required to produce the rotation is reduced by increasing the leverage of the forces exerted by the two arms, even if the force on the hands remains the same. These two equal and opposite forces are termed the force

Mount Lassen, and Mount Shasta in extreme northern California, 800 km from the main ruptures. Research is continuing on these intriguing questions of posthumous remote seismicity.

Many accelerometers were triggered in the Landers earthquake; they wrote the signature of heavy shaking. At many sites around the fault source, these records make most sense when the dominant rupture is assumed to run northward from the hypocenter near Landers. The displace-

couple. The size of this couple is called the moment; its numerical value is simply the product of the value of one of the two forces and the distance between them.

This same idea is easily extended to the system of forces that produces slip on a geological fault. In this case, the seismic moment is defined as the product of three quantities: the elastic rigidity of the rocks, the area over which the force is applied, and the fault offset that takes place in the sudden slip. An advantage of this measure is that, unlike measures based on seismic wave amplitudes, the results are not distorted by any dissipation of energy through rock friction on the propagating wave. In suitable cases, the moment can be estimated simply from the length of the surface rupture measured in the field and the depth of the rupture inferred from the depths of the aftershock foci.

Seismic moments vary over many orders of magnitude from the smallest to the largest earthquake. Between a magnitude 2 and a magnitude 8 earthquake, the seismic moment ranges over six orders of magnitude. The moment of the 1906 San Francisco earthquake, generated by rupture of the San Andreas fault over 450 km, is estimated to have been more than 10 times the moment of the 1989 Loma Prieta earthquake, in which the rupture extended over only 45 km.

THE PROGRESSION OF A FAULT RUPTURE

A fault rupture begins at the earthquake focus within the crustal rocks and spreads outward in all directions in a plane along the fault surface. The edge of the rupture does not spread out uni-

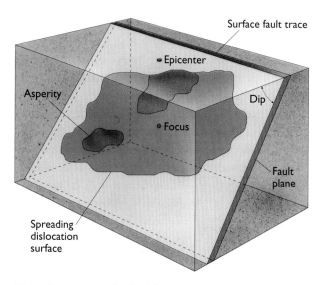

This side view into the Earth's crust shows a rupture moving outward along the dipping fault plane. At the asperities the rupture may change speed or temporarily come to a stop.

formly, but jerkily and irregularly, because faults vary in their physical properties from place to place. On the fault surface there are rough patches (often called asperities), changes in fault direction, and other structural complexities that provide *barriers* to the fault slip. Sometimes these barriers are broken by the rupture, but sometimes they remain unbroken. Then at some moment, because of the rearrangement of elastic forces, the rupture front may suddenly break free on the far side of the barrier and swiftly propagate to catch up with the rupture at adjacent points. If a barrier breaks after the principal earthquake has finished, the result is an aftershock. Observations of actual slip in the field and small-scale modeling in rock-testing laboratories have confirmed that roughness along the fault produces intermittent locking and release.

The process of earthquake generation was well described by Reid in his study of the 1906 San Francisco earthquake: "It is probable that the whole movement at any one point does not take place at once, but proceeds in irregular steps, but more-or-less sudden stopping of the movement and the friction gives rise to the vibrations [waves] that are propagated to a distance. The sudden starting of the motion would produce vibrations just as would sudden stopping." Much of the higher-frequency complexity observed in earthquake waves arises from the changes in velocity of the rupture front. These velocity changes produce bursts of incoherent waves that are dissimilar in frequency, amplitude, and phase and add to the complexity of waveforms.

In any earthquake, the extent of fault rupture depends on the history and variation in strain of the rock throughout the region and on the properties of the faulted rock and the slip surface. The rupture spreads outward until it reaches places at which the rock is not sufficiently strained to provide the energy for further extension. Then the rupture episode stops.

In its upward progression toward the Earth's surface, the fault rupture is driven by the stored energy in elastic, brittle rocks. At depths of 1 or 2 km, however, the rupture begins to encounter less rigid rocks that have been weakened by fracturing and weathering. Particularly near the surface of the fault zone there is a succession of fault gouge and shattered and sheared rock that tends to slip gradually. This material is relatively ineffective in generating seismic waves.

If a rupture reaches the surface (as happens in only a minority of shallow earthquakes), it produces a visible fault break. A scientific first

A steplike series of surface fault scarps formed in the fault rupture that caused the 1983 Borah Peak earthquake.

was witnessed in conjunction with the Borah Peak, Idaho, earthquake of October 28, 1983, when two elk hunters were amazed to see a prominent fault scarp nearly 2 m high suddenly form about 20 m in front of their road vehicle. They described, first, dizziness (perhaps P waves from the distant focus?) and then, in 2 to 3 seconds, a more or less simultaneous perception of the new fault scarp and violent rocking of the vehicle.

The elastic rebound theory of earthquake genesis is supported by the properties of seismic waves recorded on seismographs around the world. The recorded waves agree with the fault slip observed in the field in those cases where surface breakage occurs and is accessible. Among the best recorded earthquakes of recent decades that illustrate clearly the effect of the fault rupture source on seismic waves is the San Fernando earthquake that shook California in 1971.

THE FAMOUS PACOIMA DAM ACCELEROGRAM

Most people were preparing for the day's work when a strong shock struck the San Fernando Valley, just north of Los Angeles, on February 9, 1971, at 6:42 A.M. Pacific standard time, radiating seismic waves that were strongly felt throughout the Los Angeles metropolitan area. By good fortune, I was able, with a fellow seismologist, to take an early plane from Berkeley to Los Angeles and drive into the damaged area, where we were pointed toward spectacular damage and ground displacements in the city of Sylmar. On our arrival there, we immediately observed large breaks and offsets in streets, curbs, and sidewalks, which extended from one city block to another. We had clearly stumbled on the major fault rupture that had produced the earthquake a few hours earlier. Teams of geologists later determined that the fresh surface faulting extended for about 15 km along the foothills of the San Gabriel Mountains.

The fault offsets indicated both thrusting and left-lateral strike-slip motion, the strike varying from place to place, but with a mean value of N72°W and a dip of 45°N. This thrusting was such that the San Gabriel Mountains moved southward over the San Fernando Valley. Evidence of thrust faulting along the mountain

front was not uncommon in this region, although the actual faulting did not coincide with faults that then appeared on the available maps.

More than 200 strong-motion accelerometers were triggered in this earthquake, yielding records of great importance. Several of the measured peak accelerations were over 25 percent of the acceleration of gravity. The record that drew the most attention, however, was one obtained near the abutment of the concrete dam at the Pacoima reservoir, then dry. The maximum acceleration exceeded gravity on the horizontal components of ground motion at Pacoima. In other words, if this acceleration had been in the vertical direction, objects would have been hurled upward. This measurement was the first instrumental validation that accelerations of the ground could exceed that of gravity since R. D. Oldham's account of the great Assam earthquake in 1897. Despite this high peak value, the concrete dam was not damaged, nor was the chimney of the nearby caretaker's residence.

As it turned out, the Pacoima accelerometers had been placed on rock directly above the slipped fault surface. It had taken P waves about 2.7 seconds of travel to span the distance from the slip zone to the instruments. Because the ruptured fault could be well delineated, seismologists had the opportunity to determine if the fault source of an earthquake could be used to explain the ground motion recorded so near to the release of the energy. The resulting explanation brought to light some important features of earthquakes near to the rupturing fault.

The wave pattern obtained at Pacoima, shown on the next page, gives the history of the fault rupture. We start at the beginning of one of the horizontal components of ground motion and follow the onset of the various wave types

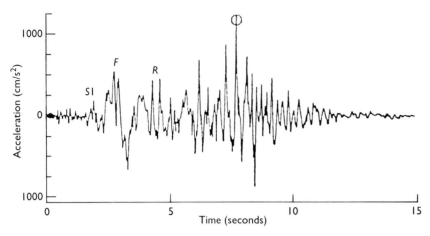

The Pacoima Dam accelerogram from the 1971 San Fernando earthquake.

through the coda waves to the end of the motion. Notice first small ground accelerations lasting for approximately 1.7 seconds. These are undoubtedly the main *P* waves, the first to reach the Pacoima site. This precursory motion is followed by a direct *S* wave, labeled *S*1 on the accelerogram. Its onset heralds the beginning of the longer-period motion. If we assume a reasonable rupture velocity of 3.0 km/s, the rupture would travel from the focus along the dipping fault to a point just adjacent to the Pacoima Dam in about 5.5 seconds. After an interval of 5.5 minus 2.7 seconds on the record, we observe the arrival of the longer-period pulse marked *F*. We can thus interpret the energetic *F* pulse as the result of the rock rebounding on the fault adjacent to the Pacoima site. The sudden displacement of the rocks (or fling of the ground) travels outward as an *S* wave. Because of its relatively large amplitude and period, this wave can be very destructive to buildings near fault ruptures.

When the rupture broke the ground surface along the San Gabriel Mountains, the earthquake entered a "break-out phase" during which

Rayleigh surface waves of various frequencies were produced. The rolling ground motion of these waves reached Pacoima about 4.3 seconds after the arrival of the *P* motion, at the point marked *R* in the accelerograms. Subsequently, waves of various frequencies and amplitudes arrived at Pacoima from successively more distant sections of the fault.

The final section of the Pacoima accelerograms, after the arrival of the *R* pulse, contains high-frequency seismic waves having some of the highest amplitudes, including the maximum acceleration spike. These late bursts of high-frequency energy were probably released from patches of roughness (the asperities on the fault surface) as the fault rupture extended from depth upward to its extremity. The last wave to arrive consisted of high-frequency energy radiated from just below the southern end of the San Fernando fault rupture. The spike with the maximum amplitude appearing on the record at about 8 seconds after the arrival of the *P* wave was probably produced by some particularly strong asperity located at some distance to the side along the ruptured fault surface.

DEEP EARTHQUAKES

There is a class of earthquake that may not be generated by simple elastic rebound along a fault. These earthquakes have foci deep below the surface of the Earth. Since 1964 the International Seismological Center in Britain has catalogued more than 60,000 earthquakes with focal depths greater than 70 km, comprising 22 percent of all earthquakes of known depth. Although these deep earthquakes are generally weaker at the surface than shallow earthquakes, sometimes they can be destructive. For example, an earthquake under the Carpathian Mountains on March 4, 1977, caused considerable damage in Bucharest, Romania, even though its focal depth was about 90 km.

The deepest seated earthquakes have foci at about 680 km. The special impact of these deep earthquakes on a number of geological theories will be discussed in Chapter 5. Because the deepest of them occur where the rocks are subjected to great pressures and temperatures (about 2000°C), they also shed light on the behavior of materials under such extreme conditions.

At present the mechanism for these very deep focus earthquakes remains speculative, although it is agreed that the elastic rebound by slip along faults in brittle rocks that explains shallow earthquakes is difficult to apply. From the early days of instrumental seismology, deep-focus earthquakes have been controversial. It took considerable time for seismologists to accept the existence of these earthquakes at all. In 1922, the Oxford professor H. H. Turner, then director of the International Seismological Summary, pointed out some discrepancies in travel times from earthquakes around the world, particularly from Japanese earthquakes. For some earthquakes, the seismic waves arrived later at the antipodal stations than was normal, and for others they arrived earlier. Turner suggested a normal focal depth of 200 km.

This suggestion gained the attention of Sir Harold Jeffreys, who for forty years was the leading theoretician in seismology. Jeffreys objected that because the heat and pressure at depths below 50 km would soften the rock from brittle conditions, it would flow rather than fracture suddenly as the strain increased. Jeffreys proposed to test the Turner view by examining seismograms for surface waves generated by the postulated deep earthquakes. According to theory, a vibration of a particular shape, such as those shown on page 36, cannot be generated if the system is disturbed at a place where that shape has no motion. It follows that because motions in surface waves are restricted to surficial depths they cannot be generated by deep sources. Jeffreys later recalled how he had "pointed out to Turner that a deep focus earthquake would excite very small surface waves or none. This could be tested by a simple inspection of the seismograms, but Turner was so satisfied by his own arguments that he would not look."

The matter was settled decisively by Kiyoo Wadati while he was working at the Meteorological Agency in Tokyo. In 1928 he published strong direct evidence that earthquake sources under Japan ranged between tens and hundreds of kilometers in depth. Soon afterward, other seismologists confirmed Wadati's results by applying Jeffreys's test. Yet there remained Jeffreys's critical objection: How is the stress released in rocks that are greatly compressed by overlying material? If a crack opened, the weight of the rock above would weld it together again.

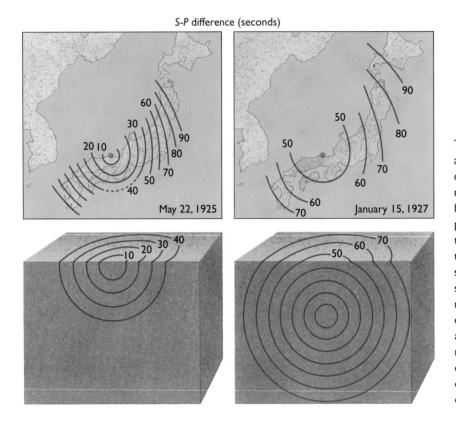

S-P difference (seconds)

May 22, 1925

January 15, 1927

The interval between the arrival of P and S waves distinguishes shallow and deep earthquakes. The contour numbers give the time interval between S and P wave arrivals at each point. A study by Kiyoo Wadati found that the difference in S and P arrival times at the epicenter of a near-surface 1925 event was less than 10 seconds, but the delay increased rapidly with distance, whereas the S-P difference in a 1927 earthquake was at least 40 seconds, but it increased more slowly. From this and other evidence, Wadati was able to assign a depth of 400 km to the 1927 earthquake focus.

If deformation took place at all at such high temperatures, it would be by plastic flow.

Seismologists began to look for more detailed clues in the form of differences between shallow and deep earthquake sources. One difference was that deep earthquakes generally have very few aftershocks. For example, in 1970 probably the largest deep-focus earthquake in over a quarter of a century occurred under Colombia at a depth of 650 km and a magnitude of 7.6. Seismographs detected no aftershocks at all following this event. After large shallow earthquakes, the foci of aftershocks usually follow close to the plane of the fault that has slipped. By contrast, even when aftershocks accompany deep earthquakes, they are more or less randomly distributed around the initial focus.

These differences suggested that the cause of deep earthquakes might be a sudden change in the volume of the rocks, resulting from a change in the phase state of the mineral material, very much as water increases in volume when it changes to ice. The sudden dilation of the rocks would produce seismic waves. This hypothesis would require that there be either an implosion or an explosion of wave energy; hence, seismographs around the world would detect only compressional or only dilational onsets, respectively, of the *P* waves. Such a consistent pattern of onsets is not found, however. The first motions of *P* waves on seismograms vary from upward to downward in various zones of the Earth, much as do the onsets of *P* waves from shallow earthquakes. In addition, as well as *P* waves, deep earthquakes produce significant *S*-wave motion, which would not be the case if an explosion or implosion were the only impulse, because such sources produce little shearing of the rocks.

Two specific mechanisms have recently been proposed for deep earthquakes. The first suggests that water fundamentally influences the brittle and plastic properties of the rock at the high temperatures and pressures of lower depths. Many minerals in the Earth's rocks contain water of crystallization, which may become mobilized at high temperatures and pressures. Indeed, in laboratory experiments, rocks that contain the green hydrous mineral serpentine are found to sustain brittle fracture under these conditions. What seems to be required is an intimate migra-

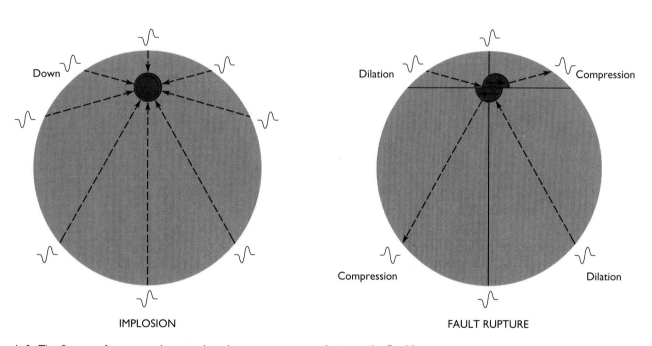

IMPLOSION · FAULT RUPTURE

Left: The *P* waves from an underground implosion arrive everywhere on the Earth's surface as a downward movement of the ground. *P* waves from an explosion would arrive everywhere as an upward movement. *Right:* The *P* waves produced by a rupturing fault initially push the ground upward in two diagonally opposite quadrants and pull the ground downward in the other two.

tion of fluid throughout the pores of the rock, which lubricates potential fractures and faults and allows slip to occur.

The second of these current hypotheses puts the unsatisfactory hypothesis of a sudden change of mineral phase into a different form. The phase transitions are thought to take place between the boundaries of rock lenses, perhaps where fluid conditions are particularly favorable for sudden transition. Along pre-existing grain boundaries the crystal structure would change rapidly, thus weakening the bonds across the discontinuity.

To test these hypotheses, conditions in the deep Earth have been re-created in the laboratory by squeezing tiny samples of rock between two diamonds like a nutcracker. A laser beam shone through the diamonds heats the rock and also allows any sudden physical transition to be photographed. Acoustic sensors detect any sudden release of energy—the analogue of an earthquake. By these methods it is hoped that the long puzzle of the causes of deep earthquakes can be resolved, perhaps even during the lifetime of Dr. Wadati, who in 1993 maintains an interest in the subject at the age of 91.

DISTINGUISHING UNNATURAL AND NATURAL EARTHQUAKES

One special class of seismic source has been of deep concern to the people of the world since the end of World War II. These are explosions of nuclear weapons in underground or underwater tests. Seismographic stations around the world made their first measurements of seismic waves from a nuclear source on July 24, 1946,

when a nuclear device was detonated underwater near Bikini Atoll in the Pacific Ocean. Although the number of recordings was meager, they gave a glimpse of the geological discoveries that could be achieved from such controlled artificial earthquakes. For example, the seismic explosion method of oil exploration, with all the experimental controls that accompany it, could be extended to problems concerning the structure and constitution of the Earth's deep interior. Even though valuable geophysical information has indeed been derived in this way, nuclear weapons testing has mainly involved seismology in quite a different way.

Because nuclear explosions yield radioactive products that can seriously harm living matter, by the mid-1950s many people around the world had become concerned about the swiftly growing amount of radioactive particles in the atmosphere being produced by aboveground tests of nuclear weapons. For this reason, the testing programs of nuclear devices were modified to minimize the radioactive fallout in the atmosphere. Underwater tests also proved to be hazardous. In March 1954, for example, the American test of a 15-megaton fusion device called Bravo exposed a number of Marshall Islanders to high amounts of radiation after it spread radioactive particles over an unexpectedly large area. Worldwide attention was ensured when two weeks later a Japanese fishing boat, ironically called the *Lucky Dragon*, docked at Yazu Harbor in Japan carrying 23 crew members who had fallen ill from exposure to radioactive fallout.

In 1958 President Eisenhower responded to the growing apprehension by suggesting that technical talks be held to discuss the policing of a test ban treaty. In July 1958, a historic conference of technical experts convened in Geneva established the basis for the design of a treaty banning weapons tests anywhere in the environment, both in the atmosphere and underground. In policing any such agreement, each side would need to be able to say with almost certainty that the other side was not cheating.

The scientists quickly came to an agreement that "the sensitivity of modern physical, chemical, and geophysical methods of measurement makes it possible to detect nuclear explosions at considerable distances. Thus, it is known that explosions of high yield which are set off on the surface of the Earth and in the lower part of the atmosphere can be detected without difficulty at points of the globe that are very remote from the site of the explosion." The committee listed a number of reliable clues for identifying atmospheric and surface explosions, such as sound waves and radioactive debris.

The only difficult problem was the detection and discrimination of underground explosions. If nuclear devices were exploded beneath the ground, the telltale signals in the atmosphere that follow aboveground explosions would not be present. However, large explosions, nuclear or chemical, under the surface of the ground do produce earthquake waves.

The main clue that such an explosive event had occurred at all would be the detection on seismographs of the seismic waves spreading out from the explosion. Detecting these waves was the first concern. However, natural seismicity is high in parts of the United States, the former Soviet Union, China, and other countries capable of producing nuclear weapons. These tectonic earthquake sources would also produce seismograms. How could the waves from man-made earthquakes be distinguished from the waves from a natural earthquake?

THE LIMITED TEST BAN TREATY

In the United States, nuclear explosive devices were tested underground largely in a remote part of the Nevada desert, which became famous as the Nevada Test Site, or NTS. Up to the present, many hundreds of underground explosions have taken place at this site. Most of them have produced seismic waves that have been recorded around the world.

When a buried nuclear device is detonated, the rock above is so shattered that often a subsidence crater forms. The photograph on page 90 shows dust clouds rising above a subsidence crater at the instant of its formation during a test of a nuclear device at NTS in mid-1969. The nuclear explosion melts and vaporizes the surrounding rock; seismic pressure waves travel outward, lifting and fracturing the rock at the surface above it. Gas pressure in the cavity then drops, within minutes or hours, and the shattered rock immediately above the spherical hole falls downward in an avalanche. As a result, a cylindrical chimney thrusts toward the surface above the debris-filled cavity. If the test device is small relative to its depth of burial, this chimney may never reach the surface. If it is large enough and if the upper ground layers prove too weak to hold their own weight, broken rock continues to cave in to the surface. In the latter case, a "sink" is formed at the surface that from the air resembles a large saucer with cracks and scalloping around the edges. Such a depression can be observed from high-flying airplanes or satellite cameras. If an underground nuclear explosion is to be kept secret, the appearance of a sink would have to be prevented by boring emplacement holes in alluvial and soft rock deep enough to secure a wide margin of

Dust clouds rise at the instant that a subsidence crater is formed after an underground nuclear explosion in mid-1969 at the Nevada Test Site.

safety. Even then, the chimney might collapse eventually, exposing the clandestine test. Even if no surface clues appear, the original explosion and the heaving of the rock produce effects that cannot be concealed by even the deepest burial. Irretrievably, elastic waves speed outward through the Earth and announce that a nuclear earthquake has occurred.

One critical difference between a natural earthquake and an explosion results because, unlike a natural earthquake, an explosion in an underground spherical cavity or underwater is a symmetrical wave source. The first P and S waves of a natural earthquake come from the focus or the initial point of rupture of the rock. At some observational points on the Earth's sur-face, the P waves arrive as an upward push of the surface rocks, corresponding to a compression of the ground; whereas at other observational points, the P waves arrive as a downward pull of the surface rocks, corresponding to a dilation. These pushes and pulls determine the direction of the first ground motion, or the polarity of the first-arriving wave. In sharp contrast, the initial P wave from a symmetrical wave source such as a nuclear explosion is recorded on seismographs everywhere as a push of the ground because the explosion drives the rock around it outward in every direction. In principle, these quite distinct patterns should expose the type of source un-equivocally. In practice, because of complicated rock structures, the P polarities from an explosion are sometimes found to occur in a jumble of directions, and especially for small events, the fault rupture mechanism does not come through clearly.

Fortunately, polarity patterns are not the only difference between the two types of sources. Because fault ruptures are relatively large, the source of the waves in a natural earthquake covers a larger area. The energy release in an explosion is much more concentrated around a point in the rock than it is in fault rupture. Thus, the P and S wave shapes of a natural earthquake are usually different from those produced by underground explosions, at least down to earthquakes of quite small sizes.

At the beginning of the research for a Comprehensive Test Ban Treaty, the snag was that, in order to employ and refine these basic differences between the two types of earthquake sources, there needed to be a leap forward in the fidelity and sensitivity of the recording systems. Of equal importance, seismologists required additional experience to see which set of clues would unequivocally distinguish one source from the other by looking at seismograph readings. Moreover, in an acceptable monitoring system the seismographs could not be operated too far from the test sites within each country. If they were only available at distant places outside national boundaries, then the effects of variations in the rock structures of the Earth might alter the P and S wave motions enough to blunt the distinctions. Such considerations led to two unnegotiable conclusions: an effective monitoring and treaty control system must be defined, and modern earthquake observatories must be built that could record uniformly both earthquakes and underground explosions around the world.

It was decided that until these steps were taken, a Comprehensive Test Ban Treaty would not be workable unless each side had free entry to the testing sites in any country. Because such on-site inspection was, at that stage of the Cold War, unacceptable, the alternative was to negotiate a limited ban that forbade tests of nuclear weapons above the ground in peacetime. The Limited Test Ban Treaty was signed in Moscow on August 5, 1963. It was the turning point in the history of the control of nuclear explosions; but, because of the earthquake confusion, it specifically excluded underground tests.

As a way to increase the ability to detect underground nuclear tests, many countries began major improvements in earthquake recording and research. Among the beneficiaries were government seismological research institutes in the United States and other countries and seismological research groups in universities. Most impressively, a global network of standardized seismographs in many countries was established, and research seismologists were given free access to the recordings obtained from it. This new earthquake recording system opened up research opportunities that hitherto had only been dreamed about. Seismologists no longer had to envy physics laboratories with their high-energy particle accelerators or astronomical observatories with their sophisticated telescopes. Ultimately, following a hectic timetable, U.S. government seismologists had installed by the 1960s much upgraded seismographs in about 120 stations distributed in 60 countries. These seismographs were the basis of a new era in the study of earthquakes and the paths along which they travel through the Earth that lasted until the new wave of digital seismographs arrived in the 1980s.

CLUES FOR DISCRIMINATION

The year 1974 saw further progress with the signing in Moscow of the Threshold Test Ban Treaty. This agreement restricted underground testing of nuclear devices to yields exceeding 150 kilotons. Seismologists continued to prepare for the eventuality of a future comprehensive treaty, which would strictly limit or even prohibit all types of nuclear weapons tests by any country. The first step toward such a treaty was to ensure that all earthquakes down to quite small magnitudes could be recorded without exception outside the boundaries of the testing country. With this restriction, it was found that seismic events could be detected down to about magnitude 3.5, which is equivalent to about 1 kiloton, much smaller than the first atomic bomb dropped on Hiroshima. Even this limit in size meant that more than 5000 natural earthquakes around the world would have to be scrutinized each year for the telltale signs of a surreptitious explosion.

After considerable research, seismologists have arrived at three preferred methods to separate the two classes of earthquakes. The most important discriminant is the depth of the source of the seismic event. Earlier in this chapter, we described why fault ruptures at depths greater than about 2 km do not generate significant seismic waves. A nation that would seek to cheat on a test ban treaty, therefore, would have to contemplate drilling holes for each secret test to depths greater than 2 km. By contrast, the usual burial depth for underground tests in Nevada is about 500 m. Drilling operations for deep emplacement would be costly and could be easily observed by surveillance satellites.

Second, although P-wave polarities cannot always be trusted, the form of the wave shapes provides a strong clue to the type of earthquake source. The complexity of the P waveforms may be dramatically different even for a natural earthquake and an explosion not far apart. The discriminant may fail, however, if the surface rock above the explosion rapidly breaks up.

A more reliable clue emerged as seismologists sorted out effective discriminants from about 1966 onward. Because of the enhanced global seismographic observatories, seismologists can now reliably calculate and compare earthquake magnitudes of different types for both natural and artificial earthquakes. The recording stations need not be near the event to provide the

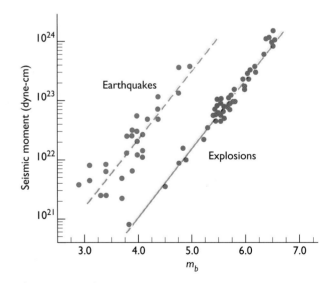

A comparison between seismic moment and one type of magnitude (m_b) calculated from distant seismograms of underground explosions and tectonic earthquakes.

needed measurements of wave amplitude. The new clue is well illustrated by the comparison of body-wave magnitudes (m_b) against seismic moment values (M). As shown in the graph on page 92, explosions produce smaller M values (smaller surface waves) than do natural earthquakes for the same m_b value (equal P waves). The contrast has been validated by comparing measurements from many North American and Soviet explosions and earthquakes. When M and m_b values from many such events are plotted, the points from explosions fall below those for natural earthquakes in the magnitude range down to at least $m_b = 3.5$.

Further work is needed to increase the confidence of discrimination when the recorded earthquakes come from small underground events with seismic magnitudes less than about $m_b = 3.5$. Sources this small might be large chemical explosions for mining and engineering purposes. Testers might be able to camouflage small explosions by firing bombs at the time of a nearby earthquake or muffle them by firing the devices in very soft rock or in a large underground rock cavity. Nevertheless, seismologists are now confident that they can distinguish between small natural and unnatural earthquakes in almost all practical cases. Even after the change in relations between the great powers, the problem remains important because of the danger of proliferation of nuclear weapons into smaller nations around the world.

5

THE EARTH'S CRUST AND PLATES

BY THE 1960S, the global network of seismographic observatories had revealed intriguing geological patterns. First, earthquakes are, for the most part, concentrated in relatively narrow belts in geologically young regions. Both earthquakes and volcanoes are common along the Pacific Rim, for example, and earthquake epicenters map out lines through the center of the oceans. In sharp contrast, other areas, such as the interior of Antarctica, are almost completely aseismic. Second, the types of faulting that produce earthquakes are also not random but have a close correlation to particular large-scale geological features. Thrust faults are common in mountain ranges, for example, whereas the earthquakes that map the connections between undersea ridges in mid-ocean are usually generated by strike-slip faults. What was still not available in the 1960s, however, was

The San Andreas fault forms part of the boundary
between two of the large plates that compose
the Earth's surface.

an overriding conception that could explain these global features and even predict others.

In revealing these patterns, the network of seismographic observatories produced its greatest scientific reward: it made a crucial contribution to the construction in the 1970s of a geophysical theory with enough breadth and depth to explain the major geological features of the Earth. Known as the theory of plate tectonics, it has to a large extent provided an evolutionary explanation for the distribution not only of earthquakes but also of volcanoes, high mountain ranges, ocean trenches, and other major geological structures. This modern view holds that the same global "tectonic" forces are the underlying cause of all these phenomena. (The word *tectonics* means simply the large-scale deformation of the Earth resulting from forces in its interior.) According to the plate tectonics theory, the locations of earthquakes and the fault mechanisms that generate them are the result of a systematic movement of the outer 200 km or so of the Earth's interior. To understand the forces that cause this movement, we first examine the structure of this outer rocky shell and the increase in temperature with depth within it.

THE CONCEPT OF A CRUST

By the end of the last century, it had been recognized that the temperature in mines and bore holes increases with depth. In 1889 the Reverend Osmond Fisher commented in his widely read book, *Physics of the Earth's Crust,*

There is no fact more firmly established in terrestrial physics than that the temperature of the rocks at the Earth's surface increases with increasing depths. Even in the frozen soil of Siberia, this increase of temperature is found to prevail although the frozen soil is congealed to a depth of 620 ft. In mining operations, this gradual increase of temperature becomes a very serious consideration, rendering labor at great depths a very severe trial for the constitution of the workmen. This increase in temperature, although universal, is not everywhere the same. The average is about 1°C for 50 ft of descent.

The increase in temperature with depth means that heat is flowing upward from the Earth's interior to its surface. In more recent years, geophysicists have measured the amount of heat flowing through the surface rocks both on continents and at the ocean floor. The flow is not measured directly but is calculated from the vertical temperature gradient and the heat conductivity, which is a measure of the ease with which the rocks transport heat. The vertical temperature gradient is obtained by measuring the temperature at various depths below the surface. Under the oceans, metal cylinders are dropped into the soft sediments and then retrieved with the mud core; along the cylinders are electric thermometers that measure the temperature at intervals. In the continents, thermometers are placed at various levels in mines or bore holes drilled into the rock. The thermal conductivity of the rock is measured from sample rock cores taken back to the laboratory.

Heat flow is usually relatively high in volcanic areas and in geothermal areas, where heat is brought to the surface by circulating water (hot springs, geysers, and so forth). It is relatively low in old, stable continental regions, which may have remained undisturbed by geological processes for millions of years. In general, heat flow decreases as the age of continental geological provinces increases and also as the age of the ocean floor increases. Usually, the heat flow ranges from 20 to 120 milliwatts per square meter, with a global average of about 60 milliwatts per square meter. Most heat flow values lie within 30 percent of the average value. Although patterns of heat flow may differ strikingly within continental and oceanic regions, the most frequently observed values are the same for oceans and continents. The sources of this interior heat are mainly the original heat from the Earth's primitive, possibly molten state and the heat produced by the decay of the radioactive atoms of unstable elements in the rocks.

Using these heat flow values, we can extrapolate the temperatures of the rocks deep within the Earth. The calculations indicate that at depths of 30 to 50 km the temperature is somewhere between 500 and 800°C. These values are high, but not extreme; the temperatures reached in blast furnaces and erupted magma are commonly between 1000 and 1500°C. Nevertheless, it was recognized early that if temperatures continued to increase at such a rate, the rocks of the Earth, rather than being rigid as observed at the surface and in deep mines, would soften and even liquefy. A common model at the time of Osmond Fisher, for example, held that the primitive Earth was wholly fluid. As heat from the surface was conducted away into space, the outer rocks cooled enough to solidify, thus forming an outer skin or crust. An analogy is the solid crust that forms on the top of molten slag in an iron furnace.

Temperature changes alone, however, cannot completely define the state of the rocks deep

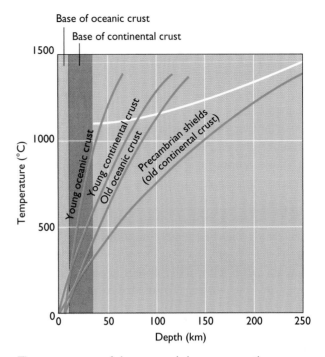

The temperature of the crust and the upper mantle increases with depth according to the age of the rock and whether it is oceanic or continental.

underground. Pressure also increases with depth, and an increase in pressure would tend to counteract the liquefying effects of higher temperatures. Surprisingly, even today the exact conditions for change from the brittle to the viscous state cannot be predicted exactly. Therefore, the melting of complicated mineral assemblages, such as are found in rocks, is not completely understood, and the temperature and pressure at the transition between solid and liquid, particularly if water is present, are uncertain.

By contrast, evidence from earthquake waves on the elastic state of rocks at depth is unequivocal. S waves from earthquakes cannot propagate through fluids, yet they are observed, with only few exceptions, traveling to depths of 2900 km. The rocks almost everywhere in the outer part of the Earth, down to depths of almost half the radius, must have significant rigidity. These rigid rocks make up the Earth's crust and, farther down, its mantle.

The first clear seismological evidence on the separate nature and thickness of the crust came at the beginning of the century, when it was inferred from earthquake recordings that there is a marked structural change at a distance of about 30 to 50 km below the surface of the continents, depending on the geographic location. This famous early work was performed by Andrija Mohorovičić of the Zagreb Seismographic Observatory in Croatia. While analyzing P and S

waves on seismograms recorded close to the epicenter of a Croatian earthquake on October 8, 1909, Mohorovičić noticed that some waves seemed to arrive later than expected for waves running along the surface of the Earth. To explain the delay, he decided that downward-heading P and S waves had been refracted along and up from a boundary at about 54 km depth. Subsequent studies showed that what has come to be called the Mohorovičić discontinuity, or Moho for short, is worldwide, although its average depth is considerably less than 54 km and it is not always a sharp transition. This boundary separates the crust from the mantle below.

EXPLORING THE CRUST

The early seismological work by only a few seismographic stations gave an impression that the crust everywhere had a bland architecture. (It is surprising that this view became widespread among geologists, who after all are very aware of the complexity of surface features.) According to early assumptions, the continental crust consisted of only two main rock layers; recent seismological observations, however, reveal more irregularity. Indeed, crustal properties may vary greatly, especially under the shallow seas and mountainous continental regions. Few regions have a crust with a geology as simple as twin layers.

Modern geophysical field measurements, in which earthquake studies have played a central part, have provided considerable detail on these crustal variations. Many studies on land, of both artificial seismic sources and natural earthquakes, have determined the physical properties of the rocks in the geologically diverse continental

Andrija Mohorovičić (1857–1936), the Croatian seismologist who discovered the sharp boundary at the base of the crust.

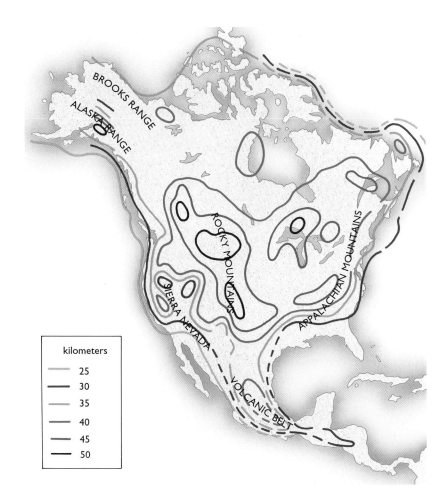

kilometers

    25

    30

    35

    40

    45

    50

Crustal thicknesses in North America, given here in kilometers, increase under mountain ranges and decrease near the ocean.

crust. The simplest structures and the most uniform thicknesses are to be found in the crusts of the ancient Precambrian shield regions, extensive blocks of rock such as occur in Siberia, Canada, and Australia that have not been disturbed since the end of the Precambrian era almost a billion years ago. Younger regions such as western North America have crustal structures composed of layers of varying thickness and dip.

Part of the effort to resolve the detailed structure of crustal rocks relies on advanced techniques developed in the oil exploration industry.

Instead of natural earthquakes, a vibration mechanism mounted on a truck and driven by a large motor serves as the source of the seismic wave energy. For about 20 seconds, the vibrators impart vertical forces up to about 30 tons over 2 sq m of ground surface. The force produced in these artificial earthquakes varies in time approximately like a sine wave, but it has a slowly shifting frequency that varies linearly from about 8 to 32 Hz during the 20-second duration of the vibrations. The signals reflect from structures in the crust and are recorded on magnetic tape by an array of many seismographs set out in a pro-file across the ground surface. In some ambitious experiments, a hundred seismographs have been spaced at intervals of 100 m along a profile 10 km long. The method eliminates the need to drill holes for explosives and allows scientists to control the characteristics of the wave sources more precisely.

The spectacular results of one such experiment are shown on this page. This work was carried out in 1976 and 1977 along the Wind River uplift in the Wind River Mountains of Wyoming by a group from the Department of Geological Sciences at Cornell University in New York. The picture of the side elevation of the Earth's crust was formed by displaying, after computer processing, the two-way travel times of the seismic P waves downward from the vibra-

tors and up to the surface again. To convert the time roughly to depth in kilometers, multiply the vertical scale by 3. If we follow the profile from the southwest to the northeast, we first see reflections from numerous layers of sediment in the Green River basin. These sedimentary rocks attain a maximum thickness of 12 km along the section and are gently folded. As we move toward the Wind River Mountains, we see steeply dipping reflectors defining thrust planes that have plunged downward into the crust (see arrow from B to D in the figure). The presence of thrust planes agrees with surface geological evidence that younger sedimentary rocks in the Green River basin have been overturned by Precambrian rocks of the Wind River Mountains. A continuation of the profile not reproduced in the figure shows that the thrust plane goes past the

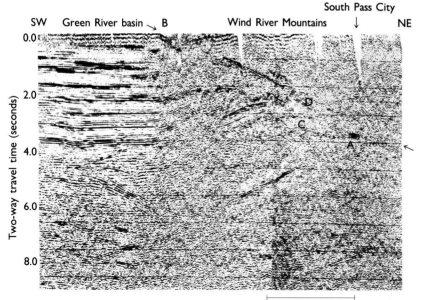

A seismic reflection "X ray" of the Earth's crust in the Wind River Mountains, Wyoming. The horizontal scale represents a distance on the surface of the Earth, and the vertical scale represents the two-way travel time of the waves downward to a reflecting layer and back to the surface.

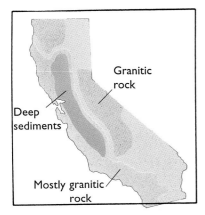

50 seconds

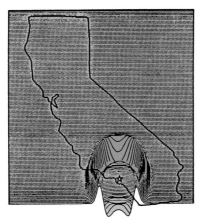

100 seconds

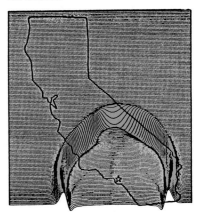

150 seconds

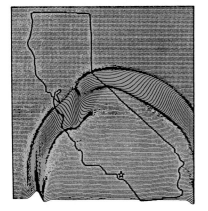

200 seconds

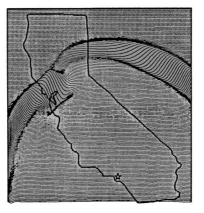

250 seconds

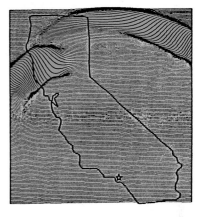

A computer simulation of a Love wave generated by an earthquake near Los Angeles, California, shows the wave being refracted by the region's main geological structures as it moves northward (time = seconds after origin time).

sedimentary basin and continues to a depth of about 25 km. Work such as this illustrates that large surface features are manifestations of deep-seated structures that can penetrate throughout the whole crust. Such displays give us a bird's-eye view of the heterogeneous nature of the Earth's crust, as though we could cut away the crust and look at it directly.

The modernized seismographic networks have enabled a remarkable recent advance in under-standing how earthquake waves are affected by crustal structure. Because the seismic waves are now recorded over a wide range of wavelengths, the wave fronts of long surface waves can be followed as they propagate through differing crustal structures, much as ocean rollers pass by a rocky headland toward a sheltered beach. A geologically simple case is shown in the diagram on this page. A computer has been programmed to show graphically the changing wave fronts of Love surface waves moving northward from the source of the Whittier-Narrows earthquake of 1985 in southern California. The wave fronts progress through three broad crustal zones: the mixed metamorphic rocks along the coast; the deep sediments of the Great Valley of California; and the granitic rocks of the Sierra Nevada. Love waves travel faster in the granitic rocks and slower in the sediments. Using these known velocities, the computer program calculates how the Love waves propagating through the Sierra Nevada race ahead of their neighbors in the valley and in the less rigid rocks to the west. This computed pattern is confirmed by the actual seismograms recorded at northern California earthquake observatories from the 1985 earthquake, and indeed the actual measurements of the wave fronts give a way to improve the crustal models used initially in the calculation.

OCEANIC AND CONTINENTAL DIFFERENCES

The largest physiographic contrast at the surface of the Earth is obviously the division into continents and oceans. Continents constitute about one-third of the Earth's surface and stand above sea level at an average elevation of about 800 m. The continents extend under the sea into a relatively shallow continental shelf a few tens of kilometers wide. From the edge of this shelf, the ocean floor drops down toward the abyssal plains of the deep ocean, where the average water depth below sea level is about 4.8 km.

For over a century there was some reason to suppose that the crust under the oceans and the

crust under the continents were not quite similar in thickness. Measurements of the pull of gravity around the world had indicated major differences between continental and oceanic areas. Such methods, using pendulums at different points on the Earth's surface, were time-consuming and unable to give quantitative crustal thicknesses for the whole globe. However, as seismographs began to record earthquake waves over long paths around the globe, these geological differences showed up as strikingly different patterns of waves for paths under the oceans and those through the continents. These wave patterns provided, for the first time, a way of discovering changes in major geological structures from remote observations.

If we knew what the properties of the Earth were, say, under a particular ocean or continent, we could predict the corresponding observed surface wave pattern. In actual practice, we observe a cryptic pattern from which we want to infer the average rock properties along the remote path. In general, surface waves roll across the terrestrial surface along tracks that intersect both oceans and continents. Some seismographic stations, however, can record pure paths through one crust or the other: those in California, for example, record waves that have traveled only across the Pacific Ocean crust from earthquakes in the South Pacific; seismographic stations in Sweden record waves that have traveled only across the Eurasian landmass from earthquakes in the Himalayas. The contrasting patterns of such waves are shown in the seismograms on the next page.

Recall from Chapter 2 that surface waves disperse into extended trains because the longer-period waves propagating through greater depths, where the seismic velocity is higher, ar-

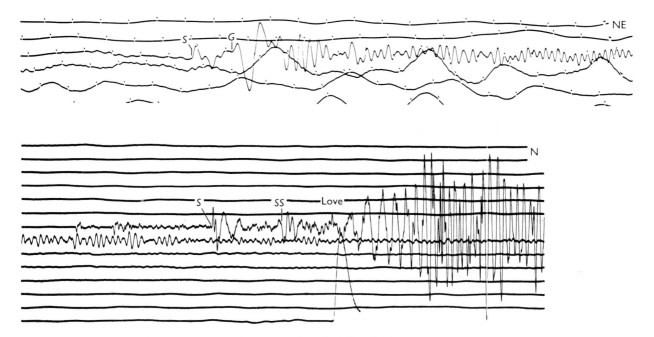

Top: A seismogram recorded by a long-period seismograph at Berkeley, California, shows the Love wave pulse (called the *G* pulse) for an oceanic path from an Alaskan earthquake. (Time ticks are one minute apart.) *Bottom:* A seismogram shows the dispersed Love wave train over a continental path from a Siberian earthquake to Uppsala, Sweden. (Time from left to right; 0.9 mm = 1 second.)

rive first. Because crustal rocks and mantle rocks have quite different seismic velocity profiles, the amount of dispersion in both Love and Rayleigh surface waves provides the telltale clues to crustal thickness. For example, the Love waves along oceanic paths appear as a single pulse of horizontal ground displacement that has traveled at a speed of 3.5 km/s from distances of more than 1000 km. At the same epicentral distances, Love waves traveling along continental paths show not a distinct pulse but rather a long wave train of steady period spread out in time. Indeed, this

sharp distinction provides a clear indication that a particular earthquake source is separated from an observatory either by almost entirely oceanic crust or by purely continental crust.

Dramatically different characteristics distinguish the oceanic and continental records of Rayleigh waves, which have, unlike Love waves, a vertical component of displacement of the ground. Rayleigh waves traveling an oceanic path disperse into a train of waves lasting sometimes for many minutes, at periods of about 15 seconds. Seismograms from earthquakes at equal distances that have followed continental paths do not show this long, monotonous wave train.

In trying to explain these differences, early researchers attempted to fit the recorded surface wave patterns to crustal models of different thicknesses. They defined a series of plausible mathematical models of the crust and calculated the theoretical wave dispersion, then ruled out those crustal models contradicted by the observed wave dispersion. This modeling indicated a definitely thinner oceanic crust; indeed, the early work with low-resolution seismographs suggested an ocean crust perhaps 20 km thick compared with 35 km for the continental areas. When the global network of seismographic stations was modernized in the 1960s, the observatories had available longer-period pendulums that could

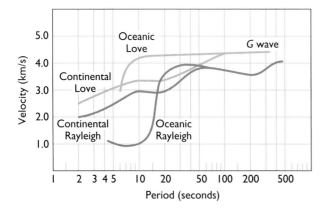

These dispersion curves explain the characteristics of Love and Rayleigh waves that have traveled along oceanic and continental paths. For example, because oceanic Love waves of most periods travel at the same speed, they arrive at the same time, creating the prominent G pulse. By contrast, the more gradual change in velocity with period possessed by continental Love waves causes these waves to be more dispersed.

accurately record seismic ground motions having periods of 10 to 50 seconds. The picture then became much better resolved: continental crustal thicknesses range between 25 and 50 km, and they are generally greater in the higher mountain ranges. In contrast, the oceanic crust varies less, ranging between 5 and 8 km; in some transitional regions and under large seas, crustal thicknesses are intermediate between those of oceans and continents. The most recent studies of the variation in the illumination of the Earth's surface by earthquake waves have revealed that the bottom boundary of the crust is often undulating. The figure on the next page dramatizes the effect of exaggerated undulations on seismic waves emanating from an earthquake focus.

The close agreement on crustal structure that was ultimately reached between many independent theoretical calculations and the observations of both Love and Rayleigh waves led to estimates of the elastic properties of the rocks that constitute the continental and oceanic crusts. Indeed, the crust under the ocean is more like a veneer of basaltic rock, produced originally as volcanic lava flows, over the deeper rocks. Finally, the definitive confirmation of the great differences in oceanic and continental crusts had a most profound geological consequence because it weakened one of the crucial arguments against the drifting of continents.

CONTINENTAL DRIFT

The notion that the continents move relative to one another can be found well before the beginnings of our own century, but the first systematic account of continental displacement was not

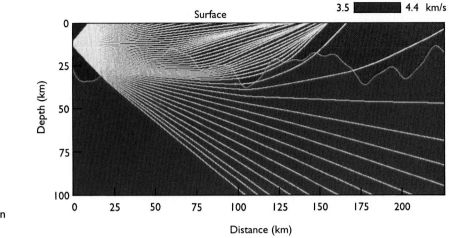

3.5 ▬ 4.4 km/s

A computer simulation shows the paths of seismic *P* waves being reflected and refracted by an uneven Mohorovičić discontinuity.

presented until 1912, in lectures by the meteorologist Alfred Wegener (1880–1930) in Germany. Probably because of World War I, the hypothesis was not taken seriously in the geological profession for about another ten years. A short unsigned review of the book describing Wegener's theory in the February 16, 1922, issue of the leading scientific journal *Nature* stated, "This book makes an immediate appeal to physicists but is meeting with strong opposition from a good many geologists." Wegener postulated that a supercontinent had broken apart about 300 million years ago and that its fragments had drifted away to form the present-day continents. As evidence for his theory, he pointed to the way that large-scale geological structures on separate continents, such as the west coast of Africa and the east coast of South America, seemed to match up. Here was a theory that would explain much of physical geology. It became a major focus of debate in the ensuing decades.

One of the founders of modern geophysics, Sir Harold Jeffreys, pointed out that the theory depended on two assumptions. The first was that any force, however small, can significantly deform the rocks of the Earth if only it acts for long enough. Jeffreys did not believe that this assumption was incorrect, although there was some evidence against it. He did, however, believe that a second assumption was wrong. Wegener thought that the drifting continents would have to be rafted through a rocky upper layer of definite strength. Jeffreys pointed out that this would not be possible unless one assumed that a small force can overcome a larger force acting at the same time in the opposite direction. Jeffreys held, correctly, that such an assumption was inconsistent with our understanding of physics. Evidence from earthquake waves that the structure of continents was deeper than earlier believed strengthened Jeffreys's objections. Most geologists were reluctant to admit the possibility of continental drift when there was no recognized natural process that seemed to have the remotest chance of bringing it about.

As we have described, by the end of the 1960s seismological studies had resolved the worldwide differences in crustal thickness. In addition, the extended study of both surface wave dispersion and the paths of seismic *P* and *S* waves had established another key piece of information: below the crust in the upper mantle there is a layer under both oceans and continents that has lower seismic velocities than the rocks above it. This decrease in seismic velocity indi-

Sir Harold Jeffreys (1891–1989), theoretical geophysicist and discoverer of the core's liquid state.

cated that the elastic rigidity of the rocky material also decreases with depth. Instead of having to explain how continents could move through rigid rock, the supporters of continental drift could seriously contemplate the concept of a soft zone supporting more rigid geological "rafts." Another serious objection to drift, that deep-focus earthquakes require strong brittle rocks to depths of almost 700 km, was also removed. The upgraded earthquake observatories provided more reliable focal depths for earthquakes all around the world, making it unequivocal that deep-focus earthquakes are generated only at very special sites and do not occur in most parts of either oceanic or continental crust.

The Earth's crust is now considered to be only the top part of the Earth's rigid upper layer. The rigid upper portion of the mechanically strong outermost shell of the Earth is called the lithosphere (from the Greek *lithos,* "rock"). The lithosphere contains the crust, but it continues as a more or less rigid layer to depths of 150 km or more, being thinner in ocean regions and thicker under older continental masses. These depths are partly suggested by the deep earthquake foci discussed in Chapter 4.

Studies of the behavior of seismic waves indicate that the base of the lithosphere is gradational rather than sharp. It merges into another layer of the Earth, called the asthenosphere (from the Greek *asthenia,* "weak"). The asthenosphere down to depths of 600 to 700 km is marked by lower seismic wave velocities and much higher attenuation of *P* and *S* seismic waves than are found in the lithosphere. It is thus concluded that the asthenosphere is softer than the lithosphere and may be approaching a molten state. The lithosphere floats on this viscous material

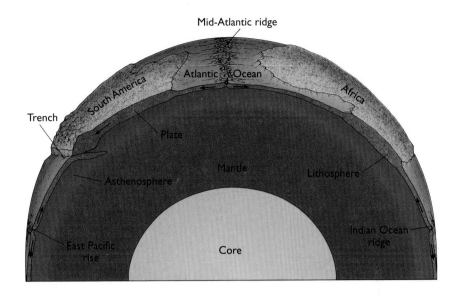

A rigid lithosphere of varying thickness floats on the softer asthenosphere. The lithosphere comprises tectonic plates moving in different directions. The African and South American plates separate along the Mid-Atlantic ridge at a rate of a few centimeters per year. The South American and Nazca plates converge to form the Andes Mountains. The thickness of the lithosphere and the asthenosphere is exaggerated so that they can be shown at this small scale.

and slowly moves along over time scales of millions of years.

With this picture of the rigid lithosphere floating on the soft asthenosphere, the essential ingredients were now available for formulating a much more satisfactory theory of continental drift—one that could avoid the debilitating criticisms that had been leveled fifty years before.

THE THEORY OF PLATE TECTONICS

The basic idea of plate tectonics is that the lithosphere consists of several large and fairly stable slabs of solid, relatively rigid rock called plates, which extend over the globe like curved caps on a sphere. There are seven large plates, such as

the Pacific plate, and many smaller ones, such as the Gorda plate off northern California, all in motion relative to one another.

Because plates are part of the lithosphere, they extend to a depth of 100 to 200 km. Each plate moves horizontally, relative to neighboring plates, on the softer rock immediately below. At the edge of a plate, where there is contact with adjoining plates, plate movement creates large drag forces that operate on the rocks of the lithosphere, causing physical and even chemical changes in them. Because the lithospheric plates are generally rigid and strong, they transmit forces throughout their interiors without buckling; the relative motion between plates is taken up almost entirely along plate boundaries, which themselves can be rather broad. At these plate edges, the Earth's geological structure is affected

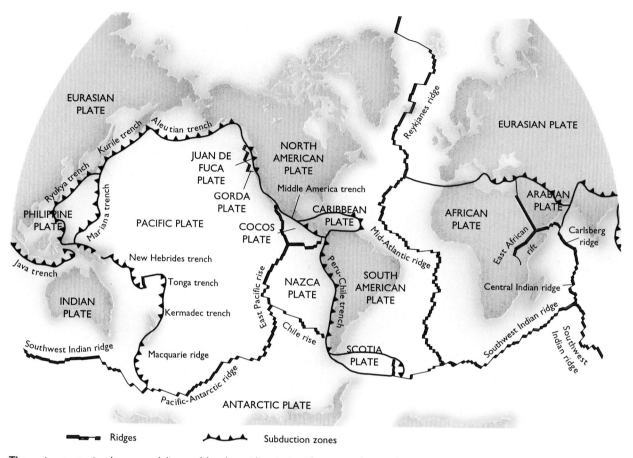

The major tectonic plates are delineated by the mid-oceanic ridges, trenches, and transform faults that form their boundaries.

by the forces of reaction between the plates, and this is where the most massive and radical geological changes occur.

The edges of the plates are clearly belts of high seismicity. This intimate relation between a plate boundary and earthquake occurrence is readily apparent in the map on the next page, showing seismicity along the California margin of the Pacific and North American plates. When the epicenters of small earthquakes are plotted, the regional mosaic is striking. The dense linear concentrations of epicenters are seen to coincide with long active faults, such as the San Andreas. Fewer epicenters, however, scatter over limited areas between the major mapped faults. The major faults are the zones of weakness in the crust along which relative plate motions occur. The slip rate along the San Andreas fault is about 5 cm per year—a typical value for large-scale faults at plate boundaries.

The theory of plate tectonics, which predicts the interactions and consequences of plates, is based on four assumptions:

1. New plate material is generated by seafloor spreading; new oceanic lithosphere is generated along active mid-oceanic ridges.
2. The new oceanic lithosphere forms part of a moving plate; this plate may or may not include continental material.
3. The Earth's surface area remains constant; therefore, the growth of the lithosphere must be balanced by the consumption of plates elsewhere.
4. Because the plates transmit stresses over great horizontal distances without buckling, the relative motion between plates occurs almost entirely along their boundaries.

More than 70 percent of the plates' area is overlain by the great oceans such as the Pacific, the Atlantic, and the Indian, where the topographic monotony of the ocean floor is relieved by seamounts, volcanic islands, and even great mountain ranges. The most striking feature is the division of the oceanic crust by a global system of active volcanic ridges, which are also the loci of significant earthquakes. The long-time puzzle was: What is the reason for this geological pattern?

The present plate structure (shown on page 108) is not permanent but is undergoing constant, gradual change. At divergent boundaries in mid-ocean, plates are spreading apart from each other. Lava is continually upwelling at

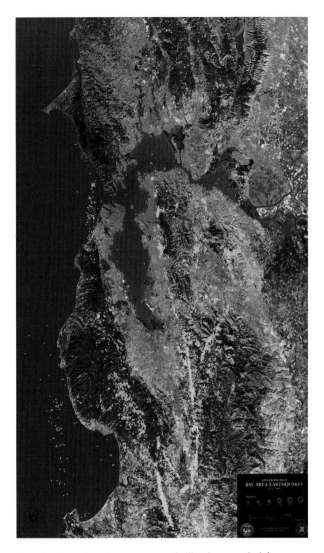

Trends of earthquake epicenters (yellow), recorded from 1972 through 1989, trace some active faults in the San Francisco Bay Area.

ridges along mid-oceanic plate boundaries, adding new plate material, derived from the rocks of the asthenosphere, to the lithosphere. As new seafloor, this newly emplaced rock then moves

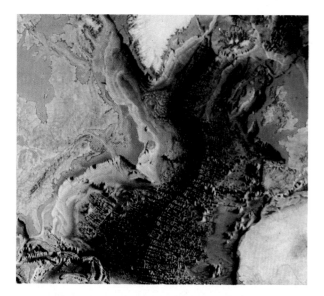

A painting of the Mid-Atlantic ridge, based on bathymetric studies, shows numerous transform faults at right angles to the ridge; offsets of the ridge along some of the faults are clearly visible.

the offset, the edges of the plates slide past each other in opposite directions. Because the slip is "transformed" by the emergence of new oceanic floor, such slips are called transform faults, and they are the sources of many earthquakes. Transform faulting occurs because the ridge lines become offset; the cause of the offsets individually is unclear.

If new plates are constantly being created, what happens to old plates? According to the plate tectonics theory, the burial ground of a plate is an ocean trench located in front of an advancing continent or island arc. At these places, called subduction zones, the surface layers of rock plunge into the Earth's interior. At the greater depths, temperature and pressure increase, and the sinking lithosphere is gradually reworked until it becomes mixed and chemically absorbed into the rocks of the deeper interior. The downgoing plate can penetrate the asthenosphere to depths of about 700 km, but often it is absorbed at much shallower depths. At present, the plates containing Africa, Antartica, North America, and South America are growing, while the Pacific plate is shrinking. The Aleutians, Japan, and the Andes are surface expressions of subduction plate boundaries, which are typified by volcanic mountain ranges.

Most convergent boundaries, where plates approach each other, are subduction zones along ocean trenches. In some cases, however, the continental edges of two plates may collide head on. The resulting compression and folding of the land create massive mountain chains, such as the Himalayas, the Zagros region (southwestern Iran and northeastern Iraq), and the Alpine belt of the Mediterranean (from Turkey to Spain). These collisions are accompanied by unremitting earthquake activity.

slowly away from each side of the ridge. In this way, plates spread and move away from each other at a generally uniform speed across the surface, like great conveyor belts, cooling and aging as they get farther away from the ridges. For this reason, mid-oceanic ridges are called spreading zones.

None of the lines of ridges appear as unbroken linear trends; instead, they are disrupted by intermittent horizontal offsets. These offsets are produced by horizontal slip between two crustal blocks; together with the spreading ridges, they represent the plate boundaries. At both ends of an offset, new oceanic floor is emerging along the ridge, causing the tectonic plates on either side of the offset ridges to move apart. Along

A dramatic example from Israel of originally horizontal, rigid layers of rock that have been folded by compressional tectonic forces applied over a long period.

Along conservative boundaries, lithosphere is neither created nor destroyed, but rather the plates move laterally relative to each other. These plate seams often take the form of transform faults such as the San Andreas fault in Cal-

ifornia, which is a long, sliding offset between two spreading ridges. Adjacent plates move relative to each other at rates up to 15 cm per year.

Although the lithospheric plates are made up of both oceanic and continental rocks, usually only the oceanic part of any plate is created or destroyed. At subduction zones, where continental and oceanic materials meet, it is the oceanic plate that is subducted (and thereby consumed). In other words, the continents are rafts of lighter material that remain on the surface while the denser oceanic lithosphere is subducted beneath either oceanic or continental lithosphere.

The rate at which oceanic portions of the plates spread apart from one another has conventionally been estimated from the observed spacing of magnetic anomalies stepping out from the mid-oceanic ridges. Every several hundred thousand years the polarity of the Earth's magnetic field reverses. When the molten rock emerging from a mid-oceanic ridge crystallizes, it records forever the Earth's magnetic polarity at that moment. As the layer of solidified magma moves outward from the ridge, the ocean floor is "encoded" with a series of magnetized stripes of opposite polarity. Because the time history of these geomagnetic reversals is accurately known, the length of ocean floor between reversals gives an estimate of the rate of seafloor spreading.

These geomagnetic observations have shown that plate separation rates over the past few million years vary from a low of 1.2 cm per year across the Arctic ridge to a high of 16 cm per year across the East Pacific rise between the Pacific and Nazca plates. Deep sea trenches are converging with the stable interiors of plates at rates ranging from a low of 2 cm per year along the southern Chile trench, where the Antarctic plate underthrusts the South American plate, to

11 cm per year along the Indo-Australian–Pacific plate boundary. Away from the oceans and deep trenches, however, magnetic measurements poorly describe the kinematics of the plates, particularly where plate motions bring continents into collision, detaching the continental crust from the lithosphere and piling it up to form mountain ranges and broad high plateaus such as in the Himalayas and Tibet.

Even though the conventional methods of measuring plate movement are usually successful for the oceanic plates, some deformation there is poorly described by a simple model of rigid plates separated by narrow structural boundaries. For example, large earthquakes occur within the equatorial region of the Indian Ocean far from the plate boundaries. Yet estimates of the seismic moments of large earthquakes there show the release of energy to be greatly in excess of the rate of energy release for large earthquakes along the San Andreas fault, which is an archetypical transform fault plate boundary. It is likely from this and other geological evidence, therefore, that the Indo-Australian plate is not a single rigid system but has some internal rifting.

In principle, the contemporary motions of plates can be measured by determining the rate of slip along the boundary faults at the plate margins. The practical problem is that plate boundaries in both continental and oceanic lithosphere are hundreds or even thousands of kilometers wide, so that it is difficult to isolate the relative plate displacements, and, of course, some plate margins are inaccessible.

The detailed motions of the tectonic plates are now being resolved by using space satellites to measure the distances between widely separated points on the broad plate margins. The

methods are based on technologies developed for radio astronomy and satellite tracking. The satellite system most widely used for this purpose is the Global Positioning System, or GPS, which employs a constellation of high-altitude (20,000 km) satellites that orbit the Earth twice a day. Signals are broadcast from these satellites specifying their times and positions. At GPS receiver stations on the ground, the distance to each satellite is estimated from the transit time of the signal. The distances from multiple GPS receivers to multiple satellites allow the location of the receiver to be estimated to within a few meters by simple triangulation, in much the same way as earthquake epicenters are located by triangulation of P and S wave travel times. When a network of GPS stations is used, errors can be reduced and relative positions can be calculated with errors of a few centimeters or less. This remarkable precision promises to allow relative tectonic motions between plates and within boundary zones to be resolved much more precisely in the next decade.

EARTHQUAKE MECHANISMS ALONG THE PLATE MARGINS

While it is now said that the theory of plate tectonics predicts the way that faults slip, it was largely seismological evidence on the motion along large faults that, together with evidence from the magnetism of rocks in the Earth's oceanic crust, convinced doubters of the correctness of the plate tectonics theory. That evidence revealed consistent patterns of earthquake source types around the different plate boundaries.

Seismological observatories record *P* waves from earthquakes along the transform faults that link offset ridges within the world-encircling mid-oceanic ridge system. These recordings indicate that the *P* waves are generated by strike-slip rebound in most cases. Such remote sensing of literally thousands of transform faults around the world established that ridges are always connected to ridges, or to subduction zones, by the same type of fracture. This horizontal strike-slip motion carries the spreading plates away from the ridges, as required by the plate tectonics theory.

At the subduction zones, where a dipping seismic region extends to depths up to about 700 km, the evidence from earthquake studies is quite different. The earthquakes there are caused by a variety of mechanisms that distinguish the conditions of the slab geometry as it makes its way downward. Where the lithosphere arcs near the top of the slab, tensional stresses pull rocks away from each other, creating normal faults. Near its bottom, the slab is being deformed by compressive forces, as the sinking of the slab is resisted by mantle rocks. There the dominant mechanism is thrust faulting, produced when compressive forces push two blocks together. Evidently the descending slab of brittle lithosphere is strong enough to enable fault fractures to exist in various orientations as the rocks accommodate the forces that pull the shallower parts of the slab downward. At depths of 650 to 680 km, below which no earthquake foci have been detected, either the plate is altogether absorbed into the rocks of the interior or it has been sufficiently softened by the higher temperatures at that depth that it is no longer brittle enough to suddenly rebound in an earthquake.

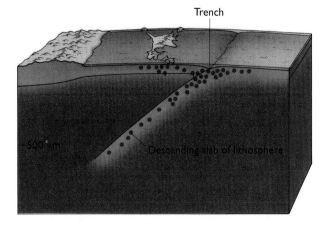

Numerous earthquakes (red dots) are generated along a subducting lithosphere.

Where plates collide, such as where the Indian plate pushes against southern Asia, the theory of plate tectonics predicts that large-scale thrusting will build mountain ranges such as the Himalayas. The prediction is in agreement with the geological field mapping of extensive thrust faults along the southern foothills of the Himalayas. Slip along these faults continues to build this enormous range against the force of gravity. Along the northern edge of the Himalayas and into Tibet, the collision of the plates is displacing Asia to the east, much as soft material is extruded out as a steel wedge is driven into unset concrete. The horizontal forces driving Asia to the east are accommodated by the transcurrent motions of strike-slip faults stretching east-west for thousands of kilometers. This plate junction to the north of India and Burma is the region of greatest earthquake activity on Earth. The underriding of the Asian plate by the Indian plate is signaled by deep-focus earthquakes beneath the Tibetan plateau.

Because the directions of forces vary across a plate, the mechanisms of earthquake origin and the sizes of earthquakes differ in different parts of a plate. Only about 10 percent of the world's earthquakes occur along the oceanic-ridge system, and these contribute only about 5 percent of the total seismic energy of earthquakes around the world. In contrast, earthquakes occurring where plate boundaries converge, such as at trenches, contribute more than 90 percent of the world's release of seismic energy from shallow earthquakes, as well as most of the energy from intermediate- and deep-focus earthquakes. The majority of the largest earthquakes—such as the 1960 and 1985 Chile earthquakes, the 1964 Alaska earthquake, and the 1985 Mexico earthquake—have originated in the subduction regions as a result of one plate thrusting beneath another.

TECTONIC PLATES AND THE DISTRIBUTION OF VOLCANOES

Most of today's active volcanoes lie within relatively narrow geothermal zones close to the margins of the Earth's tectonic plates, and in many but not all cases their sites are concentrated within the principal earthquake regions. The prevalent character of the volcanism, however, differs from one type of plate boundary to another.

By far the most voluminous eruption of lava takes place along the mid-oceanic ridges, where plates are diverging. Because hot magma is lighter than the cooler, overlying rocks, it rises through buoyancy, welling up through great

The Thingvellir Graben, a rift valley in Iceland, is actually a part of the Mid-Atlantic ridge, exposed above sea level. Rift valleys have steep sides and rugged topography produced by normal fault movement.

cracks or rifts that are produced in the ridges by the unremitting forces that pull apart the plates. In contrast, very few active volcanoes are present either at the conservative boundaries where plates are sliding by each other or at convergent boundaries where two continental plates are colliding, such as the Himalayas.

Most of the dangerous volcanoes are in convergent zones. Where oceanic plates subduct beneath either oceanic or continental plates, volcanoes lie on the overlying plate, some tens of kilometers from its edge. These volcanoes are produced by partial melting of the rocks along the top margin of the descending oceanic crust and its veneer of water-rich sediments. Because the high water content of the rocks lowers their melting temperature, melting sets in at depths of 100 km or so. The great frictional heat generated by the descending plate endows the molten rock with enough additional buoyancy to ascend to the surface. The typically explosive eruptions of volcanoes in convergent zones throw out rock fragments, called tephra; these fragments constitute about 45 to 99 percent of the volcanic products. Ash flows, mud flows, lava flows, glowing avalanches, and heavy ash fall have all been common.

About 5 percent of the world's active volcanoes lie in the interior parts of plates. One of the best examples is the Hawaiian archipelago. A popular hypothesis holds that magma formed by melting in the Earth's asthenosphere erupts onto the surface of the Pacific plate. As the plate moves northwestward, the volcano at the surface is carried away from the deeper "hot spot" and another volcano is formed behind it, and so on, until the whole chain of volcanic mountains has been formed. Most eruptions of Hawaiian volcanoes are relatively gentle, but some other midplate volcanoes are more explosive. The building of such huge volcanic mountains on the Earth's crust produces tremendous local stresses in the rocks; these stresses in turn create fractures that are prone to earthquakes, sometimes of significant size.

THE 1990 PHILIPPINE FAULT RUPTURE

As earthquakes occur, the reason for their location and mechanism can now be examined in light of the theory of plate tectonics. The role of earthquakes in adjusting for the conflicting stresses of plate movements is well illustrated by the latest damaging earthquake to shake the Republic of the Philippines. A shock of magnitude 7.8 struck on Monday, July 6, 1990, at 4:26 P.M. local time. The severe shaking from this earthquake and its aftershocks resulted in the deaths of at least 1700 people and in serious injury to 3500 others. Damage was extensive throughout the central region of Luzon, and there was sporadic damage to buildings as far distant as Manila, about 240 km away. Most seriously affected, particularly in the remote city of Baguio, were structures built on soft alluvial sediments along the river. In addition, the rain-saturated tropical soils gave way in massive landslides that buried houses and even entire villages and blocked extensive lengths of highway.

The immediate cause of the main shock and its aftershocks was slip along the Philippine and Digdig faults in the island of Luzon. The fault rupture could be measured over a distance of 110 km, but because the region is mountainous and hard to access, even more extensive faulting may have reached the surface unnoticed. Horizontal offsets on the Digdig fault were as great as 6.1 m, and vertical offsets sometimes reached about 2 m, although vertical elevations were not consistently to the north or south of the fault trace.

The Philippine Islands have long been harried by earthquakes. While working in Japan,

The two towers and atrium of Baguio's largest hotel collapsed in the 1990 Philippine earthquake.

John Milne had discussed the heavy damage to the city of Manila in the disastrous Luzon earthquake of 1895. He drew attention to the susceptibility of the Philippines to great earthquakes and pointed to the extreme seismic danger that exists there. An examination of the map on page 108 explains the high frequency of earthquakes: the Philippine archipelago lies between two of the world's major tectonic plates, the Pacific plate and the Philippine sea plate. A conspicuous fault zone, of which the Philippine and the Digdig faults are a part, runs as a rift diagonally across the islands of Luzon, Leyte, and Mindanao. In past decades, slip within this rift and along its subsidiary faults has been responsible for many major earthquakes.

The activity of this fault zone results from the interactions of three major tectonic plates. The Pacific plate pushes on the eastern side of the Philippine sea plate, forcing the western edge of the Philippine plate to subduct along the east Luzon trench beneath the eastern side of the Philippine archipelago at a rate of about 7 cm per year. The oceanic portion of the slower-moving Eurasian plate is being subducted along the western side of the islands of Luzon and Mindanao at a rate of about 3 cm per year. Thus, the Philippine archipelago is caught in a geological vise between powerful horizontal forces from the east and west; in response to these forces, the geological structure of the archipelago undergoes disruptions and shearing. The role of the Philippine fault zone appears to be to decouple the northwestward motion of the Pacific plate from the southeastward motion of the Eurasian plate. These two plates are not moving at equal rates; to adjust for the difference in speed, the strike of the major faulting is oblique to the plate motions rather than parallel to them.

To complicate the geological evolution of the Philippines, the subduction zones on each side of the island chain produce both the usual deep-focus earthquake activity of island arcs and many active volcanoes. Perhaps by coincidence, less than a year after the 1990 Digdig earthquake, Mount Pinatubo erupted. Previously regarded as dormant, this volcano had been inactive for more than 400 years. The protracted and massive eruption caused great damage on the islands, including at the extensive U.S. Clark Air Force Base, located about 180 km south of the center of the earthquake and 50 km from Mount Pinatubo. The 1990 Philippine earthquake had not been predicted, but a series of small explosions from Mount Pinatubo beginning on April 2 led to the evacuation of at least 58,000 people before the climatic eruption of June 15. Although 320 persons died as a result of volcanic activity, mostly from the collapse of ash-covered roofs, the forewarning and subsequent precautions undoubtedly averted much greater loss of life and property.

INTRAPLATE EARTHQUAKES

The general plate theory accommodates both the most obvious earthquake patterns and the systematic source mechanisms very satisfactorily. However, many earthquakes, including some large ones, occur far from the plate boundaries, and the theory does not provide a ready explanation for these intraplate earthquakes. Hinterland seismic activity has been found in all the continents except Greenland and Antarctica. Earthquake catalogues dating back to the sixteenth century cite at least 15 major earthquakes in crust that would be regarded as stable. Going back even further, throughout the 3000 years of historical record in China, scholars have recorded evidence of devastating earthquakes in that territory, away from the collision zone of the Himalayas and Tibet and from the subduction zones along the country's eastern margins. Strong earthquakes in the intraplate regions of Europe have also been described over many centuries. One notable case, the subject of many accounts and paintings, was an earthquake that occurred near Basel in 1356 with a magnitude that is now estimated from the described intensity as about 7.4.

Another striking example is the catastrophic earthquake that struck deep inside continental China in 1556. On January 23 of that year, in Shensi Province near the old capital city of Sian, there resulted the greatest loss of life ever recorded in an earthquake. The official Chinese catalogue estimates that 830,000 people died from all causes; so great was the death toll that its validity might well be questioned. In the densely populated region where the earthquake occurred, many people lived in caves excavated in hillsides of soft sediments called loess—windblown dust that compacts into thick layers but presents little resistance to earthquake shaking. When the earthquake struck at 5:00 in the morning, the cave dwellings collapsed on sleeping families. Demoralization of the population, famine, and disease following the disaster may well have accounted for a significant number of additional deaths.

The circumstances of another intraplate earthquake of exceptional size, situated in the Rann of Kutch, northwest India, in 1819, have been described in some detail. This was only the latest of many strong earthquakes in the state of Kutch, a hilly island area separated from the mainland by an extensive and uninhabited salt flat. More than 1500 people died in Kutch from this earthquake, which was perceptible as far

Woodcuts from the 1853 edition of Sir Charles Lyell's classic book *Principles of Geology* show Sindree Fort standing on a rise before the 1819 Kutch earthquake *(top)* and the fort 19 years afterward, when only the turret remained above water *(bottom)*.

away as Calcutta. Some of its effects were dramatic. A 3-m-high scarp appeared running east and west for about 25 km; it was named by local people the "wall of God." Sindree Fort, which had stood on a rise, became submerged so that the soldiers had to escape by boat from an upper turret. Careful measurements of the fault length and slip made at the time have enabled the recent calculation of the seismic moment of this earthquake. At a moment magnitude of 7.8, the Kutch earthquake was only a little smaller than the greatest intraplate earthquakes known, the New Madrid earthquakes of 1811 and 1812.

About 180 years ago, three powerful earthquakes occurred near a loop of the Mississippi River close to the boundary of Kentucky and Missouri (see the map on page 155). The dates of the shocks were December 16, 1811, and February 7 and December 16, 1812. With moment magnitudes of 8.2, 8.1, and 8.3, these are the most energetic earthquakes recorded in the contiguous United States, yet the closest plate boundary is more than a thousand miles distant. Ever since the earthquakes were first studied in detail by geologists at the beginning of this century, it has been a question why an area in an otherwise stable continent should release such enormous amounts of seismic energy. The absence of surface faulting hindered research, because there was no evidence of elastic rebound.

Very recent research may have found an answer, however, largely by examining the locations of small earthquakes in the central part of the United States, accurately determined by regional networks of seismographs, and by subsequently applying the general principles of plate tectonics. This work has led to the view that near the northern part of what is called the Mississippi embayment, the North American plate is flawed by a major rift in the old coastal rocks. The embayment of the Mississippi River is a flat region with low-lying drainage patterns and abandoned meanders of the river course. Unlike the prominent surface geomorphology of the San Andreas transform fault on the western North American plate margin, faults under the Mississippi embayment are deeply buried under river mud and marine sediments deposited on the floor of an ancient sea.

Undoubtedly, great intraplate earthquakes such as those at Shensi, Kutch, and New Madrid are the result of a transfer of stresses from the plate boundary across the whole, mainly rigid, plate. In the case of the Mississippi earthquakes, the stresses would have traveled all the way to the center of the continent from the Pacific plate margin to the west and from the Mid-Atlantic ridge to the east. Within the Mississippi embayment, the epicenters of small earthquakes lie along three lineations, which can be explained as defining three deeply buried faults. One fault zone strikes southeast from the town of New Madrid to a region of northwestern Tennessee, while a longer fault runs for more than 100 km out of Missouri into northeastern Arkansas, ending abruptly near the town of Marked Tree, 60 km north of Memphis. The third fault zone strikes north from the first fault to end near Cairo, Illinois. The shallow depth of the earthquakes along these three faults suggests that the faults are remnants of an old geological rift system, similar to the spreading center at a mid-oceanic ridge.

Once again earthquake mechanisms have provided clues to the present and past tectonic stresses—in the New Madrid case, to the stresses disturbing the stable North American continental crust. These mechanisms generally suggest the presence of compressive stresses oriented in an east-west direction, sometimes producing strike-slip earthquakes and sometimes thrust faulting. This result from seismology is in agreement with results from geodetic surveys and from direct measurements of the stress in surface rocks. All three methods indicate a general compression of the crust across the central part of the United States. The faults in the old rift system in the crust under the Mississippi embayment, perhaps inactive for millions of years, are now becoming reactivated because of changing tectonic forces. The answers proposed to the question of why this reactivation has taken place are as yet mainly speculative.

QUIET GAPS IN EARTHQUAKE ZONES

The grand scale of the plate pattern and the steady rate of plate spreading imply that along a plate edge the slip should, on average, be a constant value over many years. Thus, if two slips some distance apart along a trench produce earthquakes, we might expect that a similar slip will occur between them in due course. This idea suggests that the historical patterns of segments and time intervals between major earthquakes along major plate boundaries provide at least a crude indication of places at which large earthquakes might soon occur.

This scheme for earthquake forecasting is illustrated on the next page for the plate boundary at the Alaska-Aleutian arc. Contours on the map

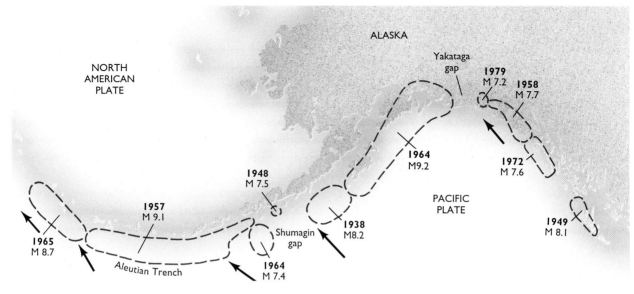

NORTH
AMERICAN
PLATE

ALASKA

Yakataga
gap

1979
M 7.2

1958
M 7.7

1964
M9.2

1972
M 7.6

1948
M 7.5

1957
M 9.1

PACIFIC
PLATE

Shumagin
gap

1938
M8.2

1949
M 8.1

1965
M 8.7

Aleutian Trench

1964
M 7.4

Seismic gaps appear along the Alaska-Aleutian arc between the rupture areas of large, shallow earthquakes (with approximate magnitudes) recorded from 1930 to 1979. The dark arrows show the direction of motion of the Pacific plate relative to the North American plate.

surround the inferred areas of seismic-energy release for some recent large earthquakes. If the seismic-energy release areas for all earthquakes in the last fifty years are plotted, many sections of the arc are covered. There remain, however, some "seismic gaps" (indicated by the heavy lines), which could be likely areas for sudden plate slip and thus for major earthquakes in the future.

At the center of the map is the Shumagin gap, for which there is evidence of rupture in 1788, 1847, and perhaps 1903. The Yakataga section, at the north of the arc, was the source of an earthquake in 1899. Surveys indicate that the North American plate converges into the subduction zone at a rate of about 1.6 cm per year in a N15°W direction, roughly perpendicu-

lar to the Alaska arc. Strain accumulation has been measured from variations in the distances between ground markers in both these seismic regions since about 1980. According to the seismic-gap theory, based on this evidence the two regions may be the most likely sites for the next great thrust earthquakes along the Alaska-Aleutian arc. Yet the surveys have not detected any significant crustal deformation in the Shumagin gap, raising the speculation that subduction is sometimes episodic—that long intervals of slow strain accumulation are occasionally interspersed by episodes of rapid accumulation. In the Yakataga gap, the surveys indicate that the rocks are being strained at an appropriate rate for the regular occurrence of another great earthquake.

In California, there is a seismic gap along the San Andreas fault between the southernmost end of the segment that slipped in the 1906 earthquake and the northernmost end of the segment that slipped in the 1857 Fort Tejon earthquake. Another example of a seismic gap is the strained area that generated the tragic 1985 Mexico earthquake, discussed in Chapter 7. In this case, the subduction zone under the Pacific margin of Mexico ruptured. On a smaller scale, the Loma Prieta earthquake, also discussed in Chapter 7, probably fits the seismic-gap theory as well. Before that earthquake, mapping of foci of small earthquakes along the San Andreas fault south of San Francisco had revealed a sparse region about 60 km long centered on Loma Prieta. The main shock and myriad aftershocks had foci that nearly coincided with the seismic gap.

We must be cautious, however, about simple applications of a seismic-gap theory, because there are known exceptions. For example, in 1979 a moderate earthquake in the Imperial Valley of California was produced by energy release along the Imperial fault in the same section that had been observed to slip in an earthquake of similar size in 1940. Thus, quick repetition of earthquakes from the same fault section cannot be ruled out.

THE HAZARD FROM PLATE-EDGE EARTHQUAKES

The moving plates of the Earth's surface provide an explanation for a great deal of the seismic activity of the world. Collisions between adjacent lithospheric plates, destruction of the slablike plate as it descends into the subduction zone beneath island arcs, and spreading along mid-oceanic ridges are all mechanisms likely to be associated with large-scale straining and fracturing of crustal rocks. Thus, the earthquakes in these tectonically active boundary regions are called plate-edge earthquakes. The very hazardous shallow earthquakes of Chile, Peru, the eastern Caribbean, Central America, southern Mexico, California, southern Alaska, the Aleutians, the Kuriles, Japan, Taiwan, the Philippines, Indonesia, New Zealand, and the Alpine-Caucasian-Himalayan belt are of the plate-edge type.

Cross sections showing locations of earthquake foci along the San Andreas fault, north of San Francisco to south of Parkfield. At top, background seismicity recorded over a 20-year period before the Loma Prieta earthquake shows that the San Andreas fault just north of San Juan Bautista had been virtually aseismic. What little seismicity occurred outlined a U-shaped area, the Loma Prieta gap. The earthquake and its aftershocks almost completely filled that gap (bottom).

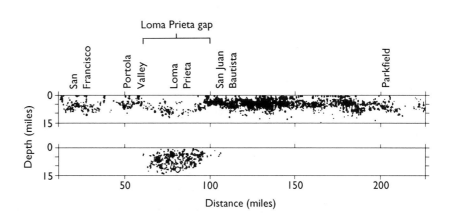

A well-defined belt of plate-edge tectonic activity, characterized by high seismicity, young mountains, volcanoes, and an ocean trench, follows the Peru-Chile coast for 7000 km from Venezuela to southern Chile. The earthquakes in this belt can be large and devastating.

On May 31, 1970, at 3:23 P.M. local time, about 25 km west of the city of Chimbote, Peru, a fault rupture began at a depth of about 50 km below the trench, producing an earthquake of magnitude 7.75. This rupture led to the most catastrophic seismological disaster yet experienced in the Western Hemisphere. The extent of the disaster did not become fully known for weeks, as rescue and relief were seriously hampered by landslides and rock avalanches that disrupted communications and blocked roads in the Andes. In an area of 75,000 sq km in west-central Peru, there were more than 50,000 deaths, 50,000 injuries, roughly 200,000 homes and buildings destroyed, and 800,000 people left homeless. Within the meizoseismal region (area of significant damage), roughly 100,000 sq km, numerous villages were almost totally demolished. Eyewitnesses said that the earthquake began with a gentle swaying, then vibrations became more intense, lasting variously from 30 to 60 or more seconds.

The grimmest result was an enormous debris avalanche from the north peak of Huascaran Mountain. More than 50,000,000 cu m of rock, snow, ice, and soil traveled 15 km from the mountain to the town of Yungay, at an estimated speed of 320 km/h. Ridges as high as 140 m were overridden, and boulders weighing several tons were projected 1000 m beyond the avalanche margins. At least 18,000 people were buried beneath the avalanche, which covered the town of Ranrahirca and most of Yungay.

A most graphic account of the Huascaran avalanche was later given by Señor Mateo Casaverde, a geophysicist with the Instituto Geofísico del Peru, who by chance was on a tour of Yungay:

As we drove past the cemetery the car began to shake. It was not until I had stopped the car that I realized that we were experiencing an earthquake. We immediately got out of the car and observed the effects of the earthquake around us. I saw several homes as well as a small bridge crossing a creek near Cemetery Hill collapse. It was, I suppose, after about one-half to three-quarters of a minute when the earthquake shaking began to subside. At that time I heard a great roar coming from Huascaran. Looking up, I saw what appeared to be a cloud of dust, and it looked as though a large mass of rock and ice was breaking loose from the north peak. My immediate reaction was to run for the high ground of Cemetery Hill, situated about 150 to 200 m away. I began running and noticed that there were many others in Yungay who were also running toward Cemetery Hill. About half to three-quarters of the way up the hill, the wife of my friend stumbled and fell and I turned to help her back to her feet.

The crest of the wave had a curl, like a huge breaker coming in from the ocean. I estimated the wave to be at least 80 m high. I observed hundreds of people in Yungay running in all directions and many of them towards Cemetery Hill. All the while, there was a continuous loud roar and rumble. I reached the upper level of the cemetery near the top just as the debris flow struck the

The city of Yungay before (*left*) and after (*right*) the massive rock and snow avalanche down Huascaran Mountain, Peru, caused by the earthquake of May 31, 1970.

base of the hill and I was probably only 10 seconds ahead of it.

At about the same time, I saw a man just a few meters down the hill who was carrying two small children towards the top of the hilltop. The debris flow caught him and he threw the two children towards the hilltop, out of the path of the flow, to safety, although the debris flow swept him down the valley, never to be seen again. I also remember two women who were no more than a few meters behind me and I never did see them again. Looking around, I counted 92 persons who had also saved themselves by running to the top of the hill. It was the most horrible thing I have ever experienced and I will never forget it.

Considerable damage also resulted from the shaking, in particular, along the coast at Chimbote and Casma and in cities and villages up to 150 km inland, where most houses and buildings of adobe construction were destroyed or greatly damaged. Along the coastline, fortunately, no tsunami was generated.

The examples of seismic gaps on pages 119–121 suggest that as the mechanics and speeds of the lithospheric plates become better understood, long-term prediction may be possible for plate-edge earthquakes. In active arcs like the Japanese Islands, it might be feasible to use knowledge of the history of large earthquake occurrence to map the current lag in elastic strain release. The question is discussed further in Chapter 8, on earthquake prediction.

6

THE IMAGE OF
THE EARTH'S INTERIOR

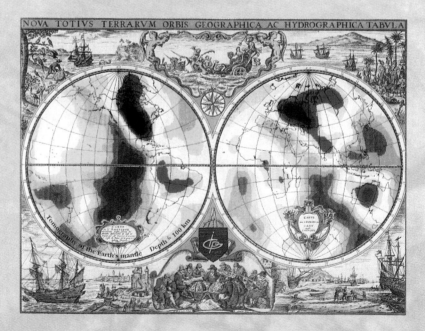

NOVA TOTIVS TERRARVM ORBIS GEOGRAPHICA AC HYDROGRAPHICA TABVLA

Tomography of the Earth's mantle — Depth ~ 100 km

IN ANCIENT TIMES, the center of the Earth was pictured as a mysterious underworld of fiery furnaces and volcanic explosions. With the growth of a more mechanical outlook after the work of Isaac Newton, early geophysicists could make more realistic inferences about the unknown interior from the properties of surface rocks. In particular, Newton's theory of gravity had a critical effect on speculations about the inside of the Earth because it provided a way to measure the Earth's density. This average property of the whole interior could then be compared with the known densities of rocks to give a first approximation of the Earth's composition. As early as 1798, Lord Cavendish in England measured the amount of twist of a torsion rod caused by the attraction exerted by two sets of leaden balls to determine a mean density of the Earth of 5.45 g/cm^3, about twice that of

A tomographic snapshot made in 1992 of the structure of the Earth at a depth of 100 km, superimposed on an early geographical map. Red is hotter buoyant rock; blue is colder denser rock.

common rocks. The odds were thus high that there were no great cavities very deep in the Earth and that the material there was very dense.

Another important clue to the state of the terrestrial interior was provided by the ocean tides raised by the gravitational attraction of the Sun and the Moon. If most of the Earth's interior were more or less liquid, the rocky surface of the Earth would rise and fall just like the ocean tides. Consequently, no tidal rise and fall of the sea would be seen at the coast. By 1887, a leading geophysicist, George Darwin (the second son of Charles Darwin), had concluded from the heights of the tides at principal ports that "the geological hypothesis of a fluid interior is untenable." He reasoned that the overall rigidity

of the deep interior is considerable, although not as great as that of steel. In a further refinement, geophysicists constructed simple curves estimating the effect on density of the great increase in pressure from the Earth's surface to its center. They then took mathematical steps to fit these curves to the sparse geological data available on the Earth's density. One early simple model of the deep interior, published in 1897, that came close to having a composition like that of the actual Earth had an outer shell of density 3.2 g/cm^3, like that of igneous rocks, and a central core of density 8.2 g/cm^3, about 10 percent less than that of iron meteorites. For the model to match the Earth's overall average density of 5.45 g/cm^3 (the modern value is 5.52 g/cm^3),

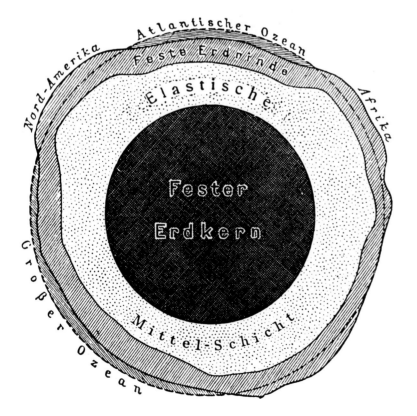

A sketch of the Earth's interior published in Berlin in 1902. This early model of the Earth has a solid crust (*Feste Erdrinde*), elastic mantle (*Elastische Mittel-Schicht*), and solid core (*Fester Erdkern*).

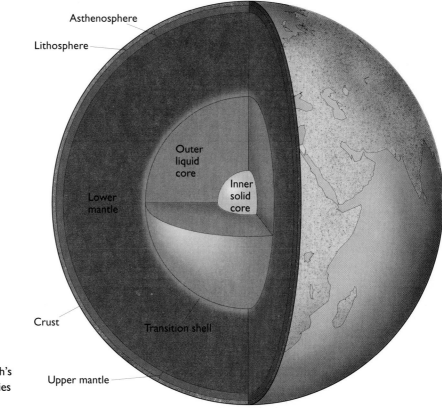

A modern cross section of the Earth's gross structure, as revealed by studies of earthquakes.

there had to be a central core with a radius of about 4500 km. (Earth's radius is 6370 km.)

Such early geophysical work relied on arguments that, although powerful, painted with a very broad brush. Quantitative variations in interior properties could not be resolved in any detail, leaving room for wide differences of opinion. There could be no final victory in the debates between those who believed that the interior was largely fluid and those who, like George Darwin, thought of it as largely solid. One speculative model of the Earth, of a type not thought outrageous at the end of the nineteenth century, is illustrated on the opposite page. The mathematical arguments on density, tides, and the Earth's shape gave a picture of a

slightly flattened planet with a solid crust (possibly quite thick) floating on an elastic or plastic substratum. Beneath this substratum there was a substantial nucleus, a few thousand kilometers in radius, that could be solid or liquid.

In the twentieth century, geophysicists have achieved a far more complete and detailed picture of the Earth's interior, and they have done so almost entirely through the use of a single tool: the analysis of earthquake waves. By examining waves from earthquakes all over the world, they have been able to locate the boundaries and define the composition of already suspected structures, and they have discovered completely unexpected structures. For example, we now know that the core inferred crudely by the nineteenth-century geophysicists is liquid, but that within it exists a solid inner core.

There is in fact no geological research technique that compares with mapping by recorded earthquake waves. Yet the seismological methods used, and their strengths and weaknesses, are not widely known. The basic question is: How can we see inside the Earth using earthquake waves? The first step in finding the answer is to look at the earthquake recordings themselves.

INTERPRETING WAVES THAT HAVE TRAVELED THROUGH THE PLANETARY INTERIOR

On the next page are reproduced seismograms recorded on March 31, 1969, at Kiruna, Sweden; they show waves from an earthquake that occurred more than 6500 km away, deep under the Sea of Japan. The novice will see little more than three sets of wiggly lines marked E, N, and Z, for the three perpendicular directions of ground motion, east-west, north-south, and up-down, respectively. Closer inspection shows offset ticks one minute apart, to mark the passage of time. The seismologist's task at the outset of any analysis is to apply the insight gleaned through years of experience deciphering such wiggly lines.

A full interpretation of the squiggles depends on correctly identifying the seismic waves of different types—*P* waves, *S* waves, and surface waves—and on making a rough determination of the paths within the Earth along which the various waves travel. As an illustration, consider the wave with clear motion on the north-south com-

ponent, marked *ScS*. An experienced seismologist identifies this wave onset, because of its position after the first *S* wave, as *S*-wave energy that has been reflected at a boundary deep in the interior that separates rocks with different elastic properties. Because the wave can be seen to arrive as a sharp peak and trough followed by little subsequent motion, we might be bold enough to infer that the reflection boundary must be rather sharp. A sharp wave onset is a sign that the reflecting surface is not spread out over a range of depths; otherwise the onset would be weak and blunt and the energy would be drawn out over several seconds. (Further, it can be argued that the mechanism of this particular earthquake source in Japan must be rather simple; otherwise the complexity of fault rupture would produce many wiggles after the first *ScS* onset.) In general, all wave onset interpretations must rely on the very extensive knowledge gathered by observatory seismologists. The observatory detective work relies heavily on knowledge of the movement of seismic waves through the elastic rocks of the Earth and on theoretical models of the fault sources of earthquakes.

Seismologists are aided in their identification of waves by their knowledge of the comparative speeds of the different wave types and the distinctive directions of shaking seen in these types. They will have learned the location of the earthquake already, and they use this information in deciphering the waves. Consider the way the main *P* and *S* pulses appeared at Kiruna in the seismogram on the opposite page. Because the compressional *P* wave travels faster than the shear *S* wave, it arrives at this distance from the earthquake focus in Japan about 8 minutes before the *S* wave. This time interval matches the

Deep-focus earthquake records made at Kiruna, Sweden, on medium-period
seismographs. A characteristic of the records, associated with the large focal depth,
is the absence of surface waves. (Time ticks are one minute apart.)

interval expected from empirical tables of seismic wave travel times that have been constructed over the past half-century. We may notice also that while the P-wave pulse is most clearly visible on the vertical component of the ground motion, the S-wave pulses are largest on the two horizontal components of ground motion. The main P wave at Kiruna emerges at the Earth's surface at a steep angle, pushing and pulling the rocks, mainly in the vertical direction. By contrast, the S wave, being mainly a transverse motion of the rocks, has its largest amplitude in the north-south horizontal direction. Because the direction across the surface of the Earth from Kiruna to Japan is closer to east-west than to north-south, the S-wave energy has been partitioned, as predicted by theory, so that the greatest amplitudes occur in the north-south direction, at right angles to the direction from which the S waves are coming.

NAMES OF THE DIFFERENT WAVES

Because P and S waves may take any of a multitude of possible paths through the Earth's interior, seismologists need a systematic notation to identify the various paths. These path symbols have been used to identify the waves in the Kiruna seismogram. The different waves are classified depending on their type and the encounters that they have made with different major boundaries inside the Earth.

The simplest notation defines waves in terms of their paths. As in the case of rays of light, it is helpful to think of seismic rays as curved lines that follow the wave paths. Like light rays falling on a water surface, seismic rays are also governed by the laws of reflection and refraction. Unlike light, however, the reflections and refractions of P and S waves at the Earth's surface and subterranean boundaries generally produce families of composite seismic rays (see page 33).

Rays that travel directly without reflection between the focus and the seismograph are designated by a single symbol *P* or *S* when the ray segment lies entirely in the Earth's mantle. Any ray segment of a *P* wave that lies in the outer core is labeled *K* (from the German *Kernwellen,* for "core waves"), and any segment of *P* type in the inner core is labeled *I*. In this scheme, the notation *PKIKP,* for example, is interpreted as a *P* wave starting in the mantle, refracted into the outer core as a *P* wave (*K* leg), and then refracted through the inner core as another *P* wave (*I* leg). Finally, the *PKIKP* wave is refracted back out of the inner core into the outer core as a *P* wave (second *K* leg); in its final leg, *PKIKP* travels as a *P* wave through the mantle to the surface.

There is no symbol corresponding to *K* for *S* waves because shear waves have not been found with paths through the liquid outer core. The symbol *J*, however, is used for the paths of *S* waves that may have passed through the inner core. The definite identification of such *S* waves would be evidence that the inner core is solid, but it should be remembered that they would have to turn into *P* waves to get back to the surface through the liquid outer core. We would thus have to look for tiny *PKJKP* waves—a fascinating search that still continues.

Earthquake waves also multiply when reflected at the outer surface of the Earth. As drawn in the illustration on the next page, reflected *P* waves with two legs are denoted *PP*, with three legs *PPP*, and so on. In the same way, we have *SS*, *SSS*, and so on, for surface reflections of *S* waves. Because seismic waves trav-

eling through solid rock are converted at rock boundaries from one wave type to another, a notation for mixed ray paths is also needed. Thus, we identify as *SP* a wave that travels its first leg in the mantle as an *S* wave and its second leg as a *P* wave. Some straightforward extensions of the ray names, such as *PSP* and *SKS*, can be followed in the diagram. When waves are reflected at a boundary, appropriate lowercase letters are inserted: for example, *PcP* denotes the *P* wave through the mantle reflected at the boundary between the mantle and core; the letter *i* denotes a reflection at the inner core boundary.

Reflected *P* and *S* waves are powerful detectors of sharp boundaries inside the Earth. A fascinating case made use of the reflected waves *PKPPKP*, called *P'P'* for short. In 1968 R. D. Adams at the Seismological Observatory in New Zealand observed small waves that arrived slightly earlier than the usual *P'P'* echoes. Ordinary waves of the *P'P'* type make the long journey from the focus of an earthquake to the other side of the Earth and are reflected back to a station in the same hemisphere as the earthquake, having passed through the core twice. Adams interpreted the precursor waves as *P'P'* waves that did not quite reach the opposite surface of the Earth but were reflected back from a discontinuity in the upper mantle.

Waves of the *P'P'* type are particularly useful for probing the Earth's structure. Their path is so long that they arrive some 39 minutes after they have begun to be generated by fault slip. Therefore, when they reach the seismograph, most of the other waves sent out in the earthquake have already arrived at the observatory, and the instrument is quiescent.

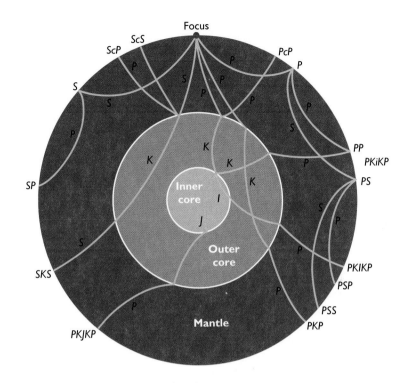

Sample seismic rays through the Earth.

A particularly striking example of multiple long-distance reflections was provided by an underground nuclear explosion at the Russian test site in Novaya Zemlya on October 14, 1970. The $P'P'$ waves passed through the Earth's core, were reflected under Antarctica, and returned to the Northern Hemisphere. In a recording made at the Jamestown observatory, the main echo $P'P'$ is the most prominent feature on the seismogram. About 20 seconds before the onset of the large $P'P'$ reflections, a train of much smaller waves begins that can be explained as reflections from the underside of layers located in the 80 kilometers of rock below the surface of

Antarctica. These forerunner waves are thus designated $P'80P'$.

As the eye scans the seismogram farther from right to left, only inconsequential waves are seen for more than a minute and a half; they are minor jiggles continuously produced by the background microseismic noise of the Earth. All at once, almost precisely two minutes before the first $P'80P'$ waves, a beautiful doublet appears: two sharp peaks, separated by a few seconds, that stand out clearly above the background shaking. These sharp pulses agree closely with the expected arrival time of rays reflected by a layer located some 650 km below the surface of

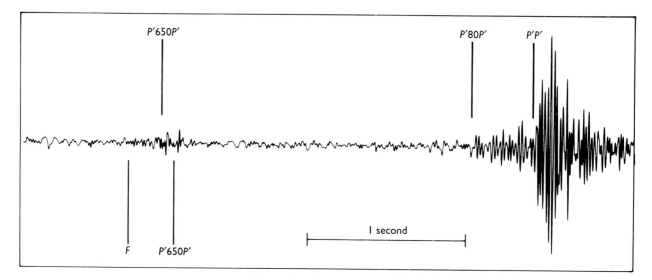

An underground nuclear test on October 14, 1970, on the Russian island of Novaya Zemlya produced this seismic trace at the Jamestown Station in California. The large waveform $P'P'$ was produced by a compressional wave reflected from the other side of the globe under Antarctica. It was preceded by an echo $P'80P'$, reflected from a structure 80 km below the surface of that continent. Two minutes earlier are P waves reflected from layers about 650 km below the surface.

Antarctica; hence they are designated $P'650P'$. The presence of a doublet means that there was only a slight variation in the paths of the two rays reflected from the 650-km layer. Perhaps one of the rays entered a transition layer within the inner solid core and the other ray did not.

TRAVEL TIMES OF EARTHQUAKE WAVES

In introducing a notation for describing earthquake waves that have been reflected and refracted by deep Earth structures, in a way we have put the cart before the horse, and we must now return to the basic question: Given the kind of wiggly lines seen in the illustration on page 129, how can the various observed pulses be used to infer the structures through which they pass or from which they rebound? The method depends on establishing, first of all, the time of travel of earthquake waves to various distances. The concept has already been discussed to some extent in Chapter 5 in relation to the exploration of the Earth's crust. The method's results are some of the great geological successes of the study of earthquakes.

Let us start with a set of earthquakes from various places around the globe. If the locations of their hypocenters and their times of origin are known, the clocks on the seismographs allow us to determine the time it has taken for the energy of the P, S, or surface waves to pass to the geographic locations of the recording seismographs on the Earth's surface. We may then plot this travel time as a function of distance. When dealing with waves through the Earth's crust, where the distances traveled are not great, it is convenient to plot the travel times against the travel distance in kilometers. However, when distances around the Earth's surface are being considered, it is much more convenient to measure the distance in terms of the angle at the Earth's center that subtends the source and the recording site. Thus, a seismic ray that passes right along the diameter of the Earth would emerge at a distance of 180 degrees. The distance between the epicenter of the Japanese earthquake and the seismograph at Kiruna, Sweden, is 63 degrees. An angular distance of 1 degree on the Earth's surface corresponds to about 110 km.

As the travel times of many earthquake waves are recorded by observatories, the scatter in the points begins to indicate an average curve. This trend can then be used to locate the hypocenters of other earthquakes from the arrival times of P and S waves recorded at numerous seismographic stations around the world. The location process is described in Chapter 3. These improved earthquake source locations can then be used to revise the travel-time tables, and these more reliable tables used to locate more accurate hypocenters, and so on. This whole process of travel-time revision is now performed automatically by computers.

After almost a century of such work, the average travel times of P and S waves through the Earth are now known to within about a sec-

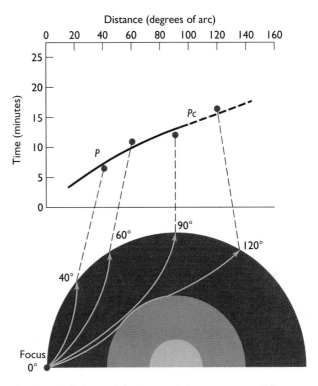

A seismological travel-time curve is here constructed from the measured travel times of P waves through the Earth's mantle. The dashed line labeled Pc corresponds to diffracted waves creeping into the shadow of the liquid core.

ond of scatter. The main effort nowadays is to determine any significant differences in travel-time curves for various regions of the world; these differences then point to departures in the physical properties of the Earth's interior from radial symmetry. Such differences can be substantial; in the case of waves traveling through the subduction zones, for example, travel times can differ by 5 seconds or more for both P and S waves.

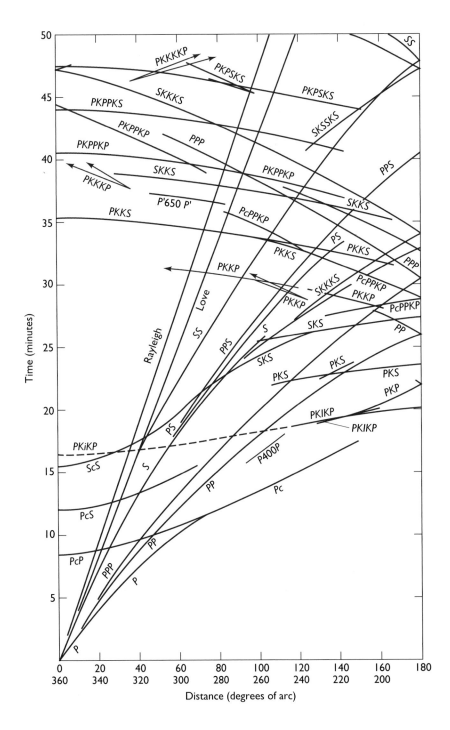

These famous travel-time curves (slightly modified by the author) were constructed in 1939 from many earthquake recordings by Sir Harold Jeffreys and his student K. E. Bullen.

The most famous set of seismological average travel times for the whole globe is shown in the graph on the opposite page. These times were constructed in the late 1930s, using the convergent approach described above, by two of the century's most outstanding seismologists, Sir Harold Jeffreys and Professor K. E. Bullen. This graph has served for more than fifty years in many studies of the Earth's interior as a standard against which deviations in wave propagation times are measured.

THE DISCOVERY OF THE EARTH'S LIQUID CORE

One of the most brilliant pieces of detective work in the history of seismology was the discovery of the core of the Earth by the British geologist R. D. Oldham, who published the result in a famous paper in 1906. Oldham's discovery illustrates well how, given travel-time curves such as those of Jeffreys and Bullen, seismologists can infer the architecture of the Earth's interior.

Following the approach outlined above, Oldham plotted the travel times of both *P* and *S* waves from a number of known earthquake sources. He called these waves the "first phases" and "second phases." Oldham's earthquake sources provided travel times for waves traversing distances from 20 degrees to almost 160 degrees, as shown in the plot on the next page from his original paper. The scale at which Oldham plotted the travel times is much compressed compared with the scale given on the preceding page.

Oldham noted two important discontinuities in the travel-time curves. First, at a distance of

Richard Dixon Oldham (1858–1936), the discoverer of the Earth's core.

about 130 degrees, the "first phase" arrivals, which we now know to be *P* waves, began to be delayed by a minute or so, on average, compared with the trend suggested by the earlier part of the curve. Second, the curve for the "second phase," which we now identify as *S* waves, could only be followed to about 120 degrees; beyond this distance the arrival of the *S* waves was delayed by 10 minutes or more. To explain the delay, Oldham hypothesized that these *S* waves had penetrated a central core that transmits *S* waves at a distinctly slower speed—about half

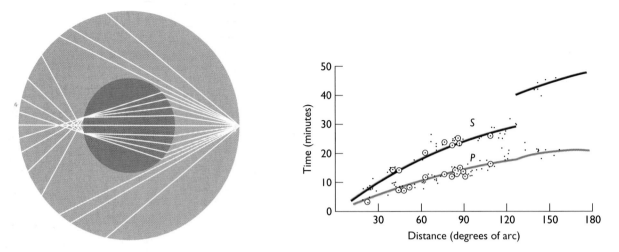

The travel-time curves constructed by R. D. Oldham for *P* and *S* waves *(right)* and the simplified wave paths he suggested for a simple two-part Earth *(left)*, from Oldham's 1906 publication.

that of waves traveling through the surrounding shell. His argument can be followed easily from the ray diagram from his paper, reproduced on this page. He stated:

> The core is not penetrated by wave paths which emerge at 120 degrees, and the great decrease [of speed] at 150 degrees shows that the wave paths emerging at this distance have penetrated deeply into it. Because the chord at 120 degrees reaches a maximum depth from the surface of half the radius, it may be taken that the central core does not extend beyond about 0.4 of the radius *R* from the center.

We know now that there are certain difficulties with Oldham's identification of the wave types, and, of course, the arithmetic is only approximate. For example, Oldham drew the ray paths as straight lines, whereas because the elastic moduli of the rocks increase with depth in the Earth, the rays actually travel along curved paths that are convex toward its center. What is a crucial test of Oldham's claim? If there is a core of the type Oldham predicted, then *P* and *S* wave reflections from earthquakes should be seen bouncing from it. Indeed, we have already noted reflections of this kind *(ScS)* on the Kiruna seismogram on page 129. More extensive observations of wave reflections led Professor Beno Gutenberg (1889–1960), working in Germany with a larger set of earthquake records than that available to Oldham, to give in 1914 the first rather precise estimate for the depth of the core. Gutenberg's estimated depth of 2900 km has stood the test of time, and modern estimates of the core depth are within a few kilometers of this value.

As knowledge of the Earth's core grew, geologists first asked whether waves that penetrated the core were delayed because the core material was fluid or because wave energy was being damped by rocks softened in the prevailing great temperatures and pressures. In the 1930s, it became clear that beyond about 105 degrees, earthquake waves propagating from the other side of the Earth were difficult to observe. Direct P waves from distant earthquakes became weak beyond this distance, and the first strong waves arrived three minutes or so later than might have been expected from a simple extension of the P travel-time curve on page 134. In addition, S waves, which do not travel through liquids, could not be identified from seismograms at the times predicted by an extrapolation of the S-wave curve beyond 105 degrees in the travel-time diagram. Thus, we may think of the core as presenting a screen to the illumination of the antipodes by direct S waves.

All these properties of the observed P and S waves could be explained by assuming that the core was liquid rock that had melted as the temperature climbed to more than 5000°C at these depths. Since this early work, telltale S waves that may have propagated through the core have been searched for many times, but none have been found. When the circumstantial and negative evidence is considered together with the tidal yielding of the whole Earth in response to the pull of the Moon and the Sun and with the way the planet as a whole vibrates after great earthquakes, it is now almost certain that the outer part of the core is a liquid.

THE DISCOVERY OF THE EARTH'S INNER CORE

Another intriguing story about the use of earthquake waves to sense deep Earth structure tells of a discovery by a Danish seismologist, Inge Lehmann, who in 1936 first published evidence that there is an inner core about the size of the Moon within the outer core. Lehmann had attended the first coeducational school in Denmark, which had been founded and maintained by an aunt of Niels Bohr. Unusually for the

Inge Lehmann (1888–1993), the discoverer of the Earth's inner core.

time, she was encouraged to pursue a scientific career, partly because, as she later recalled, at her school "no difference between the intellect of boys and girls was recognized, a fact that brought me disappointments later in life when I had to realize that this was not the general attitude." After graduating from the University of Copenhagen in Mathematics and Physical Science, she began her work in seismology in 1925. In 1928, she was appointed chief of the Seismological Department of the Royal Danish Geodetic Institute in Copenhagen, a post she held until her retirement in 1953.

Copenhagen is well situated for the recording of waves that pass through the core of the Earth from large earthquakes in the seismic zones of the Pacific Ocean. Exploiting this advantage, Lehmann obtained considerable experience reading seismograms of these waves and, by clever application of the scientific method, made the decisive step forward.

In her examination of seismograms from Pacific earthquakes, Lehmann found waves that could not be explained by contemporary models of the Earth's interior. An example of such a wave, flagged by the first indicator arrows, appears in the seismograms on this page. Lehmann believed that the arrival times of these waves could be explained if the waves had reflected off a small inner core.

Lehmann constructed an argument of several steps to support her conclusion. She first assumed a simple two-shell model of the Earth, composed of a core and a mantle. She further assumed that P waves would travel with a constant velocity of 10 km/s through the mantle and 8 km/s through the core. These speeds are reasonable *average* values for both regions. She then introduced a small central core, which, again, was taken to have constant P-wave speed. Her simplifying assumptions allowed her to take the seismic rays to be straight lines (chords), as

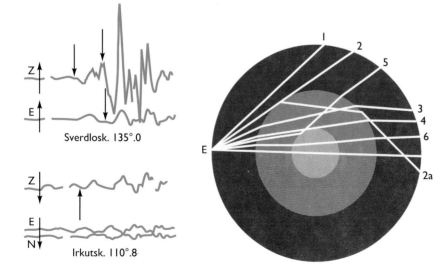

Sverdlosk. 135°.0

Irkutsk. 110°.8

In her 1936 publication, Inge Lehmann referred to these seismographs recorded from a New Zealand earthquake of June 16, 1929, at two Russian stations. The core wave arrivals are marked by arrows. She proposed that the earliest core waves had bounced off an inner core, as wave number 5 does in her diagram of the simplified wave paths for a simple three-part Earth.

Oldham had done; thus, she could calculate the theoretical travel times for this model by elementary trigonometry. She then proceeded by successive calculations to show that a reasonable radius of the inner core could be found that agreed with the observed travel times of the early core waves. Her hypothesis was that the early core waves were reflected from a hypothetical inner core having a radius of about 1500 km. The reflected waves would emerge at earthquake observatories at distances shorter than 142 degrees from the earthquake source, at times close to those actually observed. Lehmann published these results in a paper with one of the shortest titles in seismology; namely, "*P′*." She was careful to state in the paper that she had not *proved* the existence of the inner core but had put forward a model that had a high likelihood of being correct.

Until the early 1960s, it was not clear whether the boundary of the inner core is sharp or is spread out over a distance of up to 100 km. A fundamental property of wave reflections is that gradual and indistinct boundaries will turn back the wave energy weakly, with broad indistinct waveforms, especially at higher angles of incidence. The standard Jeffreys-Bullen travel-time curves of the day had been constructed under the assumption that a zone of gradual transition exists between the inner and outer cores. Thus, these curves predicted that no *PKP* waves would be seen arriving at distances less than 110 degrees from the earthquake source, because waves reflected at those higher angles of incidence would lose energy in the transition zone and become too weak to reach the surface.

In 1963, I undertook with a student, Mary O'Neill, to study core waves recorded by the seismographs of the Berkeley network of stations. We observed *P* waves arriving at distances shorter than 110 degrees from the earthquake source, precisely those distances forbidden by the travel-time curves of the day. Furthermore, these wave pulses were of very short duration, indicating that they had wavelengths as short as 5 km, compared with the more usual 10 to 100 km. Consequently, we were seeing waves that had been reflected from a sharp boundary to the inner core—no thicker than about 5 km. The measured travel times of these waves indicated that the reflecting surface was at a radius of 1216 km from the Earth's center.

ECHOES FROM THE CORE

If the sharpness of the boundaries of the inner and outer cores remained at all uncertain after the study of core waves recounted above, any doubt was put to rest in the 1970s by evidence from artificial earthquakes. During this decade, an array of seismographs operating in Montana recorded waves from underground nuclear explosions in Nevada at an angular distance of only 10 degrees. These seismographs were thus able to capture reflections at a very high angle of incidence from deep inside the Earth, producing seismograms such as those on page 140. These onsets had travel times corresponding to those predicted for *PcP* and *PKiKP* waves. Undoubtedly, they were earthquake echoes that had bounced steeply from the boundary of either the outer core *(PcP)* or the inner core *(PKiKP)*. There were two immediate conclusions. First, the two core surfaces are sharp; second, their radii are within a few kilometers of those that had been predicted by the Jeffreys-Bullen tables.

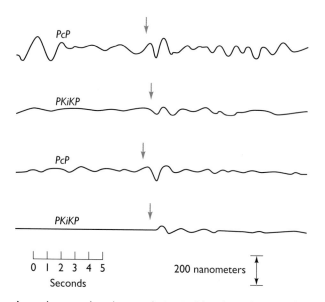

PcP

PKiKP

PcP

PKiKP

|_|_|_|_|_|_|
0 1 2 3 4 5
Seconds

200 nanometers

Nuclear test in Nevada   Seismic array in Montana

Mantle

PcP

Outer
liquid
core

PKiKP

Solid core

An underground nuclear explosion in Nevada on January 19, 1968 (code-named "Faultless"), produced these traces on seismographs in Montana. The vertical scale shows the magnitude of ground movement involved; 200 nanometers is only half the wavelength of violet light. Echoes bounced back from the outer core (PcP) and inner core (PKiKP) at an angle of only 10 degrees.

The second line of evidence on the nature of the outer core boundary is one of the most spectacular in seismology. If the outer core boundary is sharp, then the P waves that travel through the liquid outer core should bounce back into the liquid at appropriate angles when they reach the opposite edge of the core. After reflecting, they travel back through the outer core until they again encounter its edge and are bounced back once more. At each bounce, some of the energy is reflected back into the fluid, and some is refracted into the mantle, finding its way to the surface where it is recorded by seismographs. Modern sensitive seismographs, at quiet sites, detect those very minute signals that have been trapped inside the core and reflected there many times. The waves are denoted by symbols such as P4KP and P7KP, which indicate four and seven reflections of P waves within the core, respectively. The wave paths are checked by a computer to produce a realistic model of the Earth, such as the one shown on this page.

With this behavior in mind, it was a treasured moment for me one day in 1973 when I scanned a seismogram made at the Jamestown seismographic station in California, on which was recorded an underground nuclear explosion at a weapons test site at Novaya Zemlya in the Soviet Union. At the second predicted for a *P7KP* wave to arrive, I could see an unmistakable wave pulse nestling in the microseismic background noise. Rarely before had such a seismic wave been unequivocally identified. Exotic earthquake waves of this type have been observed now in many seismograms. Up to 13 legs have been recorded within the liquid core.

We can immediately draw important conclusions about the physics of this part of the Earth's interior. First, the damping of the *P* waves in the liquid core must be very small because they are able to continue to bounce backward and forward with so little attenuation. This low damp-

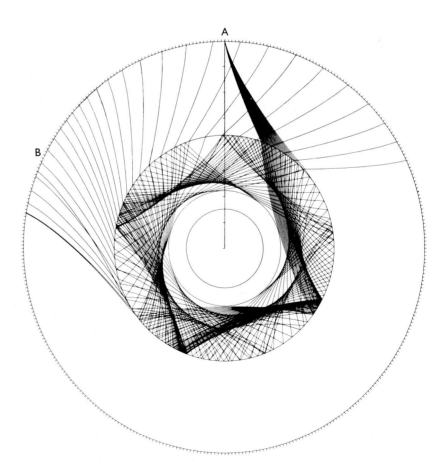

Multiple reflections from *P* waves trapped inside the Earth's liquid outer core. This computer plot depicts the paths of waves, generated by a seismic event at A, that have bounced inside the core seven times before reaching the surface; for example, at station B.

141

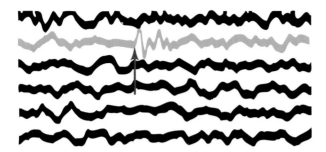

The faint pulse of the *P4KP* echo can be seen in this seismogram made at Jamestown, California, of an underground explosion on Novaya Zemlya, Russia, in 1970.

THE INVERSE PROBLEM

In carrying out the first stages of their pioneer work, Oldham and Lehmann solved what are called in science "direct problems." In specific terms, they proposed tentative models of the Earth, which they defined by adopting radii for the internal boundaries and by assuming plausible seismic wave velocities. Then, using simple formulas such as "velocity equals distance divided by time," they predicted a theoretical travel time, which they could compare with the observed travel times. This type of problem is said to be direct because the properties of the Earth's interior are assumed to be known, and direct calculations from these properties predict when the waves would be observed on the Earth's surface. In the second stages of their arguments, they used trial and error to improve the agreement between model and observation.

In fact, problems in remote sensing of the deep interior of a planet must be solved by both "direct" and "inverse" arguments. Seismologists often begin with observations of the travel times to given distances, and from these they derive the distribution of velocities and hence the geological structure. Problems of this kind are "inverse problems." They arise in many scientific contexts, from medicine to industrial engineering, and constitute one of the most fascinating parts of modern scientific work.

A typical example comes from the study of earthquake fault sources. If the distribution of rough patches along an active fault were known, then a simple calculation would give us the appearance of the seismogram at the Earth's surface. In fact, we never know the distribution of asperities directly. We must infer it by arguing backward from the pattern of seismic waves re-

ing indicates that the rocks of the outer core, perhaps an alloy of iron, do not have the viscous solid-state properties of the solid mantle. Second, the wave onsets remain sharp even after many reflections. This is a sign that the reflecting surface is not spread out over a range of depth; thus the underside of the mantle-core boundary must be a sharp discontinuity.

Third, the mantle-core boundary cannot, even if sharp, vary in its radius very significantly. If there are any undulations or bumps on the inner surface of the core, they must be small. Otherwise, as the successive *P7KP* waves are generated, they would be scattered and arrive at times different from those predicted by a smooth core boundary. By this argument, we can infer that any bumps on the underside of the mantle-core interface are less than 10 km in height, if they exist at all. Such smoothness is a rather remarkable feature of a zone so deep within the Earth, where very hot plastic mantle rock and liquid core rock are in contact and where the liquid rock of the core moves under convection.

corded by strong-motion seismographs at the surface. We will take up this question again in Chapter 8.

The basic method used in determining the deep structure of the Earth's interior is to translate curves of measured travel times of seismic waves, like those shown on page 134, into a distribution of average seismic wave velocity throughout the Earth. A radially symmetric Earth model is assumed as a first approximation, a step that makes the P and S speeds a function only of depth and greatly simplifies the calculations. The method makes use of a powerful numerical scheme worked out in the mid-1930s for computing, from the travel-time curves, the variation in P or S velocity $v(r)$ as a function of the radius r. The scheme relies on mathematical transformations also used in inverse applications in optics and acoustics. In the graph on this page is plotted a recent set of curves for the P and S velocity distributions in the Earth based on this numerical inversion. Because these velocities are mathematically connected to the density and elastic properties of the rocks through which they pass, the curves provide a reliable way to infer the rock types present at any depth in the Earth.

Abrupt changes in velocity clearly define the gross structures of the Earth's interior, but the velocity distribution curves also reveal more subtle variations in structure within the mantle, the great shell that extends from the base of the crust for a distance of about 2900 km to the boundary of the liquid core. The mantle can be immediately divided into two large regions. The upper mantle, which extends down to a depth of about 670 km, is characterized by rather rapid changes with depth in the average velocities of the P and S waves traveling within it. Its lower

boundary is the same boundary revealed by the reflection of $P'650P'$ waves, discussed on page 132. This section of the mantle includes the lithosphere and asthenosphere, and it is of great importance because the bottom of the lithosphere separates the overlying rigid part containing the tectonic plates from the more mobile flowing portion of the mantle.

The lower mantle makes up the bulk of the Earth. The P and S velocity curves show that, on average, the speed of earthquake waves within the lower mantle increases gradually with depth. These increases in P and S velocity can almost

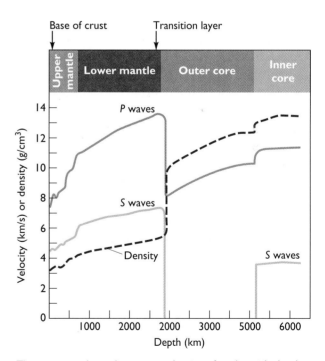

These curves show the average density of rocks with depth through the Earth and the speeds of P and S waves traveling through them.

certainly be explained by the greater and greater compression of the rocks by the overlying material as the depth increases. The lower mantle consists of dense silicate rocks, and because *S* waves as well as *P* waves travel through almost all parts of it, we know that the mantle is solid and strong, at least on short scales of time. However, the mantle rocks also flow slowly over intervals of millions of years because they have viscous properties that are enhanced by the high temperatures at these profound depths.

A closer scrutiny of the travel times of earthquake waves through the mantle in different geographical regions has indicated that there are two marked deviations from this simple picture. First, the travel times of different wave paths may vary by 10 to 15 percent from the average travel times for other paths to equal distances. This disparity in travel times indicates that the mantle is not entirely homogenous but contains within it a lumpiness, particularly in the upper mantle but also to some extent at greater depths. Second, in a zone 100 to 200 km wide above the boundary between the mantle and the core, there is an anomalous region in which the speeds of the seismic *P* and *S* waves are not what would be expected if the rock properties continued uniformly all the way to the boundary. Because this thin transition layer is so close to the liquid core, its physical properties, when unraveled, should give a key to the interactions between the solid mantle and the liquid rock in the core.

THE EARTH'S OSCILLATIONS

Since the massive Chilean earthquake of May 1960, it has been known that very great earthquakes are energetic enough to shake the whole Earth in a manner that would produce motions of the ground perceptible to seismographs. One modern method of central importance for inferring the properties of the Earth's interior looks at the different tones at which the Earth rings after it is set into vibration by an earthquake.

I well remember my own delight in carrying out a search for the Earth's fundamental frequency of oscillation following the 1960 Chilean earthquake. My method was to look mathematically for the vibrations hidden in the seismo-

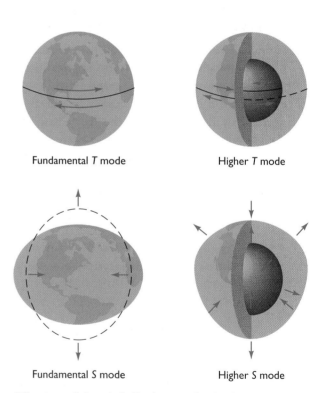

Fundamental *T* mode

Higher *T* mode

Fundamental *S* mode

Higher *S* mode

Vibrations of the whole Earth may take the form of *T* modes, caused by solely horizontal displacements of the Earth's rocks, and *S* modes, caused by displacements along the Earth's radius together with horizontal displacements.

grams of this earthquake recorded by a very long period pendulum in the Grotta Gigante near Trieste, Italy. The longest periods of vibration I measured were 54.0 and 44.0 minutes for the global motions drawn in the first column of the illustration on the opposite page. But I also found many overtones of the motion, such as those illustrated in the second column. These Earth harmonics arise just as musical harmonics do when a guitar string is plucked. It has long been known that the frequencies of the resonant vibrations of an elastic string or of a tolling bell can be calculated directly from the physical properties of the elastic body. By analogy, if we knew the physical elastic properties inside the Earth, as we might know the density and elasticity of a brass bell, we could calculate the expected frequencies and amplitude pattern of the resonant vibrations following a great earthquake. This direct problem, however, is the opposite of what we need to do: we start with the observed vibrations and try to construct a model of the inaccessible interior having a structure and elastic properties that will produce tones with frequencies in agreement with the observed ones.

Although this inverse problem is recalcitrant because many workable models are possible, progress is being made. Each time a great earthquake sets up the free vibrations of the Earth, the global system of seismographic stations produces a fruitful harvest of measurements of these resonances. Even in 1960, the measurements of the Earth's vibrations were used to confirm the general structure of its interior already inferred from the *P* and *S* wave travel times.

The measurements of the whole Earth vibrations also give us another important insight into the properties of the rocks deep inside the Earth. Because the vibrations die away over many hours, they measure the damping properties of the rocks in the Earth. These damping values, in turn, provide an estimate of the viscosity of the rocks at various depths. In the future, reliable measurements of these viscosities will help in modeling the convective motions of the mantle that drive the surface tectonics of the Earth.

THREE-DIMENSIONAL IMAGES OF THE EARTH'S INTERIOR

We have seen how earthquakes are used to probe the deep structures that would be found in any slice through the Earth: the mantle and the

MAIN SHELLS OF THE EARTH'S INTERIOR

Descriptive name	Range of depth (km)	Physical state
Crust	5–11 (oceans)	Solid
	0–40 (continents)	Solid
Upper mantle:		
Noncrustal lithosphere	Moho to 150 km	Solid
Asthenosphere	150–670	Solid (upper part near melting)
Lower mantle	670–2780	Solid
Transition shell	2780–2885	Solid (lower velocities)
Outer core	2885–5155	Liquid
Inner core	5155–6371	Solid

outer and inner cores. The resulting picture of the Earth, illustrated on page 127, is of concentric shells of spherically symmetric structures. Although it is a simplification, this picture was a necessary basis for understanding the history and evolution of our planet. As discussed in Chapter 5, the outer surface and crust of the Earth are, of course, anything but radially symmetric. That is, they have different properties along different slices through the Earth's crust. For this and other reasons, we might expect that there will also be lateral variations in rock properties even at profounder depths. For a complete architectural map of the interior, we need to pass from a two-dimensional to a three-dimensional image of the whole Earth.

In the last ten years, there have been striking advances in resolving these lateral variations, particularly in the upper mantle but also around the Earth's core. Geologists have even found hints of nonsymmetries in the inner core. These exciting developments represent the culmination of the dreams of the early geophysicists such as Oldham, Milne, Jeffreys, Gutenberg, and Lehmann. They are made possible through the cooperation of the network of appropriate seismographs encircling the world. Such a network of digital instruments, able to record remote earthquakes above magnitude 6 within a broad band of frequencies, is now largely in place—at least on the land surfaces of the Earth.

Scientific disciplines often turn to technologies and techniques of analysis developed in another area of science. So it is with the efforts to use earthquakes to probe the deep interior of the Earth. In this case, the powerful new exploration method, called tomography, was pioneered in medicine to observe the human body and in engineering to study flaws in materials. In modern medicine, this technique, used by doctors to obtain images of anomalous growths in the body, goes by the name of CAT scanning, for "computerized axial tomography." Sensors placed on one side of the body indicate the way that variations in the density or absorption of human tissues affect the intensity of X rays or atomic particles applied from the other side. Similarly, in geophysics, waves generated in earthquakes are observed after their passage through the interior of the Earth at seismographic observatories around the Earth's surface.

When preparing to scan the human body for abnormal organ variations, medical tomographers carefully design the placement of the detection instruments around the organ. Unlike their medical counterparts, seismologists cannot control the source of the tomographic probes; they must make do with those large earthquakes that happen to occur in the rather limited seismic areas of the world. Nevertheless, the two techniques are basically very similar. In both cases, a numerical image of the internal structure is reconstructed from the properties of the waves that have traveled through the structure from source to receiver. The seismologist has available the deeply descending P and S waves as well as seismic surface waves traveling along different paths in the surficial part of the Earth.

A conventional medical X ray captures a two-dimensional projection of the living organ on film; the overlapping structures make interpretation difficult. In a CAT scan, the X rays are sent along different paths that intersect the target organ; slices of the body's interior can be imaged and stored in the computer memory. By adding up these slices in appropriate ways, an image of the three-dimensional structures is formed. Geophysical tomography uses analogous

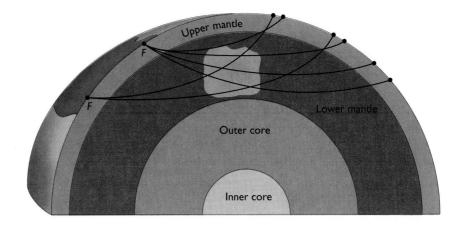

Seismic paths passing through the colored region in the lower mantle provide a tomographic scan of the region.

methods to visualize three-dimensional heterogeneities within the Earth. Waves are examined from many earthquake sources, chosen so that the waves have paths that pass through the region where the anomalous geological structure is being mapped. Very fast computers enable a large number of wave measurements taken at the global seismographic stations to be compared, not only from one earthquake but from many seismic sources. *P* waves, *S* waves, and the reflections—such as *PP*, *SS*, and *ScS*—can all be considered in a joint mathematical and statistical analysis.

The application of tomography to the Earth's interior differs significantly from its application to medicine in one other respect, the physical quantity being measured. In most medical body scans, the anomalous tissue structure absorbs more of the energy of the X rays or other radiation than does normal tissue. Therefore, it is the absorption of the waves that is measured. In the

seismological case, while anomalous structures may absorb more energy, further attenuating the wave, it has not yet proved possible to make much use of this difference in attenuation. Instead, the variation in the *velocity* of the seismic waves along their path is measured. The results are thus described as "fast" and "slow" geological structures in the mantle of the Earth. For an Earth varying only along its radius, a mesh of crisscrossing seismic wave paths indicates locations where the individual paths have deviated from the average velocities. The method's strength can be understood by considering that a deviation from the average rock velocity along one ray path could occur anywhere along it. If, however, the ray path is intersected by another ray path, which has the same deviation in travel time from the expected value, then the two wave paths probably intersect at the place where the anomalous region occurs.

Three-dimensional terrestrial tomography may also be performed using surface wave dispersion. In the graph on page 134 are also shown lines that indicate the average speed of the Rayleigh and Love surface waves. Because these waves travel around the Earth's surface, the curves represent the average speeds along great circle paths between an earthquake source and the recording station.

Soon after surface wave speeds began to be measured, they were found to vary from great circle path to great circle path, indicating that, at least in the outer parts of the Earth, geological structures have significantly different properties from region to region. We saw in Chapter 5 how the dispersion curves of surface waves were used to infer that the crust under the oceans is thinner on average than that under the continental masses. With the new generation of digital seismographs, which allow the recording of much longer wavelengths, it is possible to estimate more detailed structural variations in the mantle by comparing the dispersion properties of surface waves along many intersecting paths around the globe.

THE CONVECTIVE MOTIONS OF THE MANTLE

Such tomographic studies result in maps of the interior showing regions where the earthquake waves travel faster or slower than average. These maps immediately throw light on one of the most debated issues in the exploration of the Earth's interior: the convective motions of the mantle.

The partially liquid or plastic interiors postulated in the early models naturally led to speculation that there is very slow circulation of the viscous rock in the mantle, like the convection currents set up in a pot of boiling oil. Within the Earth, heat from deep in the mantle would be transferred upward in convection cells thousands of kilometers across. By means of these cells, heated viscous rock would flow in a circuit from the hotter deep regions to the cooler surface ones. Because buoyancy would keep the lighter rocks, whether liquid or solid, toward the surface, the silicate rock in the crust was thought to be less dense on average than the rock (probably rich in iron) in the substratum. These speculations, ultimately shown by earthquake studies to be true, were reinforced by observations of lava lakes at volcanoes like Vesuvius and Kilauea, where a crust would often solidify on top of the viscous molten lava.

This concept of vast, slowly churning convection cells in the upper part of the Earth fell into disfavor in the first half of the twentieth century, although it was readily adopted for the core. The easy propagation of S waves through the mantle argued against its being liquid, as was thought necessary for convection. Recently, scientists have again considered the possibility of very slow convection of the plastic but solid rock in the upper substratum and below it, and most now accept that convection does occur. These swings in beliefs about internal motions have depended crucially on evidence from earthquake waves.

Because cooler rocks have contracted and are therefore denser than average, seismic waves travel faster in them. Thus, because tomographic studies can map regions of differing wave velocity, they are able to reveal the warmer rocks moving upward and cooler rocks moving downward in the great mantle convection cells. Consequently, for the first time, the three-dimensional tomographic images deep under continents and oceans, under mid-oceanic ridges and island arcs, provide evidence for ancient and present dynamics of the planet.

To extract the most information from the tomographic results, scientists must display the wave velocity variations in imaginative ways. They must be able to visualize adequately the full three-dimensional shapes and sizes of the anomalous regions, and they must be able to indicate the variations in seismic velocity. Many innovative color graphic schemes with variable perspectives are now available to make possible such scrutiny. Striking examples can be found from recent work based on measurements of earthquake surface waves between pairs of global digital stations.

The image on the next page of deep three-dimensional variations was selected from the still rather restricted number of studies that have produced accessible color diagrams. Because the subject is a hot topic of research at the moment, and because tomographic methods are becoming mastered, many other examples will surely become available in the next decade. The present example is from the published work of Professor Toshiro Tanimoto, now at the University of California at Santa Barbara. Working alone and with colleagues, he has made about 18,000 measurements of surface waves recorded by global broad-band seismographs. He then divided the upper mantle, down to about 500-km depth, into 10,000 small volumes, called volume elements. The next step was to describe the S-wave velocity perturbations from the average for each volume element. These velocity perturbations were defined by 1000 initially unknown parameters that are easily calculated for each volume element from the surface wave measurements using modern computer workstations. This method is able to map anomalous zones with a resolution of about 7000 km laterally and 100 km vertically.

In the image on the next page, visualization of the three-dimensional variations is helped by a special color rendering. Surfaces drawn through volumes of constant S-wave deviations are plotted on a Mercator projection map. Red denotes a deviation of -1.1 percent and blue a deviation of $+1.9$ percent from the average S-wave velocity. Prominent correlations can be seen immediately. The low-velocity (red) zone more or less encircles the Pacific Ocean; the decrease in speed arises from hotter-than-usual rocks in the upper 400 km of the mantle. The Hawaiian Islands also are underlain by a relatively hot asthenosphere. In sharp contrast, the old Precambrian shields of Canada, Australia, and South America are underlain to a depth of 400 km by large patches of rock with higher-than-average earthquake wave velocities. This difference would indicate that the rocks in the upper mantle under the oldest continental masses are colder than rocks found elsewhere.

It is not easy to overdramatize the radical improvements that the x-raying of the Earth's interior using three-dimensional tomographic methods has brought to the process of geological discovery. The heavy constraints imposed by using models of the Earth that allowed only radially symmetric changes in physical properties have now been broken. Perhaps the clearest ex-

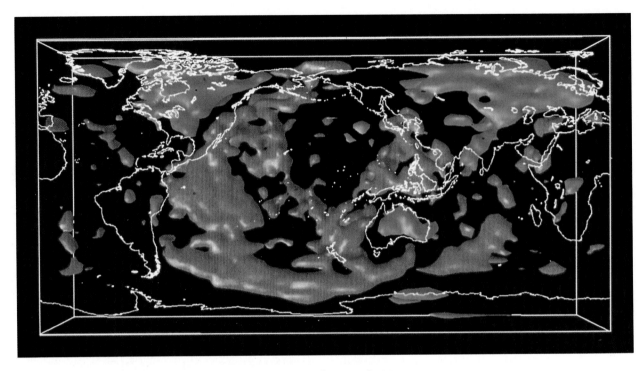

Red blobs show regions where the rock properties give lower S-wave velocities (hot rock) and blue blob regions where they give higher S-wave velocities (cold rock), in this three-dimensional perspective of the upper part of the Earth down to 410 km, drawn using a Mercator projection. The hotter rock around the rim of the Pacific basin is prominent.

ample of progress lies in the growing ability to construct a more realistic picture of the great convection cells within the Earth's interior. Although the plate tectonics theory provided explanations for many major geological features, including the patterns of earthquakes and volcanoes around the globe, a driving engine was lacking. Why did the plates form as they did? Why do they move in the directions they do? And why do they move at the speeds measured? Early attempts to answer these questions by proposing

mantle convection as a driving mechanism used only simple one-dimensional or crude two-dimensional models. For example, rocks might be assumed to flow in a single vertical plane from a mid-oceanic ridge to the downgoing subduction slab. Yet a glance at the world map of tectonic plates on page 108 underscores the great variety of their size and direction of movement.

Through the analysis of huge numbers of wave paths from many earthquake sources, it has already been shown that the convection cells vary in size and location in the mantle. The hot material and the cold material move relative to each other in many lateral directions. There is not always an exact correspondence between the center of the moving plates and the top of the cells, and the cooled rock in the mantle does not necessarily flow back to greater depths along simple vertical sheets.

Tomographic methods are also starting to answer the question of whether the convective circulation of material in the Earth's mantle extends without interruption from the boundary of the core right to the lithosphere or if there is a division at the base of the asthenosphere 670 km below the Earth's surface that separates the larger flow patterns in the lower mantle from small convective cells above. The future of this type of research appears bright. It is well known that the additional tomographic resolution needed can be obtained by installing more broad-band digital seismographs around the globe, particularly in the spaces in the deep oceans from which there are now no recordings. We can expect that within the next decade the main patterns of flow inside the Earth will be well understood.

7

PREDICTING STRONG GROUND SHAKING

WHEN MOST PEOPLE think of earthquake prediction, they think of efforts to forecast the time, location, and magnitude of future earthquakes. But it is equally important to predict the strength and duration of the ground motion. Not only is such forecasting a mark of a mature scientific discipline, but the predictions are crucial for understanding how the intensity of an earthquake varies from place to place and what patterns of damage are likely to result.

In earthquake country, all critical structures such as hospitals, large bridges, dams, high-rise buildings, power stations, and offshore oil platforms must be constructed to withstand the ground motion of large earthquakes. When designing an earthquake-resistant structure for a particular area, engineers rely on predictions of ground motion to tell them the strongest ground shaking that a structure is likely to experience during its lifetime.

Workers digging for the trapped occupants of a concrete building after the 1985 Mexico earthquake.

MAPPING SEISMIC INTENSITY

The first and still most widely used yardstick of the strength of earthquake shaking is seismic intensity, a measure of the damage to structures, of disturbance to the ground surface, and of how strong the shaking felt to people. The intensity is assessed not by reading instruments but by observing the effects in the meizoseismal zone, the area of strong shaking. Thus, intensities can be assigned even to historical earthquakes.

The first intensity scale to achieve general use was developed by M. S. Rossi of Italy and Francis Forel of Switzerland in the 1880s. This scale, which assigns values from I to X, was used to map the intensity of the 1906 San Francisco earthquake. To determine the value for a particular earthquake, a seismologist evaluates many easily observable results of the shaking: the proportion of people who felt it, their physical reaction (did they run outdoors, for example), the movement of household objects, the damage to chimneys and nonreinforced masonry, and so on. These descriptions are then compared with descriptions attached to each of the values on the intensity scale, and a value is selected that makes the closest match.

A more refined scale was devised in 1902 by the Italian volcanologist and seismologist G. Mercalli; its range extends from I to XII. A version is given in the appendix, as modified by H. O. Wood and Frank Neumann to fit building and social conditions in California. (It does not fit all conditions there, however. After an earthquake in the remote northern Sierra Nevada, a disturbed resident telephoned me to ask, "What rating on the modified Mercalli scale would be earthquake noises like a bear climbing on the roof?") Other intensity scales are used in Europe and countries such as Japan where conditions differ from those in California.

Intensities at different locations in the affected area are rated numerically according to the descriptions on the particular scale used, and the sites that have been assigned different values are then separated by contour lines to form an isoseismal map. These maps provide crude but valuable information on the distribution of strong motions, the effect of soils and underlying geological strata, the extent of the fault rupture, and other factors pertinent to engineering problems.

Because eyewitness reports are subjective and because the extent of damage depends on the social and construction practices of a country, they have obvious drawbacks as quantitative measures of seismic wave motions. In particular, they say little about the frequencies of the waves, the duration of strong shaking, the ratio of vertical to horizontal energy, and the ratio of translational to rotational motions—information needed by structural designers. Clearly, instrumental records are required to achieve a complete picture of the ground shaking.

SPECIFYING EARTHQUAKE MOTION

Since their design in the 1930s, strong-motion accelerometers have been able to record the heavier shaking near the source of large earthquakes, where the acceleration of the ground can exceed

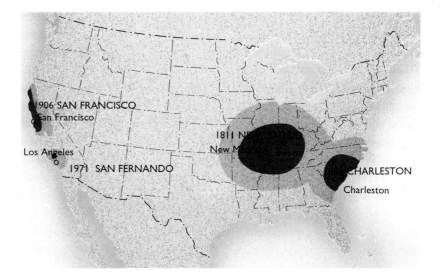

The isoseismal contours for the 1906 San Francisco, the 1971 San Fernando, the 1811–1812 New Madrid, and the 1886 Charleston earthquakes. The contours connect sites having the same modified Mercalli intensity. Each red area corresponds to an intensity of VII or greater and each blue area to an intensity of VI. Ground shaking extends over a much larger area in the eastern United States.

that of gravity at frequencies between 5 and 20 Hz. The number of such accelerometers in earthquake countries around the world grew gradually until the 1960s, when the need for more information on strong ground shaking by both seismologists and engineers stimulated the rapid deployment of such instruments, which now number about 5000 installed throughout the world. At present, California alone has more than 600 strong-motion instruments in the field, and linked sets of accelerometers operate in or on more than 50 buildings, bridges, and dams. The first and most numerous group of accelerometers measures the actual earthquake waves, unaffected by the shaking of nearby large structures. These accelerometers are separated from one another by distances of tens and even hundreds of kilometers. By contrast, the interconnected instruments in a structure are spaced only a few tens of me-

ters apart so that they can measure the detailed vibrations of the structure caused by the shaking of its foundation in the earthquake. Both types of measurements are essential to earthquake-resistant design.

Instrumental records alone, of course, are not sufficient to predict future earthquake intensity. The recorded ground motions must be interpreted. At a considerable distance from an earthquake source, seismograms of ground shaking are generally rather simple in character, consisting of a number of well-separated types of waves. In sharp contrast, the ground motion of a large earthquake near its source is usually quite complicated. It is often difficult even to begin to interpret the complex seismic waves, except in a general way. Because the boundaries of research follow the unexplored problems, seismology now focuses a great deal of attention on seismic

155

strong motions. Scientists around the world are attempting to improve their ability to forecast the strength of earthquake shaking for a given geological setting. From the beginning, strong-motion accelerometers provided two pieces of information that could be read easily from the record: the maximum or "peak" acceleration and the duration of shaking. Both are simple numerical measures that structural engineers may refer to instead of long descriptions of the complexities of actual seismic ground shaking.

A building at rest has no acceleration; it is in a state of equilibrium under the downward force of gravity and the resistive stresses in its supporting frame. When an earthquake occurs, seismic forces are applied to the building supports at the foundations. Because these forces are proportional to the ground acceleration, the peak acceleration of the seismic waves has become the simple parameter most commonly used by engineers to define ground motions. The ground accelerations, and hence the seismic forces, are impressed on the foundations simultaneously in both horizontal and vertical directions. Because buildings have been designed to resist the downward pull of gravity, and thus vertical forces in general, it is the horizontal ground acceleration that is crucial in causing damage.

The use of peak acceleration as a measure evolved in the 1960s when there were few strong-motion records available. In many countries with earthquake risk, certain records became standards for setting design requirements. The most famous of these standards is the strong-motion record obtained in the 1940 Imperial Valley earthquake, magnitude 6.7, by an accelerometer situated at El Centro, California, about 6 km from the ruptured fault source. So common was its use as a standard that I was never surprised when visiting an engineering research laboratory in a foreign country to be presented with "the El Centro record." The peak acceleration of the ground obtained horizontally was $0.33g$ (or 33 percent of the acceleration of gravity), and the strong shaking had a duration of about 30 seconds.

In more recent years, after the deployment of strong-motion accelerometers throughout the world, instrumental measurements were obtained in many moderate-sized and a few large earthquakes. A peak acceleration of $0.5g$ was recorded in the Parkfield, California, earthquake of 1966, and in the years since even greater peak accelerations have been measured in a few cases. For example, in the Imperial Valley, California, earthquake of October 15, 1979, there was a peak acceleration of about $1.7g$ in the vertical direction.

Even as this book was being written, the world record was broken by a magnitude 7.0 earthquake that struck in May 1992 near Cape Mendocino in northern California. During this earthquake, a spike of vertical ground acceleration of at least $1.8g$ was measured. In most cases, such very high acceleration values are represented on the record by only one or two high-frequency waves that are not characteristic of the overall wave pattern. In any case, these narrow spikes cause little vibration in ordinary engineered structures, although such a sharp jolt could throw down smaller objects or affect mechanical and electrical equipment.

As the number of ground motion measurements has increased, another property of the peak motions has come to light. Strong-motion instruments often record high accelerations near the source of even quite small earthquakes. An example was observed in the earthquake that

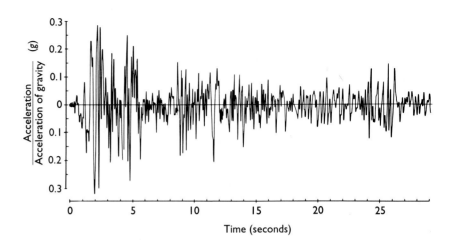

The famous El Centro record of ground acceleration in the 1940 earthquake in southern California.

struck Ancona, Italy, on June 24, 1972. This sharp shock had a magnitude of only 4.5, yet it still damaged older, unreinforced structures in the city. The recorded peak horizontal acceleration was 0.61g, twice that recorded near the fault source of the 1940 El Centro earthquake of magnitude 6.7. Observations such as these demonstrate that the size of earthquakes cannot always be correlated with peak acceleration.

In practice the peak acceleration does not provide enough information to engineers because the peaks tend to be found at high frequencies, which are often the least destructive to sizable structures such as bridges, dams, and high-rise buildings, as explained on page 176. Damage is often much more attributable to the velocity of back-and-forth motion of the foundation and particularly to the foundation's displacement. For these reasons, engineers also consider the maximum velocity and maximum displacement of the ground when designing earthquake-resistant buildings.

Both parameters can be obtained from the recorded peak accelerations by mathematical calculation, specifically by applying the technique of calculus called integration. First, the seismologist plots the peak accelerations at each moment during the earthquake against the time, creating an acceleration time history. Integrating the acceleration time history produces a velocity time history, showing the peak velocity at each moment in time. The square of the velocity is directly proportional to the seismic wave energy that is entering any building. This energy is dissipated in the building by the resistive structural forces working to vibrate the structure elastically or in the worst cases by the bending and breaking of the supporting frame. Integrating the velocity time history in turn produces a displacement time history.

Engineers have tried to counter the effects of high ground acceleration by building structures on foundations that allow some decoupling of the earthquake from the structure itself. This goal goes back at least a century, when many patented anti-earthquake devices were proposed to "isolate" structures from ground shaking. Indeed, such a scheme was attempted by Frank Lloyd Wright in his Imperial Hotel in Tokyo, illustrated on page 21. The essential idea is to allow the structure to displace significantly in the earthquake but at the same time to reduce the high-frequency accelerations that pass upward into the structure by placing damping devices between the ground and the building frame that work like automobile shock absorbers. In such designs, peak displacement rather than peak acceleration is of critical importance. Only a few such base-isolated structures have yet been tested in large earthquakes, but the results have been encouraging.

A structure that withstands the brief moment of peak acceleration may yet be crippled as the shaking continues. Thus, another important measure describing ground motion is the length of time that strong shaking continues at a site, technically termed earthquake duration. It is crucial in predicting the overall energy of the ground motions and in understanding the degree of damage suffered by a structure.

Duration is also a measure of the dimension of the source of the waves. As described in Chapter 4, the seismic waves are radiated from a dislocation that moves across the full dimensions of the faulted surface. The dimensions of the fault are thus connected directly to the total time that seismic waves are radiated from the fault.

The duration tends to increase with magnitude, a trend confirmed by plotting measurements taken in many earthquakes to form a curve. The duration used in constructing the curve is that of the strong acceleration that is significant in affecting structures. This time interval is usually much shorter than the duration of shaking perceived by people in the earthquake, because people are sensitive to motion having accelerations as low as $0.001g$—far too small to damage buildings.

When plotted against time, the parameters of peak acceleration, peak velocity, peak displacement, and duration encapsulate well the history of ground motion in a strong earthquake. The time histories characterized by these four parameters represent the view offered by the time domain, one of the two windows through which we may picture an earthquake. But seismologists and engineers also turn to an alternative representation of earthquakes provided by recordings of the ground motion at various frequencies, known as the frequency spectrum. The motion of an earthquake may be treated conveniently in either the time domain or the frequency domain.

The frequency spectrum of wave motion allows us to look at each component of the total wave pattern: it shows both the amplitude of the wave of each frequency present in the motion and the position (or phase) of each wave making up the overall pattern. The best-known example is the rainbow spectrum formed by a glass lens dispersing white light into the colors from red to violet, each with its own amplitude (or brightness) and phase. A spectrum of strong ground motion also consists of two parts: the amplitude spectrum and the phase spectrum. Normally, only the amplitude spectrum is considered in strong-motion seismology and earthquake engineering, because the wave amplitude at each frequency is directly related to the way the structure vibrates at that frequency. The phase spectrum, however, is also critical in many ways. It defines the pattern of the seismic waves.

We stressed in Chapter 2 that the various waves will arrive in a sequence that depends on the speed of the wave type, whether P, S, or surface wave. On a strong-motion record, therefore, there will be pulses of energy arriving at a site at times defined by the wave type and by the position of the site relative to the rupturing fault. The entire wave pattern is presented in the phase spectrum.

The pattern of wave arrival, or phasing, is an important factor in structural damage, such as cracking concrete. If the structural systems affected showed linear behavior, the response of a structure would be identical even if the waves were to arrive at the structure in reverse order. However, many types of structure behave nonlinearly in heavy shaking. For example, if strong shaking occurs at the beginning of the earthquake, initial cracking and elastic failure cause loss of structural strength. Continued shaking, even at a lower acceleration or velocity, can collapse the weakened structure. If the weak ground wave motion arrived first, on the other hand, it would shake an undamaged structure and have no deleterious effect.

THE BEGINNINGS OF MORE COMPLEX WAVE INTERPRETATION

In the 1940s, it was almost impossible to interpret the wiggly lines on the El Centro photographic record as P, S, and surface waves or to understand their generation by the rupturing fault. The wave types in a complicated seismogram are often most easily identified by comparing wave patterns at neighboring points. This cross-correlation of the waveforms allows an estimate of the speed and direction of waves. Because no adjacent recordings were obtained and because a definitive scientific description of the 1940 earthquake was not available, seismologists were not comfortable using only El Centro motions to predict future ground motions elsewhere by theoretical or numerical modeling.

The importance of installing groups of closely spaced accelerometers was demonstrated in an earthquake of magnitude 5.5 that was generated by a slip on the San Andreas fault near Parkfield, California, in 1966. A straight line of accelerometers extending outward from the San Andreas fault captured a striking change in wave pattern with distance from the fault.

The instrument nearest the San Andreas fault showed that the rocks had heaved back and forth mainly in a single pulselike motion in a horizontal direction perpendicular to the strike of the fault. On instruments farther away from the fault, this pulse became less intense and the duration of strong shaking increased. For the design of engineered structures located near an active fault trace, the question then became whether such a pulse or heave of the ground was typical of earthquake motions near the fault rupture. If the answer was yes, special allowance would have to be made in the design.

Seismologists recognized the variability of the wave pattern at Parkfield as a source of intriguing insights on wave radiation and fault source properties. Subsequent studies indicated that the large horizontal pulse might be expected near all

159

fault ruptures and that it was probably an *SH* wave associated with the fling of the elastic rebound of the strained rocks along the fault.

One of the drawbacks of the Parkfield measurements, however, was that the individual accelerometers, typical of the time, did not provide absolute time. Because of this deficiency, no precise temporal intercorrelation could be made between the waveforms of the various stations. When digital accelerometers able to record the absolute time became available in the 1970s, they could resolve clearly and in detail the complete wave pattern. Seismologists could seriously consider how best to arrange their instruments to disentangle the complicated motion near the earthquake source.

SEISMOGRAPHIC ARRAYS: THE MODERN EARTHQUAKE TELESCOPE

In 1978, in response to the growing interest in obtaining accurate measurements of strong earthquake intensities, a number of organizations convened an international workshop in Hawaii to discuss instrument arrays for recording strong motion. Interested seismologists and engineers from many countries were invited to participate, and some seminal recommendations emerged. The conference report remarked:

Isolated single instruments provide insufficient information to give a clear understanding of the factors influencing strong ground motion. What is required are multiple-instrument, two- to three-dimensional arrays with configurations tailored to the specific

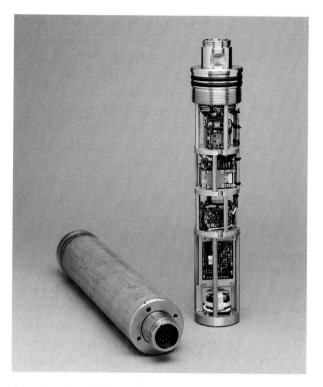

A modern down-hole accelerometer. The inertial mass lies within the yellow bands at the bottom of the tube, under a stack of electronic circuits.

information desired. At the present time, the number of such arrays is inadequate. Only when a greater number of such arrays are operational and data has been gathered will it be possible to improve significantly the accuracy of predictions of the major strong ground motion at a particular site.

The workshop also recommended that arrays be specifically designed for favorable locations in seismically active regions of the world. Out of these deliberations there emerged in the 1980s a body of seismological observations that would have been regarded as extraordinary by seismologists only twenty years earlier. In a short time, the scientific insights into strong ground motion increased sharply, in terms of both theory and observation.

The Hawaii conference concluded that the recording instruments needed to be spaced to capture waves of the frequency appropriate for the seismological problem at hand. For example, high-frequency waves have very short wavelengths; only 100 m would separate the peaks of a 2-Hz wave traveling through soil. To follow the changing waveforms, the instruments would have to be placed at most 100 m apart. For a study of ground motion from a very long fault rupture that produced long-period waves up to 100 seconds, the distance between the stations in an array would need to be on the order of 10 km. However, for the design of critical stiff structures such as nuclear reactors, frequencies of about 10 Hz are important. Such high frequencies would require spacings between the accelerometers of a few tens of meters.

Because seismic waves emerge from their passage through the Earth's interior at various angles to the ground surface, instrumentation is also needed along a vertical line—for example, at intervals down a bore hole—to measure the upward and downward passage of the waves. Unfortunately, "down-hole" arrays are expensive to install compared with surface instrumentation, so this facet of the program progressed more slowly at first, except in Japan. The installation of down-hole arrays did not gather momentum in California, for example, until after the 1989 Loma Prieta earthquake.

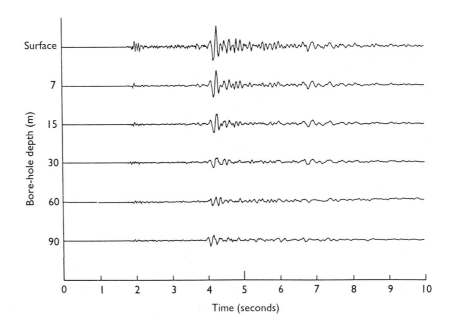

Records from down-hole accelerometers show the intensity of shaking decreasing with depth.

The first large array of digital strong-motion seismographs was installed on the northeast coast of Taiwan in September 1980. Because of its location, the array is designated by the acronym SMART 1, for Strong Motion Array, Taiwan, No. 1. The choice of Taiwan, a highly seismic area, proved to be most productive. Since its inception, SMART 1 has recorded more than 3000 accelerogram traces from over 50 earthquakes, of magnitudes from 3.6 to 7.0. The epicentral distances of these earthquakes from the array center ranged from 3 to 200 km, and the focal depths to 100 km. Thus the sample of

earthquake types and distances of wave propagation has been a very wide one. Moreover, the recorded earthquakes have resulted from all types of focal mechanisms ranging from the strike-slip type, common in California, to the thrust type more typical of other seismic areas and particularly associated with subduction zones.

The SMART 1 array, illustrated on this page, consists of 36 digital accelerometers arranged in three rings of radii 100 m, 1 km, and 2 km, and an additional, 37th recorder in the center. Seismic signals are recorded on ordinary magnetic tape cassettes in a digital form that al-

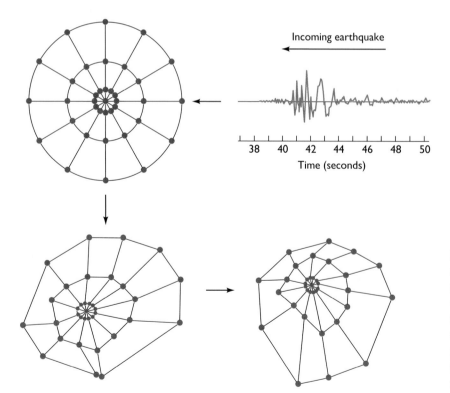

Dots denote the sites of strong-motion seismographs operating as an array in Taiwan. Incoming seismic waves produce a set of records like that shown at top right. Each site is slightly displaced by the waves, producing distorted rings like those at two separate times shown (highly magnified) at the bottom.

162

lows the signals to be directly transferred to the memory of a computer.

The designers of SMART 1 decided to arrange the array in three concentric circles because the earthquake sources in eastern Taiwan are not restricted to a particular fault but are distributed in many azimuths around the array. The circular symmetry of the array enables it to respond equally well to earthquakes coming from any direction and from any distance. Because of its flexible design, SMART 1 can be used for both engineering and seismological studies.

In the former type of study, the array is used to analyze the response of structures to seismic waves. An incoming wave front consisting of P or S waves is recorded in turn by successive accelerometers. As the earthquake waves move outward from their source, they slightly displace each instrument site in SMART 1 in a way that depends on the types of seismic waves and their amplitudes and phases. The resulting deformation of the rings can be illustrated by making a plot on a desktop personal computer from the digital records. The bottom left of the figure on the opposite page depicts the wave displacements recorded by the 37 accelerometers at a single moment in time during a strong earthquake. The wave displacements at many moments may be plotted to produce a series of snapshots of the actual variation of ground displacement over time.

The distorted rings in the figure (highly magnified) indicate how large buildings also deform when excited by earthquakes. For example, the two frames shown at the bottom of the figure highlight the manner in which strong ground shaking deforms the foundation of a large structure in a continuously changing way.

In the case shown here, relative displacements of up to 5 cm occurred within a distance of 200 m.

From one point to another over a short distance, earthquake waves may be similar in frequency, amplitude, phase, and direction of shaking, or they may be quite different. The correlation between wave patterns at nearby points is termed wave coherency. The SMART 1 array has provided many recordings demonstrating the degree of likeness of high-frequency waves over short distances and graphing the coherency at various wave frequencies for the various types of seismic waves.

Coherent waves may be exceptionally damaging to a structure or relatively harmless, depending on their wavelengths. The effects of wavelength can best be described by analogy with a rubber float on a swimming pool surface. When the waves on the water have wavelengths longer than the length of the float, the float follows the crests and troughs of the waves almost exactly. On the other hand, if the waves are in the form of ripples, then these much shorter wavelengths do little to excite the motion of the float. In the same way, the excitation of a structural foundation may be either exaggerated or reduced, depending on the wavelengths of the traveling coherent waves. For this reason, wave coherency has become an important consideration in the design of large buildings. Studies with SMART 1 have indicated that over some frequency bands the structural response to coherent ground motion is reduced by up to 20 percent.

Arrays like SMART 1 are also needed to determine the variation of intensity throughout the area of strong shaking, which is affected both by the attenuation with distance and by changing geological structures.

THE FACTORS THAT DETERMINE STRONG GROUND MOTION

As earthquake waves move outward from their source, the peak accelerations, velocities, and displacements generally decrease. Thus, plotting the peak values against the distance from the seismic source provides a way of mapping the attenuation of the ground motion at sites at various distances from the source, for a given earthquake magnitude. The attenuation with distance is found to vary significantly from region to region, depending on the properties of the crustal rock. For example, attenuation is much lower in the western United States than in the eastern part. The younger crustal rocks of the western North American plate dampen the wave energy more quickly than do the older, more rigid rocks in the east.

Peak accelerations do not, however, decrease smoothly with distance from the source but are

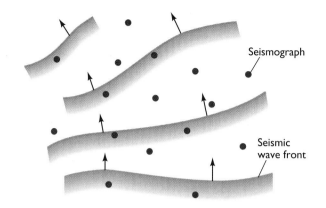

An earthquake wave traveling across an array of seismographs is distorted by geological structure.

much affected by several geological circumstances. First, where the walls of the slipping fault are particularly rough, the rupture will produce bursts of high-frequency wave energy. Second, the high-frequency earthquake waves with wavelengths of only hundreds of meters are scattered and amplified by irregularities in the crustal rocks and by steep topography such as ridges and gullies. Third, thick alluvial soils may amplify some waves and dampen others, depending on the soil and rock structures and the frequency of the waves. Extended geological structures, such as alluvial basins, set up multiple propagation routes for the seismic waves; the waves may reflect from the basin margins and reinforce one another at various places. Thus, the intensity of the ground shaking at any site is determined by three factors: the mechanism of the seismic source, the inhomogeneities and structural variations in the rock between the source and the site, and the soil and other geological conditions at the site. Using arrays of

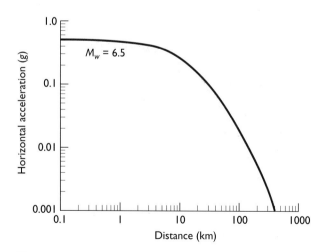

The average attenuation of horizontal acceleration with distance from the earthquake source, for an earthquake of moment magnitude 6.5.

both strong-motion accelerometers and more widely spaced regular digital seismographs, seismologists have been able to analyze how all three factors combine to produce areas of exceptionally destructive shaking.

Consider first the reconstruction of the faulting process. Because the energy recorded at distant stations is often greatly modified by the variations in geological structure that occur over long distances, the closer the instrumentation is to the source, the better. If an array of strong-motion instruments is operated near a rupturing fault, the waves will pass across the array in a particular direction. The front sweeps from one station to the next, causing each in turn to record the ground motion. The time of passage from one side of the array to the other provides a measure of the velocity of the waves, whereas their direction of travel is determined by the sequence of stations hit by a front. Because each wave has its own particular velocity, the different types of seismic waves can be distinguished from one another. The P waves arrive first, for example, and the predominantly S waves second. Thus, the direction and azimuth of each wave front can be determined by comparing the signals from each sensor of a seismic array. The actual correlation of the successive recordings is, of course, performed most efficiently by a computer.

As the rupture proceeds down a fault, the direction from which the wave fronts come to the array will change. Thus, successive measurements of the directions of, say, the main S wave can be mapped into a series of successive foci along the fault rupture. In this way, the strong-motion seismic array is analogous to a group of radar receiving dishes tracking a moving satellite across the sky.

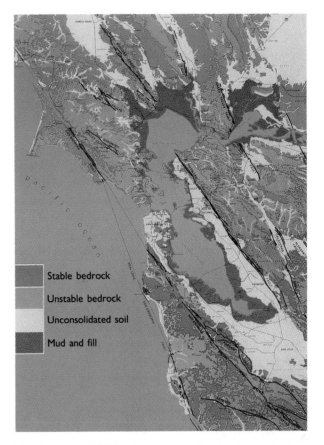

Stable bedrock
Unstable bedrock
Unconsolidated soil
Mud and fill

The intensity of shaking in an earthquake should vary in the San Francisco Bay Area according to soil type. The shaking is least intense on stable bedrock, but landsliding is likely when the bedrock has been made unstable by decomposition, saturation with water, or its location on steep slopes. Unconsolidated soil is prone to moderate shaking, particularly if it is thick and water-saturated. Mud and fill magnify earthquake waves, like a shaking bowl of Jello.

The second factor in strong ground shaking is the effect on the earthquake of the inhomogeneities and structural variations in the rocks between the source and the site. Actual seismograms differ profoundly from the bland records that are computed theoretically for a homogeneous, elastic rock layer. Real waves contain high-frequency fluctuations produced by the scattering of the seismic waves by various geological obstacles. This wave scattering is similar to the scattering of sunlight by the molecules of air that produces the blue sky. The scattering obstacles in the Earth's crust range from a few meters up to kilometers in diameter.

Each seismogram can be regarded as a series of bursts of energy, each of which comes from an obstacle within the crust. A comparison of the array recordings can detect the change in direction of pulses of energy at various frequencies as the recorded train passes across the set of instruments. In this way, the location of the main scatterers in the crust can be inferred.

In many seismically active regions of the world, the geology is particularly complicated. For example, in the San Francisco Bay Area of California, a broad zone of crushed rock runs along the San Andreas fault; on one side of the fault lie granitic rocks and on the other thick sequences of sedimentary rocks. The sedimentary rocks in particular contain fractured and layered sequences. This abrupt juxtaposition of contrasting geologies had a profound effect on the patterns of damage created by the Loma Prieta earthquake of 1989.

THE "WORLD SERIES" EARTHQUAKE

At 5:04 P.M. Pacific daylight time on October 17, 1989, thousands of fans were making their way to Candlestick Park, south of San Francisco, for the third game of the baseball World Series.

In other parts of the San Francisco Bay Area and central California, people were finishing work or departing for home, many to listen to the upcoming baseball game. It was not to take place as planned.

Over a quarter of a century before, I had given up the seismic calm of my native Australia to live and work in earthquake country. On my arrival at Berkeley, my predecessor, Professor Perry Byerly, had told me, "You will be lucky as a seismologist because you will experience personally a great earthquake sometime in your career. Perhaps like the 1906 San Francisco earthquake." In my ensuing 27 years as director of the Seismographic Stations at the University of California, one of my main concerns was to keep the seismographs operating, upgrade them, and stay prepared for the "big one." But the big one had not yet occurred when I retired as director in 1988.

Then, on the afternoon of October 17, 1989, in my Berkeley home a kilometer from the university campus, I suddenly felt violent shaking. Fortunately, my house was not damaged, although in Berkeley some chimneys fell and seismically weak structures incurred some minor damage. From the reaction of the house and the time between the initial P and the later S waves I could tell that the earthquake was large and about 80 to 100 km from Berkeley. At the Seismographic Station, the university campus staff and students immediately began to calculate the exact position and size of the earthquake source. Within 20 minutes they had called me at home to report a magnitude 6.5 to 7.0 earthquake south of San Francisco Bay in the Santa Cruz Mountains, about 100 km away. This estimate confirmed my own crude calculation.

Another eyewitness of the October earthquake, Professor Leonard Nathan of the University of California, Berkeley, wrote some thoughts after the shock:

We were driving home when the car rocked sharply as though hit by a gust of crosswind. When we opened the front door of the house we saw every picture on the wall was skewed and cloisonne vases atop the kitchen cabinet had tumbled to the floor. We turned the television on and our ignorance ended. But however sharp and vivid, the images on the television were just pictures. My sister-in-law had been high up in the Oakland Kaiser building when it began to twist and yaw and went on twisting and yawing for what seemed like a very long time as she and her fellow workers slowly wound down the stairway to street level. Our younger daughter rushed home from work to find her apartment a shambles, everything spilled and scrambled, the building itself losing its brick facade. What my daughter and sister-in-law brought home was firsthand dread. Now and then we felt an aftershock reminding us the danger, perhaps, was far from over.

Now on the television there were directions on how to get relief or assistance. There were human interest stories, especially the intensifying drama of the search for possible survivors buried in the ruins. We badly needed examples of heroism and miracle. The most authoritative new voices were those of the experts. The quake scientists were the first to be brought in and they tried to put, if not a human, at least an intelligible face on nature. Next the engineers arrived to ex-

As a result of the 1989 Loma Prieta earthquake, the upper roadway of the Cypress Street interchange on interstate highway 880 collapsed onto the lower roadway.

plain why things fell down and how they should have been or could be built so that they wouldn't fall down. To this vast chorus was soon added the resonant voices of the national networks. Only when the national anchorman reported from the smashed Cypress Street interchange could the whole country join in.

167

THE SOURCE OF THE LOMA PRIETA EARTHQUAKE

The source of the Loma Prieta earthquake turned out to differ somewhat from expectations. The slip was only partly as predicted for large earthquakes generated along the San Andreas fault; but, not for the first time in science, hindsight allows a reasonable explanation of the mechanism. The map of the aftershocks defines the section of the San Andreas fault that ruptured in the main earthquake, a segment about 40 km in length and 20 km in depth. The focus of the main shock was unusually deep for this tectonic region, about 15 km, and the rupture extended to within a few kilometers of the surface but did not break it. Reports from the 1906 earthquake had suggested a surface ground breakage along this stretch of fault, so geologists were surprised when, observing from helicopters flying over the area on the morning of October 18, they could find no continuous fault offsets in the San Andreas fault zone. There were many landslides and much ground cracking on hillsides, but the telltale signs of a major fault slip were not visible.

Another surprise was the direction of displacement of the crust in the area of the ruptured fault. The foci of the aftershocks clearly indicated a fault dip to the southwest at an angle of about 70 degrees. From seismographic records and later geodetic surveys, geologists calculated that the crust on the southwestern side

The earthquake was officially named for the highest peak in the Santa Cruz Mountains, Loma Prieta, or "dark mountain." At a magnitude of 7.1, it was the largest earthquake to hit the San Francisco Bay region, home to more than 5.9 million people, since the 1906 San Francisco earthquake. The shaking was felt for approximately 1,000,000 sq km, from Los Angeles in the south to the Oregon border in the north and to western Nevada to the east. The earthquake resulted in 62 known deaths and more than 3700 injuries, and it left more than 12,000 people homeless. It created over $6 billion of property damage and greatly disrupted lifelines, including freeway structures, the San Francisco Bay Bridge, utility lines, communications, and power.

A large number of strong-motion accelerometers recorded the motion throughout the Bay Area. These recordings gave a unique measurement of the way the seismic waves varied, both with azimuth relative to the source and with distance, and as a function of the local geological conditions. One striking finding was that the seismic waves that shook the region near the city of San Jose, at an intermediate distance from the source, were not as high in amplitude as were the waves at more distant sites in San Francisco and the East Bay, where the damage was the most dramatic of the earthquake.

After the earthquake, it was soon reported that the San Francisco Bay Bridge—the main artery of traffic between San Francisco and East Bay cities such as Oakland, Berkeley, and Wal-

of the fault plane had moved northwestward about 2 m and upward about $1\frac{1}{3}$ m with respect to the northeastern side. This deformation was puzzling, because such an elevation of the Santa Cruz Mountains on the western side of the San Andreas fault would eventually uplift the peaks there higher than the now higher eastern side! The offsets also differed significantly from the mainly horizontal displacements along the San Andreas fault that had been seen in 1906.

There were no clear earthquake precursors in the Loma Prieta earthquake, although there had been two moderate earthquakes recently in the vicinity, one a year before and the other a month before. The inability to predict the earth-

quake was a crucial demonstration that much of the recent optimism about specific earthquake predictions was misplaced.

The rupture began in the center of the 40-km-long fault and spread north and south simultaneously. Because the rupture speed can be assumed to have been about 2.5 km/s, this rupture would have been completed in about 8 seconds. If the slip had begun at one end of the zone, it would have slipped twice the distance, and hence the seismic waves would have been generated for up to 16 seconds. In other words, the strong shaking in the Loma Prieta earthquake lasted only half as long as it might in another earthquake of equal magnitude.

nut Creek—had failed. In addition, there were reports of a massive collapse of a two-story concrete freeway structure that ran on top of bay fill from the east side of the San Francisco Bay Bridge through the city of Oakland. Along a $2\frac{1}{2}$-km section called the Cypress Street interchange, the freeway's massive upper deck dropped onto the lower one, crushing the cars below. Because commuter traffic on the freeway

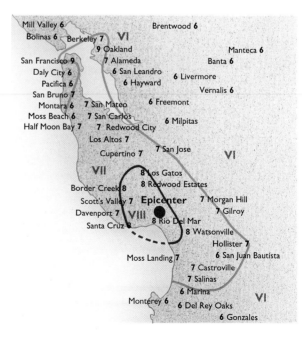

This map showing the modified Mercalli intensities of the Loma Prieta earthquake places the highest intensities in San Francisco and Oakland, 100 km from the epicenter. Arabic numbers indicate the intensity value for localities where observations were made; roman numerals represent the intensity level between isoseismal lines.

is normally bumper to bumper at that time of day, it was feared at first that many thousands of lives would be lost. In fact, because of unusually light traffic, there were only 26 deaths at the Cypress Street interchange. Modified Mercalli intensities of IX were judged appropriate for these pockets of heavy damage in Oakland and San Francisco, whereas a lesser intensity rating of VIII was assigned to an area 50 km long and 25 km wide near the epicenter, including the towns of Los Gatos, Watsonville, and Santa Cruz.

Dramatic new findings based on accelerometer recordings explained these counterintuitive variations in intensity. First, it has been demonstrated that many of the waves that traveled

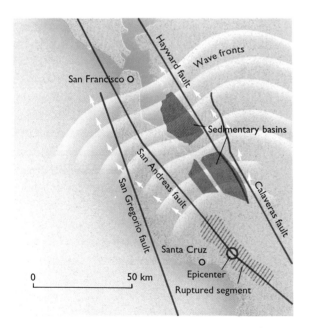

During the 1989 Loma Prieta earthquake, differing geological structures in the San Francisco Bay Area focused the seismic waves toward San Francisco.

downward from the Loma Prieta source were reflected back at the base of the Earth's crust and reached the surface at distances of 80 to 100 km. This distance happened to coincide with that of San Francisco. The reflected waves, however, skipped underneath the cities at the southern end of San Francisco Bay. Second, numerical models show that the seismic wave fronts traveling to the north from the earthquake source in the Santa Cruz Mountains were refracted away from their great circle paths by the major changes in geological structures that occur in the Bay Area. The largely granitic rocks on the west side of the San Andreas fault and the marine sediments on the east side transmit the seismic waves at different speeds. The effect was to swing wave fronts that were first headed northwest toward Alaska back toward San Francisco. In the same way, wave fronts headed toward Reno, Nevada, were turned back toward the east side of the bay (see page 32). Similar mathematical computations will enable geologists to forecast the focusing of seismic energy for potential earthquake sources in other areas.

San Francisco and Oakland were unlucky in the 1989 earthquake. They received a double dose of energy: shaking was severe not only because of the refracted waves but also because of geological conditions at the most damaged sites themselves.

DISASTER IN THE MARINA DISTRICT

One of the most damaged areas in the Loma Prieta earthquake lay in the city of San Francisco, almost 100 km away from the epicenter.

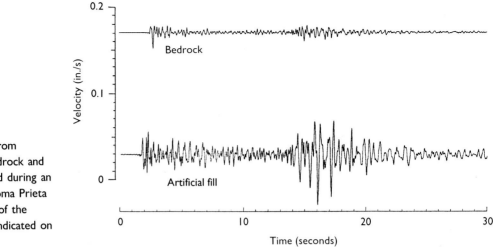

These two seismograms from temporary stations on bedrock and artificial fill were recorded during an aftershock of the 1989 Loma Prieta earthquake. The location of the station on artificial fill is indicated on the map on page 35.

During the great San Francisco earthquake of 1906, the shores along the lagoon that later became the Marina district experienced shaking of high intensities. This area was subsequently filled, partly with beach sand and partly with rubble from buildings damaged in the 1906 earthquake, to prepare for the Panama-Pacific International Exhibition of 1912. Over the years it became one of the most attractive areas of the city.

Because of its ground composition, the Marina district was vulnerable to a common hazard in earthquakes: the liquefaction of sandy soil. During shaking, fine-grained soil that is saturated by water takes on a liquid character after a number of cycles of varying shearing stresses. When the Loma Prieta earthquake struck, the filled ground in the Marina area settled more than 5 inches during the main shock. The ground lurched, and sections of water-saturated sand liquefied. Buildings were shifted from their

foundations, and some collapsed. After the earthquake, recorders were placed on the filled area and on nearby rock to compare the ground motions from large aftershocks. The results demonstrated that the landfill had amplified the seismic ground motions as much as eight times. The extent of the damage in the Marina district was heightened by structural problems. Many of the residential buildings were constructed so that their first floors were fronted by or made up entirely of garages without shear resistance to shaking. Inspectors found that more than 70 percent of the buildings located on the filled land were unsafe for occupancy after the quake (see the photograph on page 34).

The sandy soil liquefied in recently deposited sediments elsewhere around San Francisco Bay and along the Pacific coastline near the earthquake source as well. The downward compression of the overlying soil squeezed the liquefied sand upward through cracks and fissures, often creat-

Liquefied sand produced this "sand volcano" in the 1989 Loma Prieta earthquake.

These effects emphasize how important it is to incorporate the results of geological surveys into land-use plans and building codes. The effect of liquefaction can be minimized by densifying the sands or by incorporating special building foundations. Soil fills along the bay shore that had been placed by modern methods under the supervision of engineers performed well during the shaking. Despite the presence of bay muds and other adverse subsurface conditions, no damage was reported to building foundations on these well-emplaced fills.

The Loma Prieta earthquake illustrated that the local condition at a site, as mentioned earlier, is the third critical factor determining the intensity of shaking. Special research programs are now exploring the effects on ground shaking of local geological and soil conditions, such as the presence of a sharp ridge or the existence of a thick layer of soil in an alluvial basin. The dangerous effects of alluvial basins in particular were dramatically illustrated by an earthquake that devastated part of Mexico City in 1985.

ACTION AT A DISTANCE: THE MEXICO EARTHQUAKE OF 1985

California has had 5 earthquakes of magnitude greater than 7 in this century. In contrast, Mexico has had 42, many of which took a great toll in human lives. The largest of these earthquakes, at a magnitude of 8.1, was the tragic earthquake of September 19, 1985. This earthquake had its source in the subduction slab under the Pacific coast of Mexico. It occurred in a seismic gap that had been pointed out by seismologists for more than a decade (see the map on page 185).

ing striking features descriptively called sand boils and sand volcanoes. These features, along with lateral spreading of the ground and settlement and cracking of the soil, were observed not only in the Marina district but also at the Port of Oakland, Oakland Airport, Alameda Island, and other locations along the shoreline characterized by loose sandy soils derived from hydraulic fills and by a shallow groundwater table.

The earthquake severely damaged many buildings used for businesses and schools. Thus, it was fortunate that the shock struck in the early morning, at 7:17 A.M. local time, when these structures were not fully occupied. Even so, casualties in Mexico City, more than 350 km away from the focus, amounted to more than 8000 dead and 30,000 injured. About 50,000 people were left homeless. The severe damage to or destruction of about 500 buildings created an estimated $4 billion worth of damage. Yet be-cause Mexico City has a population of over 18 million people and about 800,000 buildings, these statistics indicate that the shaking severely affected only a small fraction of the city. Dam-age along the coast nearer the source was also significant but much more limited, partly be-cause of the types of buildings and geological conditions there.

A network of accelerometers provided exten-sive measurements of the strong ground motion of this earthquake, both in Mexico City and

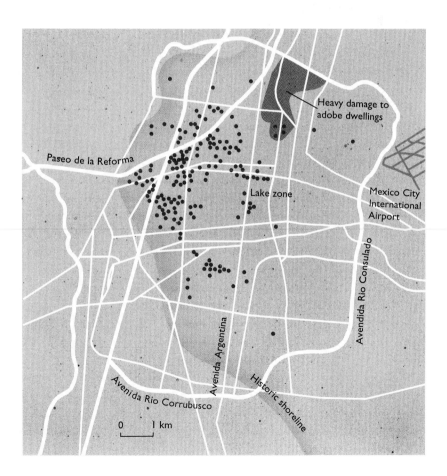

Heavily damaged and collapsed major structures were concentrated in the old lake zone of Mexico City. Each dot represents a heavily damaged or collapsed building.

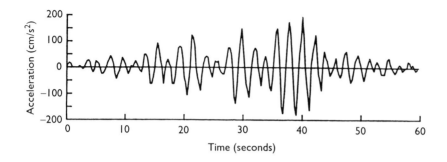

These horizontal ground accelerations were recorded over the soft lake zone in Mexico City during the 1985 earthquake. The ground shaking was spread out into more than 15 cycles of motion with a period of about 2 seconds.

along the part of the Pacific coastline most affected by the shaking. The instruments along the coast had been installed at specially selected locations in response to the recommendations of the international workshop held in Hawaii in 1978, which had proposed placing arrays of accelerometers in the most seismic areas of the world, including Mexico, in order to obtain essential missing data on strong shaking of the ground. About seven months after the workshop, an earthquake of magnitude 7.8 struck along the coast of Mexico. Seismologists from both Mexico and the United States, in a cooperative program, then evaluated the hazard probabilities at different sites and decided to install additional accelerometers in the states of Guerrero and Michoacan northwest of Acapulco, where there were seismic gaps. During the subsequent 1985 earthquake, the stations provided 16 digital records of strong ground motion very near the seismic source.

By the time the seismic waves had traveled the 350-km distance between the earthquake source near the coast and the Valley of Mexico, their amplitude had been greatly reduced. Few structures built on firm soil and rock suffered damage. In one part of Mexico City, however, the near-surface geology of the alluvial basin cre-

ated particularly hazardous conditions. Over recent geological time, rains had carried gravel, sands, and clays into the basin and deposited them in Lake Texcoco, which had been drained by the Spanish after the conquest of the Aztecs to allow growth of the city. Modern Mexico City is to a large extent built on the higher ground surrounding the old lake bed, but near the city center there are parts underlain by a thick deposit of very soft sands and clays having a high water content. It was this zone of the basin that contained most of the buildings that collapsed during the September 19 earthquake. The map on page 173 shows the striking concentration of structural damage. (A similar pattern of damage had resulted previously in Mexico City from an earthquake in 1957.)

What is the explanation? Let us start with the radiation of the seismic waves from the sudden movement along a fault in the subduction zone of the Michoacan coast. Locally, seismic waves radiated upward to the surface through distances of 20 km or more. Accelerometers along this part of the coast showed ground shaking amounting to 0.16g in a horizontal direction, a moderate intensity for such a large-magnitude earthquake. As the waves traveled through the crustal rocks toward Mexico City, they spread out in space, and their average amplitudes decreased. Those that shook the firm surface materials in the higher parts of Mexico City, such as at the National University of Mexico, were reduced to horizontal accelerations of only 0.04g, and no damage resulted. In the lake zone, however, surface waves with about a 2-second period were preferentially amplified by the clay layers.

It is a basic law of physics that when an elastic system, such as a guitar string, is forced to move at one of its natural frequencies, the amplitude of the movement will grow in preference to motions at other frequencies. An alluvial basin also has natural frequencies at which the seismic motions will grow or resonate. The actual values of the resonant frequencies depend on the shape and size of the soil layers and of the alluvial basin. These geological structures in effect trap the incoming seismic waves and amplify some of them. In the soft lake sediments of Mexico City, strong-motion instruments on the surface measured peak horizontal accelerations of up to 0.40g. Moreover, the ground continued to

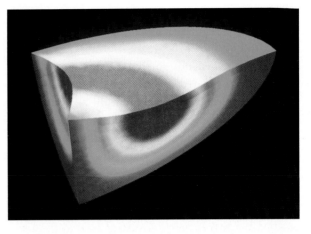

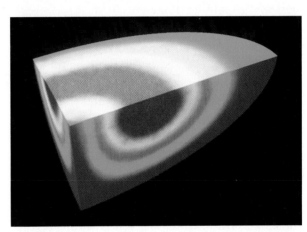

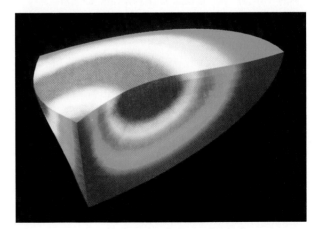

A computer model can predict the seismic vibrations in one-quarter of an ellipsoidal basin filled with soft, alluvial soil—a simplified version of the type of basin that so amplified shaking in the 1985 Mexico City earthquake. The standing waves modeled here rotate about the vertical axis. As the cycle of motion begins, the basin is deflected clockwise in a horizontal direction *(top)*. It then rotates back toward its rest position *(middle)* and is deflected counterclockwise *(bottom)*. The ground displacement will be greatest in the red area and least in the dark blue area at the center, edge, and bottom of the basin.

vibrate at modal frequencies even when the underlying seismic wave train had passed on. Thus, the S and surface waves arriving at Mexico City became stretched out so that there were over 15 cycles of this motion in the dispersed wave train.

The seismic waves were amplified again by the vibrational properties of certain buildings. Like the basins, buildings and other structures have natural frequencies of vibration. When their foundations are pushed sideways by waves of these frequencies, they will sway back and forth like inverted pendulums. In the Mexico earthquake, the waves were amplified by buildings between 10 and 14 stories high. In these buildings, the resonance effects led to large displacements and structural failures. Even in the most heavily shaken zone, however, most buildings in Mexico City were not structurally damaged. Left intact were most short buildings and high skyscrapers, such as the Latin American Tower of 37 stories, which had been constructed in the 1950s. Its extreme height produced a vibration period of 3.7 seconds—above the period of the most intense seismic surface waves.

Many earthquake disasters have resulted from the amplification of seismic waves within depressions containing layers and pockets of soft soils and clays. Such basins underlie many heavily populated areas of the world, including Los Angeles, Mexico City, Tokyo, Shanghai, and the margins of San Francisco Bay.

SYNTHETIC EARTHQUAKES

Many hundreds of strong earthquakes have now been recorded by accelerometers around the world. Nevertheless, the sample is still not adequate to predict the strong ground motion close to a source under different rock and soil conditions and for any specified fault mechanism. Many of the accelerograms have been obtained from the large California earthquakes of the last two decades, and most of these were recorded at distances of more than 20 km from the fault source. This important library of records is not homogeneous; although it contains many types of soil conditions and earthquake mechanisms, not all geological conditions are represented well in the record sample.

Thus, there are practical reasons, as well as a purely scientific interest, to produce so-called artificial or synthetic ground motions for specified situations. These synthetic ground motions are not physical reproductions of the shaking, as the term *synthetic* might imply, but are estimates of ground shaking arrived at through a formal analysis. While writing this book, I have been involved in estimating the likely ground motions that would occur in the maximum credible earthquake on the Hayward fault. This active fault runs through the University of California, Berkeley, campus. A large, damaging earthquake was last produced by slip on this fault in 1868; its magnitude has been estimated at between 7 and 7.25.

My colleagues and I were especially interested in estimating the ground motion from such an earthquake at the San Francisco Bay Bridge, which stretches east-west across the bay from Oakland on the east side to San Francisco on the west. These estimates would aid a group of engineering colleagues who, under contract with the California Department of Transportation, are investigating the earthquake resistance of the Bay Bridge. Although a span fell from its supports in the 1989 Loma Prieta earthquake, it was not vitally damaged; the crucial question is how it would fare in a closer, larger earthquake.

To begin our construction of the synthetic ground motions, my colleagues and I estimated, from recent observations, the peak accelerations, velocities, and displacements that are likely from a magnitude 7.25 earthquake on the Hayward fault at a distance of about 10 km, the distance to the Bay Bridge. We now know from the 1989 Loma Prieta earthquake, for example, that an earthquake of this size, in this area, would rupture a length of fault of about 40 km, to a depth of about 15 km.

Next, we used attenuation curves to adjust the peak motions to fit those 10 km from the source. We found expected values at the Bay

Bridge of 0.7g acceleration, 25 cm/s velocity, and 30 cm displacement. Of course, there will be variations around these peak values in any particular earthquake, depending on the actual distance from the Bay Bridge of the rupture along the fault and also on geological and seismogenic factors on the Hayward fault—factors that are presently unknown.

With the peak values in hand, we could proceed to obtain a full picture of the shaking. The next stage was to select a record of an already observed earthquake having similar peak values, if one was available. The best that we could find was the record from the town of Capitola, 15 km from Loma Prieta, taken during the 1989 Loma Prieta earthquake. These Capitola ac-

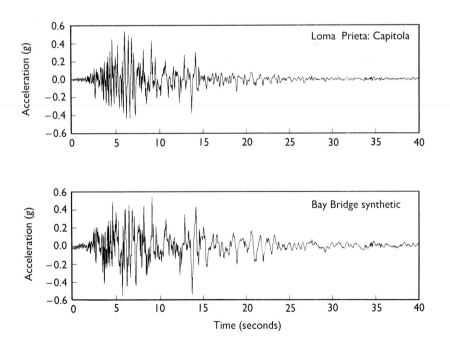

The Capitola records (top) were used in constructing a synthetic seismogram (bottom) of the shaking that would be expected under the San Francisco Bay Bridge in a hypothetical earthquake along the Hayward fault.

celerograms were not quite large enough to satisfy our peak parameter conditions, so we had to scale their amplitude upward. The duration was also adjusted to about 30 seconds, the average value expected for a magnitude 7.25 earthquake. Finally, ground motion spectra appropriate for earthquakes of this size were chosen from past studies, and the record was adjusted to have a similar spectrum. The resulting synthetic seismogram is given on page 177.

Because earthquake sources are of various types and depths and occur in different geological structures, this method requires a great deal of interpretation and extrapolation between recorded ground motions. Consequently, seismologists are attempting to develop less empirical methods of constructing artificial ground motion. Numerical methods of modeling the strong seismic ground motion produced by realistic seismic sources have recently advanced by leaps and bounds. The massive increase in computing power has, of course, been essential to this flourishing part of seismology.

The heart of a successful numerical modeling scheme is to specify the length and width of the proposed fault slip, divide the area into small elements, and allow each element to slip by a certain amount calculated according to the computer code. Slip at specified rupture velocities is initiated in all directions at the seismic focus. The shaking of the surrounding rocks in response to each of these slips is calculated from the theory of elastic response to sudden cracking. By further computer calculations, these motions are transferred through the complex of rock structures between the fault and a specified surface point and then summed to form a synthetic seismogram. The mathematics is similar to that

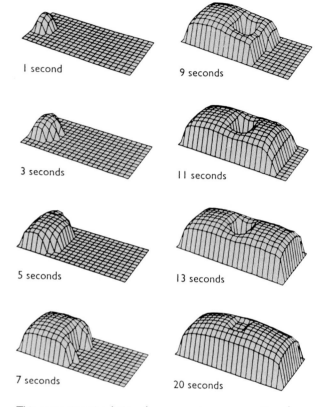

1 second	9 seconds
3 seconds	11 seconds
5 seconds	13 seconds
7 seconds	20 seconds

This computer simulation shows a rupture propagating along a fault having a strong patch at the center.

used to predict the motion of a piano string at one end in response to a blow by a hammer along some portion of the string.

The uncertainty in the results of these methods arises mainly from simplifying assumptions, some of which are rather arbitrary, such as the actual process of rupture propagation over the fault plane and the detailed time history of the slip. In addition, often little is known about the physical conditions of the rocks along the fault (that is, the distribution of roughness or asperities) and about the places where the fault rupture stops at its bottom, top, and end.

After computing seismic waves radiated from a specified fault source, seismologists are able to produce maps of the expected seismic intensities in vulnerable regions such as San Francisco, Los Angeles, Boston, Tokyo, and Quito. As we will see in Chapter 9, these maps are the first requirement for planning future development in earthquake country, assessing the vulnerability of older structures, designing earthquake-resistant new structures, and otherwise reducing the risk from earthquakes.

8

FORECASTING
EARTHQUAKES

THE ABILITY TO make predictions is often taken as a hallmark of a well-developed scientific discipline. For example, the theory of gravitation developed by Newton enables astronomers to make highly accurate quantitative predictions of planetary orbits and spacecraft trajectories. Or, given observations of the temperature, pressure, and water content of the atmosphere, meteorologists can apply the theoretical equations of atmospheric movements to make reasonably accurate, though short-term, predictions of currents and the weather.

Scientific predictions usually give the size of the phenomenon and the location and time of its occurrence. Similarly, in seismology, there has always been a desire to use the knowledge of the forces within the Earth to forecast the size, place, and time of future earthquakes. Very accurate

The laser beams of a geodimeter measure ground deformation in Parkfield, California, the site of an earthquake prediction experiment.

forecasts could allow strict and extensive precautions to be taken that might drastically reduce loss of life and property damage. If the prophecies were known to be very uncertain, however, only cautious and limited arrangements could be made in advance of an impending earthquake.

People have attempted to foresee earthquakes since ancient times. One common belief, for example, was that a certain type of weather precedes an earthquake; another was that animals show prescience in their behavior before a seismic event. In earthquake country even today, one hears accounts of such correlations from local citizens, who make various claims of the ability to predict earthquakes from observations of natural changes in the environment. In assessing the validity of such claims, it must be remembered that there is always a chance that any predicted future event will occur—even if the forecast is made by picking a date at random.

It is generally accepted that a serious prediction must also specify the location, the origin time, and the magnitude within specific narrow limits—for example, "an earthquake of magnitude about 7.0 will occur in the next seven days within 50 km of city A." Such an absolute statement, however, is impossible to justify. Because a prediction will always be based on a limited number of measurements and other observations, themselves somewhat imprecise, the place, time, and size can be given only with some degree of likelihood. Thus, besides stating place, time, and size, an earthquake prediction must state the probability of occurrence.

There is another, more fundamental difficulty inherent in earthquake forecasting. Suppose that seismological measurements indicate that an earthquake of a certain magnitude may occur in a seismic area during a certain period of time. By chance alone, the odds are not zero that an earthquake will occur during the period suggested. Thus, if an earthquake occurs, that cannot be taken as decisive proof that the methods used to make the prediction are correct, and they may fail on future occasions. Of course, if a firm prediction is made and nothing happens, that must be taken as proof that the method is not valid, at least universally. For this reason, a prediction must also specify the odds that the earthquake would occur by random chance, independently of the argument set out for the particular prediction.

Perhaps the most popular notion about earthquake prediction is that animals can sense earthquakes before they happen. As early as 373 B.C. in ancient Greece, there were stories of rats and centipedes moving to safety before destructive earthquakes. Two decades or so ago in China, much was made of reported premonitory animal behavior. More recently, a bizarre theory was advanced by one geologist in the south San Francisco Bay Area that when an extraordinarily large number of dogs and cats are reported in the "Lost and Found" section of the local newspaper, the probability of an earthquake striking the area increases significantly. The missing animals were taken to be a sign that an earthquake of Richter magnitude 3.5 to 5.5 would occur within a 110-km radius of downtown San Jose within a designated time period. The geologist claimed a success rate of 80 percent over the last twelve years. Yet no theory was advanced to explain this strange correlation, and the predictions made did not work out over a period of fifteen years or so.

This strange case illustrates the difficulties in testing the validity of any claim that anomalous animal behavior presages seismic activity. Despite the availability of sensitive measuring instruments like microphones, electric voltage meters, and thermometers, the actual stimulus that might cause the claimed animal reaction has never been determined objectively. Animals exhibit erratic behavior from time to time that arises from many natural causes. Control is thus next to impossible, and seismologists are deeply skeptical of claims that animal behavior can predict earthquakes.

A careful comparison of the earthquake predictions published in scientific journals with the actual seismological record indicates that no proclaimed methods can yet be taken as proved. Indeed, the extensive and often imaginative research on earthquake prediction of the last two decades has raised doubt about whether earthquake prediction within strict bounds of time and place will ever be possible for most earthquakes, particularly the large, damaging ones. Three examples of predictions that meet some of the desired criteria and that were made by persons with scientific training will give a flavor of the problem.

In seeking to predict earthquakes, efforts have often been made to find forces, either outside or inside the Earth, that would trigger a fault rupture, like the straw that broke the camel's back. These forces have been attributed to severe weather conditions, volcanic activity, and the tidal forces produced by the gravitational attraction between the Moon and Sun and the Earth. In the late 1950s, the leading scientific journal *Nature* published a seismologist's claim that the gravitational attraction of the planet Uranus had induced periodicities in earthquake occurrence. This theory appeared odd: since Uranus is one of the most distant planets, its attractive force on the Earth is quite tiny compared

with that of the Moon. Yet the published formal statistics seemed to indicate that the periodicities claimed were dependable.

The difficulty lay in the scientific method that was followed. Although correlations of this kind are sometimes useful in bringing to light actual interactions between forces and events, they are notoriously untrustworthy and require careful testing. If we search for correlations between one set of observations and another, without any physical connection being stated, sooner or later some correlation at a high level of significance will be found *by chance alone*. Thus, if we plot the birth rate of babies in New York against the fall of heavy rain in the Himalayas, sooner or later we will find a period in which the two measures correlate closely. In the Uranus case, the search for a link between great earthquakes and the gravitational pull of the planets had begun with the near planets and worked outward until by luck there was a correlation.

The second example comes from a popular book written by two astronomers in 1974. The book's authors created an extraordinary chain of logic to relate the *alignment* of the planets to the occurrence of large earthquakes. To begin, they pointed out that an approximate alignment of the planets takes place every 179 years. The gravitational attraction on the Sun is thereby increased, and the additional gravitational force produces heightened sunspot activity. In turn, the greater solar activity increases the solar wind, which is formed of charged nuclear particles that continuously flow outward from the Sun. The more intense solar wind then significantly changes the weather patterns on the Earth. These new weather patterns, containing unusual atmospheric disturbances, increase stresses on the surface of the Earth; for example, high wind pressures might press on mountain ranges. These additional stresses, it was argued, may trigger tectonic movements, including catastrophic earthquakes.

The theory's authors selected the San Andreas fault as a likely candidate for cataclysmic ruptures during the next planetary alignment in 1982. The case was made that because the San Andreas fault had not ruptured in the south since 1857 and in the north since 1906, the strain in the rocks was particularly large and the situation ripe for an earthquake to be triggered by planetary alignments.

Fortunately for California, there were serious flaws in the argument. In the first place, global catalogues of earthquakes showed that the years 1803, 1624, and 1445, which fit the 179-year planetary cycle, were not periods of unusually dramatic seismic activity. California history records no memorable earthquake in the year 1803, for example. Elsewhere, only one great earthquake, which happened to occur in Japan, is catalogued in 1445, and only one is listed for 1624, an event in the West Indies. By contrast, four great earthquakes are given in the global catalogues for 1448 and five for 1604, although neither of these years fits the periodicity of the speculation.

Actually, the scientific case against this prediction method, with its very remote series of connections, is quite strong. Calculations based on Newtonian gravitational theory show that the additional pull of the more distant planets on the Sun is quite insignificant compared with that of the Earth and Venus. As a consequence, this line of argument would require that we consider many more periodicities in addition to the 179-year planetary alignment, each corresponding to an alignment of the closer planets.

The third case of misguided earthquake forecasting set off a public debate concerning the imminent likelihood of a massive earthquake that would have wreaked havoc in the cities of Peru. In 1976, articles appeared in a European scientific journal describing how earthquake waves are produced when rock cracks under pressure. This theoretical work was held to be applicable not only on a small scale to the failure of rocks in mines but also on a very much greater scale to the slip of a geological fault. Further, it was suggested that the theory would provide the precise time, place, and size of a coming large-scale fault failure and, hence, of an accompanying earthquake.

Shortly after the article's publication, two scientists applied the rock fracture conjectures to their study of two large earthquakes that had struck near Lima, Peru, in 1974. As a result, they came to believe that a serious seismic hazard had developed near that city. They envisaged that a "preparation phase" for a massive earthquake had begun in the region, and their calculations suggested that approximately six years after 1974 a major earthquake of 8.4 magnitude would occur. Because the scientists involved worked for the U.S. government, they had immediate credibility. Their forecast created consternation in Peru among the public and in the government.

A searching inquiry into the speculations was undertaken by the National Earthquake Prediction Evaluation Council, a group that had been set up under the auspices of the U.S. Geological Survey to investigate serious predictions. The council's report deflated the forecast, and as it turned out, no massive earthquake hit Peru either in 1980 or any time to date—fortunately for a country where many structures were not

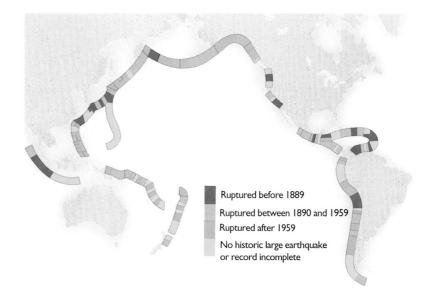

Ruptured before 1889

Ruptured between 1890 and 1959

Ruptured after 1959

No historic large earthquake
or record incomplete

These seismic gaps were mapped for
the Circumpacific region in 1989.
Where faults have not ruptured
recently there is more potential for
an earthquake.

built to withstand the forces of a strong earthquake. Because Peru is situated on the seismically active subduction margin of the Nazca tectonic plate, there is little doubt that slab
thrusting will produce great earthquakes there in
the future. But we do not know just when.

In an important broad sense, studies of historical seismicity patterns, particularly along the
margins of tectonic plates, have made it feasible
to predict the probable locations of damaging
earthquakes. However, such records do not enable us to forecast a precise time of occurrence,
except in unusual geological circumstances.
Earthquakes do not appear to take place on a
regular schedule. Even in China, where 500 to
1000 destructive earthquakes have been catalogued over the past 2700 years, statistical studies have not revealed clear periodicities of major

earthquakes. Rather, they indicate that great
earthquakes may be separated by long, seemingly
random periods of quiescence.

THE CHINESE AND JAPANESE EARTHQUAKE PREDICTION EXPERIENCES

During the 1970s, world attention was caught
by a highly publicized program of earthquake
prediction in China. In one well-reported episode, on February 4, 1975, officials of the Man-
churian province of Liaoning issued an urgent
warning, based largely on the occurrence of
many small earthquakes in the area, of a strong
earthquake within 24 hours. That evening a

high-intensity earthquake did strike the region near the town of Haicheng, but fortunately most of the population had left their homes and were unharmed.

The Chinese claimed to have forecast the time of several earthquakes correctly: not only the 1975 Haicheng earthquake but also a pair of earthquakes of magnitude 6.9 that occurred 97 minutes apart, near the China-Burma border in western Yunnan on May 19, 1976. Yet in assessing the history of the Chinese program, it is only fair to cite its failures as well as its successes. On the one hand, some forecasts of impending earthquakes turned out to be false. For example, an alert issued in August 1976 in Guangdong province (normally not very seismically active) near Guangzhou and Hong Kong convinced many people to sleep outdoors, yet no

earthquake took place. On the other hand, catastrophic earthquakes have struck with no forewarning. The tragic earthquake of July 27, 1976, almost razed Tangshan, an industrial city of 1 million people situated 150 km east of Beijing. Official reports estimated that about 250,000 persons died in the most heavily shaken area. About 100 persons were killed in Beijing, where some mud walls and old brick houses collapsed. Moreover, it is estimated that an additional 500,000 persons were injured. When the enormous industrial loss was added to this human calamity, it is no surprise that the economic aftermath for the whole country was severe. The Tangshan earthquake also had political implications: a traditional Chinese view maintains that natural disasters are a mandate from heaven, and earthquakes have been claimed to

This collapsed bridge was destroyed in the 1976 Tangshan earthquake.

Buckled railroad tracks are a sign of the widespread ground deformation that occurred in the Tangshan earthquake.

mean trouble for governments as far back as the Sung dynasty (A.D. 960–1280).

In Japan, where there are also many centuries of earthquake statistics, vigorous research aimed at earthquake prediction has been under way since 1962 but so far without definite success. One hurdle in testing the Japanese prediction methodology is that no great damaging earthquake has struck the Japanese Islands during recent years, although there have been a number of moderate shocks.

The Japanese program, drawing on the contributions of hundreds of seismologists, geophysicists, and geodesists both in universities and in many government research institutes, has progressed through five well-funded five-year plans. The program began by observing short-term changes in the geological properties of the seis-mogenic regions: the geology of active faults was mapped; crustal deformations were continuously monitored using improved geodetic instruments and tide gauges; and dense networks of simple seismographs were installed to map uniformly even very small earthquakes. In addition, instruments at selected earthquake observatories continuously measured variations in the Earth's magnetic field and in the electric currents in rocks, chemical and temperature fluctuations in geothermal areas were sampled, and groundwater levels were catalogued. Most recently, studies of historical earthquake cycles in the vicinity of Tokyo, together with local measurements of crustal deformation and seismicity, have suggested that although a repetition of the great 1923 Kwanto earthquake centered near Tokyo is not now imminent, damaging earthquakes in neighboring areas cannot be ruled out. In particular, the heavily industrial Tokai district, along the coast of Honshu near the Izu Peninsula, has been closely watched for anomalous geological changes for more than fifteen years.

As the Japanese program and similar observational programs elsewhere mature, the burning question becomes: What patterns revealed by the measurements are relevant to seismological forecasting? If a detailed theoretical understanding were available of the physical processes that lead to fault rupture, it would define the measurable anomalies that precede an earthquake. Because this theory is lacking at present, research on prediction in Japan and elsewhere has relied mainly on the hope of finding serendipitous clues. In 1982, a senior Japanese seismologist, Z. Suzuki, reviewed earthquake prediction around Japan and abroad: "The present state of the art is very chaotic. . . . A remarkable variety of earthquake precursors have been reported so far. Some reported precursors seem very strange and open to doubt. Even excluding these ambiguous cases, no general and definite way to successful earthquake prediction is clear." This judicious statement holds true a decade later. Consequently, strong debate is leading to a rethinking of what has been perhaps the most ambitious and certainly the best-funded program on earthquake prediction in the world. A revised program has been proposed that will emphasize basic research on the still mysterious short-term physical processes that are forerunners to any major fault slip.

Although we do not yet have the precisely formulated theory of earthquake genesis needed to make reliable predictions, the elastic rebound theory of fault sources does allow us to make crude forecasts of when to expect the next extensive rupture on a known active fault. In fact,

after the 1906 California earthquake, H. F. Reid used the rebound theory to argue that the next great shock near San Francisco should strike about a century later. His argument was simple. Survey measurements made across the San Andreas fault for about fifty years before the 1906 earthquake indicated that the relative displacement of mountaintops to the west and east of the fault had reached 3.2 m in those fifty years. After the rebound on the fault on April 18, 1906, the maximum relative displacement at the fault rupture itself was about 6.5 m, or about twice as much as the displacement measured across it at remote points. Therefore, about one hundred years would elapse before 6 m of strain in the crustal rocks would again accumulate, thus setting the stage for the next great earthquake. The credibility of this conclusion rests on the somewhat tenuous assumptions that the regional strain continues to grow uniformly over time, that the fault properties before the 1906 earthquake were not altered by the earthquake itself, and that the accumulated strain is not released by a series of moderate earthquakes.

PROGNOSTICATION EVIDENCE

Several of the more promising harbingers of impending earthquakes have already been discussed, such as the detection of strain in the rocks of the Earth's crust by geodetic surveys (Chapter 4) and the identification of suspicious gaps in the regular occurrence of earthquakes in both time and space (Chapter 5).

In recent years, the major earthquake prediction effort has been aimed at more precisely measuring fluctuations in the physical parameters of

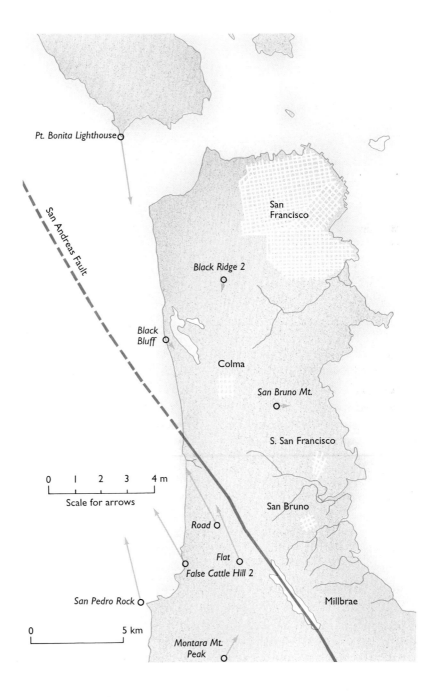

Arrows show the length and direction of relative displacements measured in crustal rocks across the San Andreas fault, after the 1906 rupture.

San Andreas Fault

Pt. Bonita Lighthouse

San Francisco

Black Ridge 2

Black Bluff

Colma

San Bruno Mt.

S. San Francisco

San Bruno

Millbrae

0   1   2   3   4 m
Scale for arrows

Road

Flat
False Cattle Hill 2

San Pedro Rock

0   5 km

Montara Mt.
Peak

crustal rocks in seismically active continental areas. Special sensing devices have been installed to observe long-term changes in these parameters. The number of measurements is still limited, and the results so far have been conflicting. Sometimes unusual behavior has been recorded before a local earthquake; in other cases, nothing significant has been seen. Alternatively, variations in the parameters may occur that are not followed by earthquakes. Five measurements that have been thought to be particularly auspicious, listed in the figure on this page, are *P*-wave velocities, the uplift and tilt of the ground, the emission of radon gas from wells, electrical resistance in the rocks, and the rate of earthquake occurrence.

Just as the weather changes before a hurricane, elastic rock properties change just before a major fault slip begins, over a period ranging from hours to many months before the catastrophic rupture. Laboratory studies of rock fracture show that as the pressure on the water-saturated rocks grows, tiny cracks and pores fill with water and spread throughout the specimen, weakening the rock. Several consequences may be observable in the field: the volume of the rock swells; pathways are created for the escape of water-soluble gases to the surface; the velocity of the compressional seismic *P* waves changes differently from that of the shear *S* waves; and the water diffusion alters the electrical resistance of the rocks.

How can each of these parameters be employed in a prediction scheme? First, precursory changes in the *P*-wave velocities are of particular interest to seismologists because variations of one-hundredth of a second in the travel times of *P* and *S* waves are easily measured with modern seismographs and chronometers. The *P* and *S* waves measured may originate in smaller earthquakes within the focal region, in larger earthquakes outside the focal region, or in explosions or the actions of mechanical thumping devices.

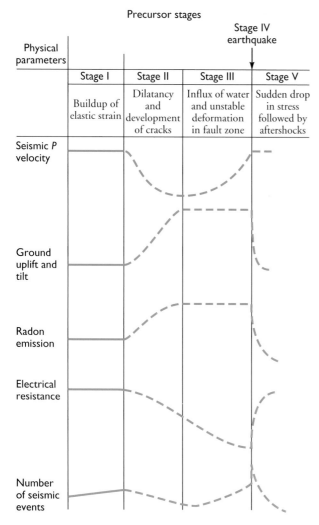

It has been suggested that changes in several physical parameters may precede earthquakes and serve as precursory clues in earthquake prediction.

The scheme has been tested in a number of countries with mixed results. In the United States, for example, fluctuations in travel times before a number of small to moderate earthquakes along the San Andreas fault have not been found to be significant.

The second parameter is change in ground level, such as ground tilts near active faults. Again, the few uplifts of the required regional scale that have been studied give rather cryptic inferences on the reliability of such measurements.

The third parameter is the release of radon and other gases into the atmosphere along active fault zones, particularly from deep wells. It has been claimed that significantly increased concentrations of radon were detected just before earthquakes in some parts of the former Soviet Union. Normally, in a quiet time, high concentrations of several gases are found in active fault zones, especially at structurally weak sites such as fault bends and intersections. Variations in radon concentrations in the ground, in the air, and in groundwater have been plotted at such favorable locations, both within a few kilometers of large earthquake epicenters and hundreds of kilometers away. The same levels of fluctuation, however, have been found both before and after earthquakes and in many studies without any earthquake occurring at all. Because the geological environment varies so much, it has been impossible to determine whether earthquake-associated increases are exceptions to the normal variations in gas concentration.

The fourth parameter, to which a good deal of attention has been given, is the electrical conductivity of the rocks in an earthquake zone. It is known from laboratory experiments on rock samples that the electrical resistance of water-saturated rocks, such as granite, changes drastically just before the rocks fracture in a high-pressure device. A few field experiments to check this property in fault zones have reported decreases in electrical resistance before an earthquake; others have not. Again, more studies of this kind are needed before this method can be embraced.

Variation in the seismicity rate is the fifth parameter. More information is available on this method than on the other four, but the present results are not definitive. In brief, from time to time a strong change in the normal background earthquake occurrence in a region is noted—usually an increase in the rate of small earthquakes. Sometimes these tremors prove to be foreshocks of a damaging earthquake. An apparently successful forecast based on this scheme has been described by Italian seismologists. After the tragic principal shock of May 6, 1976, in the Friuli region of northern Italy, the number and size of aftershocks were monitored. In early September 1976, it was noticed that the number occurring per day in the region had increased significantly. On this basis, authorities issued a general warning that people living in buildings of dubious strength might be advised to sleep elsewhere, even in tents. On September 15, 1976, a major aftershock ($M_s = 6.0$) struck at 5:15 P.M., collapsing many weakened buildings. Yet few were killed in this earthquake.

PALEOSEISMOLOGY

Although these five parameters so far have not proved to be reliable predictors, there is another, more promising method of earthquake prediction

This Jeffrey pine tree, called the Pool tree, has been growing near the San Andreas fault in southern California for more than 370 years. The top was broken off in the large 1812 earthquake centered nearby. The root system was so damaged that, as its tree rings show, growth slowed for years afterward.

that gives a longer-term probability of the earthquake hazard in a region. The new research field of paleoseismology discovers "fossil earthquakes," whose patterns of occurrence suggest the future rate of seismic activity. The field draws heavily

on geological evidence of long-term crustal deformation, and it relies on the general concepts of plate tectonics for its justification.

In the 1906 San Francisco earthquake along the San Andreas fault, a witness described seeing "limbs snapped off, trees uprooted" and reported that a "forest looked as though a swath had been cut through it 200 ft in width." Trees sway violently in seismic shaking; branches and even trunks break off. In assessments of earthquake intensity by the modified Mercalli scale, light shaking of trees is a measure of intensity V and strong shaking a measure of intensity VII; broken branches and trunks rate intensity VIII+. Often trees lose their crowns because the ground shaking is amplified as it progresses up a tree. (In the same way, the upper stories of 12-story buildings were damaged by shaking in the 1985 Mexico City earthquake.)

These observations suggest that, by analyzing tree rings, we may be able to determine the locations, dates, and even intensities of earthquakes in the distant past. The idea is that local seismic shaking might have disturbed the growth pattern of the tree, perhaps by loosening or destroying the root system or by causing the loss of many branches or even the entire crown. The disturbances in growth would show up as alterations in the width or shape of tree rings. The method is to take wood cores from trees, either living or dead, in an area that is subject to earthquakes. Disruptions in the rate of growth are correlated from place to place to give a measure of the size of the area of high seismic intensity.

Many other events, including droughts, may affect the growth rate of tree rings. Thus, hiatus in the growth near a fault can be attributed to earthquake damage only when all other disturbing mechanisms have been ruled out. For example, tree rings were found to have changed in size at the time of the great 1857 earthquake in Fort Tejon, southern California. But meteorological data indicated an extreme drought that same year. In such cases, it is necessary to decide whether the rings most resemble the narrow rings produced in drought years or the sequence of nonuniform rings that indicates an extended period of growth recovery after earthquake damage.

It is of special interest to sample trees close by the causative fault because, when the fault type is known, this evidence will verify that an earthquake caused the tree damage. Dip-slip faulting would lead to a broad zone of soil disturbance, whereas strike-slip faulting would normally affect only those trees within a few meters of the actual fault rupture. The key to such validation is to count the number of rings over a fixed radial distance along the tree core and endeavor to match these numbers for at least two trees in the area. The chronology of tree rings near the suspected earthquake source must then be compared with that of trees farther away. A drought would give the same chronology for trees in a whole region, for example, whereas ground shaking would not.

A number of geochronologies of earthquakes from interesting tree ring studies have been published. The "Rosetta stone" of such studies is shown on this page. Very old pine trees near the San Andreas fault at Wrightwood, California, had grown in a zone of high-intensity ground shaking produced each time the fault slipped. The wood core in the photograph was taken in 1986 from the stump of a tree that had died in 1957 and subsequently been cut down. The rings of the disturbed tree clearly narrowed in 1857, the year of the last great rupture of this segment of the San Andreas fault. The uniformity of the growth pattern was also disturbed in 1812, the year of another damaging southern California earthquake. Unlike the widely felt and well-described 1857 earthquake, the 1812 earthquake is documented by only scanty geological evidence. Another convincing case comes from the enormous 1964 Good Friday earthquake in Alaska. Sitka spruce trees on the beach at Cape Suckling, which was uplifted 4 m by the thrust faulting of the crust, were tilted in the shaking and their roots were exposed. Field sampling of

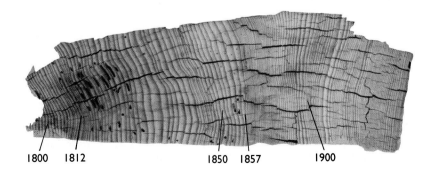

Narrowed tree rings are evidence of both the 1812 and 1857 earthquakes in this section from the stump of a white fir that grew on the San Andreas fault near Wrightwood, California.

1800   1812   1850 1857   1900

tree cores again showed that the tree rings narrowed in 1964 compared with the average width before and after this magnitude 8.6 earthquake.

We turn now to a more widely used and perhaps more reliable method of extending back the record of seismicity along active faults. This method depends on geological field studies of soil layers in the ground. These studies ascribe dated features in the stratigraphic record to specific large historical earthquakes. Under favorable circumstances, they reliably track sequences of great earthquakes back to the start of Holocene time, 10,000 years ago. For example, about 50 km northeast of Los Angeles, the trace of the San Andreas fault transects a low-lying area that becomes a swamp during the rainy season as the waters of Pallett Creek rise. Trenches excavated by geologists across the fault in this area exposed a well-marked sequence of layers composed of silt, sand, or the brownish, partly decayed plant matter called peat. Geologists believe that the displacement and liquefaction effects of great earthquakes are often preserved in such beds of sand and peat.

During the strong shaking of the ground, water-saturated sand layers at some depth below the surface become liquefied. The overpressure of the rocks and soil above then causes the lighter and more buoyant water and sand to rise to the surface, forming a layer of sand. As the cycle of wet and dry seasons continues, grass and other vegetation grows in the sand, and Pallett Creek and other neighboring streams carry down gravel and silt. The deposition of these sediments covers up the sand layer formed in the intense shaking; the deposited silt now contains peat created from the organic remains of dead plants. After the passage of time, another great earthquake occurs, again liquefying the sand and creating

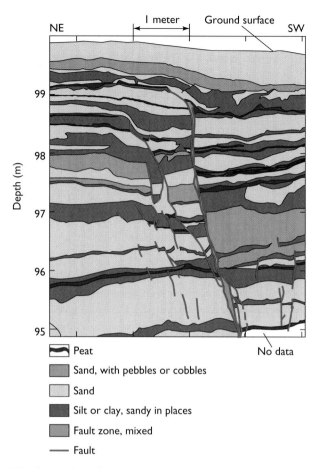

The San Andreas fault appears exposed in the southwest wall of a trench at Pallett Creek, California. The peat layers (dark brown) show increasing amounts of vertical displacement with depth, owing to the cumulative slip from repeated earthquakes. The uppermost, unfaulted strata were deposited after the 1857 earthquake; the lowermost peat bed on the southwest side of the fault was deposited about A.D. 800.

sand flows at the surface. These are, in turn, also covered up. Thus, a sequence of alternating layers of sand and of silt and peat forms as younger layers are created over older ones. The plants or other organic materials within each layer are dated by radiocarbon methods.

At Pallett Creek, evidence was found for at least nine earthquakes extending back more than 1400 years to A.D. 545. The dates, all but one of them approximate, are as follows:

1857, 1745, 1470, 1245,
1190, 965, 860, 665, 545

The year 1857 marks the directly documented Fort Tejon earthquake of January 9, the last major earthquake produced by rupture of the nearby section of the San Andreas fault. There is thus a direct check on the method. The main conclusion from the work at Pallett Creek is that the average time between past earthquakes in the area is approximately 160 years, but there is a large variation. The greatest time interval was nearly 200 years and the smallest as short as 55 years.

Similar studies on liquefaction have since been carried out across other active faults in many places, including China and Japan. It should be noted that damaging earthquakes may occur, perhaps during a dry season, when the ground is not moist enough to liquefy significantly even in a large earthquake.

THE CASCADIA SUBDUCTION ZONE

How well can forensic seismology unravel the record of past great earthquakes? And, further, how well can such paleoseismological evidence predict future earthquake hazard? A case history of the Cascadia region illustrates how modern geological studies are meeting such inquiries.

In the Pacific Northwest of North America, a belt of volcanic mountains, called the Cascade Range, runs from California through Oregon and Washington states into British Columbia. These volcanoes are the result of a subducting slab, which takes the Juan de Fuca plate and the adjacent Gorda plate down beneath the North American plate. The entire region, called the Cascadia subduction zone, stretches northward from Cape

Trench excavations in the Tanlu fault zone of Anhui province, China, exposed this solidified "pipe" originally formed during an earthquake by upward-rising sand and water.

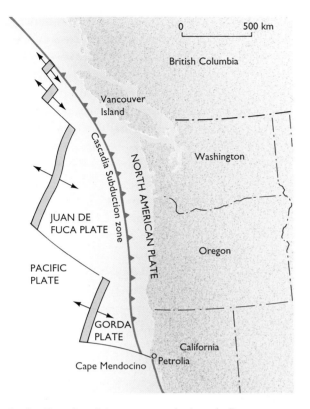

At the Cascadia subduction zone, the Juan de Fuca and Gorda plates plunge under the overriding North American plate.

even one as large as the immense 1964 Alaska earthquake, which was generated by the subduction of the Pacific plate under Alaska along the Aleutian trench.

Measurements of the recent motions of the Pacific and North American plates indicate that the plates are still converging along the zone at an average rate of about 4 cm per year. As the Juan de Fuca plate is overridden by the North American plate, material at its margin melts deep beneath the North American plate. Molten rock in the form of magma is still rising to the surface, producing active volcanoes such as Mount St. Helens. Along the continental margin itself, geodetic surveys confirm that the Cascade Range is being compressed and that portions of the Washington coast are being uplifted. Yet despite the geological activity, essentially no earthquake activity has been recorded in historical times along the Oregon portion of the Cascadia subduction zone.

Whether there is a significant seismic hazard in the northwestern United States depends on whether the subduction process is still vigorous enough to generate damaging earthquakes within a limited span of years. Only a few years ago, because of the historical absence of major earthquakes, geologists believed the Cascadia zone to be almost aseismic. Recently, however, several lines of evidence have led to a profound revision of this picture of quiescence. First, by analogy with other subduction zones, the undoubted convergence of the North American plate against the offshore Pacific plates must require a downward movement of oceanic crust under the Cascades; there is nowhere else for the rock to go! Second, there is recent direct evidence of deformation of water-saturated ocean floor sediments of Holocene age (the last 10,000 years) along a

Mendocino, where the San Andreas fault swings westward into the Pacific, to north of Vancouver Island. Over the last few million years, the two Pacific plates have been gradually sliding downward beneath the western margin of the continental plate at various rates. From evidence gathered at other subduction zones, we expect periods of smooth sliding to alternate with periods when the subduction slab is locked, until eventually the strain exceeds the strength of the rocks. At that time, the strain is released in a sudden slip that can produce a major earthquake,

belt of crustal rocks that contain large, folded layers, called a fold-and-thrust belt. On land as well, many folded structures of relatively young age have been discovered in the uppermost crust of the southern part of the Cascadia zone. The horizontal shortening by both submarine and subcontinental folding is consistent with the continued pushing together of the two plates.

Third, there is evidence that the ground surface along the coastline has experienced cycles of uplift and subsidence. Along estuaries and tidal inlets in a number of places, metal cylinders have been bored into the water-saturated muds down to depths of tens of meters. The long cylindrical mud cores so obtained show lengths of soft, mottled, gray mud interspersed with thin-

ner layers containing the fossil remains of tree stumps, driftwood, and particularly peat. The peaty layers must have been deposited when the land surface was above high-tide level and covered with marshes of salt-tolerant plants, much like those common along the Pacific coast today. To produce each thin peaty layer, the marshes must have suddenly dropped beneath sea level, to be covered with sand and fine sediments. The organic material in these peaty beds can be dated to accuracies of a few tens of years using radioactive carbon techniques. On the coast of Washington State, extensive marshy lowlands have sunk 0.5 to 2 m at least six times in the past 7000 years. The coast most recently subsided about 300 years ago.

In this trench, the uplift and subsidence of a coastal salt marsh at Mad River slough, Humboldt Bay, California, are recorded by alternating layers of peat, deposited after uplift, and mud, deposited after subsidence. The labels refer to modern marsh (A), the base of a modern peat layer (B), and the top of a buried peat layer (C) dated to 300 years ago.

A

Peat

B

Mud

C

Peat

The subsidence of the coast caused flooding after the 1964 Alaska earthquake. The coast later rebounded, as is apparent in a photograph of the same area today.

Such changes in coastal elevation are common in the large subduction zone earthquakes of Alaska and Chile. For example, the coastal uplift and subsidence in the 1964 Alaska earthquake amounted to many meters. In both areas, subsidence of the coast has caused fertile lowlands to be replaced by water-covered estuary and flats. Over tens of thousands of years, fertile coastal marshes were repeatedly drowned and then reformed by the slow uplift and redeposition of soils. The drowning of fertile coastal areas has at least sometimes been coincident with large thrust earthquakes.

In light of these arguments, the earthquake hazard along the Cascadia subduction zone has been reevaluated. One extreme conclusion is that essentially the whole Cascadia subduction slab could slip beneath the continent in one episode, generating a mega-earthquake. A less extreme assessment is that, given the admittedly slow convergence rate and the lack of seismicity in Oregon and southern Washington along the subduction slab at present, sudden slip will occur on only limited segments of the slab. Moderate earthquakes can be expected intermittently along the Cascadia zone, particularly on the portion adjacent to the Juan de Fuca plate.

The adjacent Gorda plate segment off northern California differs from the Cascadia zone to the north in that many earthquakes, including shocks up to magnitude 7.5, occur relatively frequently within it. Thus, the ocean crust of the small Gorda plate must contain many active faults on which elastic strain is released. In the Gorda segment, the belt of deformed crustal rocks follows the shoreline down to a point near Cape Mendocino where it intersects the northwest-tending San Andreas fault with its strike-slip displacements. In this region, three quite different tectonic features merge: the San Andreas fault, the underwater Mendocino escarpment, and the Cascadia fold-and-thrust belt. The adjustment of stresses around this "triple junction" might be expected to affect the timing of large earthquakes in all three systems.

In fact, a recent event has removed some of the speculation about present-day seismogenic slip on the Gorda subduction slab. On April 25, 1992, a thrust of the subduction slab at shallow depth under Cape Mendocino near Petrolia produced a substantial earthquake ($M_s = 6.9$). Two damaging aftershocks followed the next day. In the town of Ferndale especially, many older wood-frame houses were thrown off their foundations. A very high spike of horizontal ground acceleration, over $1.8g$, was recorded on rock foundation near Cape Mendocino. Although this acceleration is probably now the world's record high, most other accelerometers in the region showed seismic waves of only average amplitudes.

The tidal zone along the coast near Cape Mendocino was surveyed immediately after the earthquake, but little change in elevation was found. In this case, the key geological evidence took a few days of tidal cycles to become clear. A week or so after the main tremor, geologists were contacted by local residents who complained of a stench along the seashore from rotting seaweed and other tidal zone life. Revisits to the coast clearly showed that a reach of over 100 km had been uplifted by a meter or so relative to high tide. The uplift above the high-tide line had killed off marine life in the elevated foreshore, leaving a visible band of discolored shells on the rocks.

The recent studies along the Cascadia subduction zone illustrate well how diverse geological and geophysical evidence can throw light on earthquake hazards in a tectonic region where, unlike the San Andreas fault system in California, there is no historical evidence of great earthquakes. At the moment, geologists cannot offer any definite forecast of when or if a great Cascadia zone earthquake will strike in the next hundred years. The studies do mean, however, that significant seismic hazards in the northwestern part of the United States and the Vancouver Island region of Canada cannot be ruled out.

The thrust of the Cape Mendocino subduction slab in 1992 produced a coastal uplift of 1.2 m. The uplift killed a layer of intertidal plants raised above the high-tide line, shown in this photo taken at Devil's Gate six weeks after the earthquake.

CALCULATING THE ODDS OF AN EARTHQUAKE

In the case of natural hazards such as floods and windstorms, the best strategy has been to state the statistical odds that such an event will happen. The same approach is now used in some earthquake-prone areas, where seismologists are making public announcements on the probability of damaging earthquakes. In particular, after the 1989 Loma Prieta earthquake a working group established by the U.S. Geological Survey estimated the probability of future damaging earthquakes in northern California. They concluded that the chance of an earthquake of 7.0 (M_w) or greater occurring in the San Francisco Bay Area in the next 30 years was 67 percent. Their method relies both on an analysis of past earthquakes and on the calculation of stored strain.

Probability is a measure of the chance that some event will occur. The probability may range from *zero,* which means that there is no chance the event will occur, to *one,* which means that the event is certain to occur. Numbers between these values give a measure of the relative probability of the event. For example, the probability of tossing a head in one throw of a coin is .5 (50 percent), and the probability of drawing one heart from a deck of playing cards is .25 (25 percent). Of course, if the coin is unbalanced or the deck is irregular, these odds will differ.

From experience, most people have a reasonably correct idea of the probabilities involved in games of chance and in many common circumstances in life. Thus, few people would question that the odds of injury from driving on a crowded freeway are higher than from walking on a sidewalk. Similarly, there would be wide agreement that the probability of injury from an earthquake is higher, in general, in Los Angeles than in Texas. It would also be widely accepted that the chance of such injury would depend on whether a person was in an unreinforced brick building or in a timber-frame house bolted to the foundation. The challenge is to give such beliefs the same definite numerical form as is achieved in calling the toss of a coin.

A useful formulation is to specify the odds of an anticipated earthquake or to specify the sizes of earthquakes that will occur in a certain area in a given time. If we know the number and magnitude of the earthquakes that have occurred in a region in 100 years, we might hope to calculate the average magnitude that is expected in the area, or the odds that a specified magnitude will be exceeded every 10 to 20 years, say. In the San Francisco Bay Area, for example, in the 55 years from 1936 to 1991 there have been five earthquakes with a magnitude of $6\frac{3}{4}$ or greater. We can then calculate that if these earthquakes occur randomly, another earthquake of the same magnitude or greater might be expected in the next $55/5 = 11$ years with a high probability.

A serious problem mars this type of probability calculation: earthquakes in a given tectonic region do not occur exactly at random but usually in clusters or separated by gaps, according to systematic trends. Examples of long-term gaps were given in Chapter 5. This variation in time and space renders the concept of the average odds of an earthquake occurring above a given size unsatisfactory for short-term planning.

An alternative method of determining probability is based on the elastic rebound theory, which explains earthquakes as the result of sudden slip on faults, segments of which rupture

because they can no longer sustain the elastic strain that has built up in neighboring rocks. The more the strain increases, the more probable it is that another earthquake will be generated. Geological or geodetic measurements allow scientists to estimate which segments are most likely to slip in the future.

The first step is to define where fault segments begin and end; this is usually done by mapping bends or offsets in the fault or by mapping its intersections with other faults. The assumption is then made that the largest-magnitude earthquake that could be produced by any segment is that produced by the rupture of the whole segment. Smaller lengths will produce earthquakes of smaller magnitude, and larger lengths will produce earthquakes of greater magnitude. Thus the sudden rupture of a 40-km segment of a fault like the San Andreas, as occurred in the 1989 Loma Prieta earthquake, generated an earthquake of about magnitude 7.

The second step in assessing probability is to determine which fault segments along an active fault zone have slipped in the past and to measure the rate at which strain is accumulating in the region. As an illustration, we may consider the information available in 1989 on the section of the San Andreas fault in the Santa Cruz Mountains that ruptured in the 1989 Loma Prieta earthquake. From the long-term geodetic measurements, the average rate of relative displacement across the San Andreas fault in central California is about 1.5 cm per year. As a comparison, in the 1906 San Francisco earthquake, the Santa Cruz segment of the fault is believed to have slipped only about 1.6 m while the segment north of San Francisco slipped more than 5 m. Thus, given the constant rate of slip, the probability of earthquake rupture on the Santa

Cruz Mountains segment, was, at least until the rebound in the 1989 earthquake, higher than the probability of rupture on the segment to the north.

The earthquake resulting from each episode of slip along a fault segment is assigned a magnitude. Thus, we can measure the intervals of time between earthquakes greater than a given

magnitude. We then determine what magnitude of earthquake occurs within a specified time—at intervals of 50 years, 60 years, and so on. These numbers can be plotted in a histogram that shows the frequency of earthquakes above a given magnitude. From the histogram, we can calculate, for example, the most probable recurrence interval by finding the line that divides the area under the histogram into equal right and left areas.

This type of probability calculation, based on the amount of slip that has occurred on fault segments, is applicable only to seismic regions where active faults are observable at the ground surface. The limitation is a serious one. One of the few seismic regions of the world where faults active at the surface are well mapped is along the San Andreas transform system of California. A recent probability plot for this area is shown on the opposite page. There are many assumptions underlying the published odds, and the numbers given have large uncertainties. Nevertheless, such calculations should become more reliable as further geological and geodetic surveys are carried out.

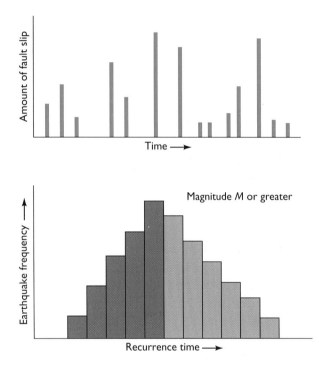

Top: From the study of geological strata, scientists can obtain a record of the various amounts of slip along a given fault. Each slip is proportional to the magnitude of the earthquake generated. Thus, the time intervals between the recurrence of earthquakes above a fixed magnitude can be counted, leading to the histogram below.
Bottom: A histogram showing the number of earthquakes, with a given magnitude M or greater, that occurred with specified recurrence times since the last earthquake.

THE PARKFIELD EARTHQUAKE PREDICTION EXPERIMENT

One particular case history illustrates the expectations and frustrations of the modern program designed to forecast earthquakes of significant size. The case concerns the Parkfield area in central California along the San Andreas fault. In this region of rolling, open ranch land, remote from highly populated areas, the San Andreas fault traces are clearly visible; its seismological

CALIFORNIA

San Andreas fault

10% North Coast

Expected magnitudes

8+

7–7.9

6–6.2

San Francisco Peninsula

San Francisco

20%

90% Parkfield

Southern Santa Cruz Mountains

30% Cholane

30% Mojave

Coachella Valley

10% Carrizo

40%

Los Angeles

San Bernardino Mountains 20%

San Diego

Bars on the map of California give rough estimates of the odds that major earthquakes will be centered on different segments of the San Andreas fault in the next thirty years.

properties along a 25-km section are among the best understood in the world.

Seismographs installed from 1887 onward at the University of California have recorded moderate-sized earthquakes (magnitude 5.5 to 6.0) on the San Andreas fault near Parkfield in 1901, 1922, 1934, and 1966. The reports of nineteenth-century inhabitants indicate that similar earthquakes occurred in 1857 and 1881. The earthquake dates immediately suggest a cyclical pattern: the earthquakes recur with an almost constant period of 22 years. The sole exception is the 1934 fault slip. Furthermore, seismograms show that the earthquakes of March 10, 1922;

June 8, 1934; and June 28, 1966, are similar in their wave shapes, indicating that the same segments of the San Andreas fault had ruptured in all three cases in much the same way. A plausible conclusion was that the Parkfield segment of the San Andreas fault rebounds time and again with a characteristic mechanism. Thus, like a mechanical engine, a regular cycle of behavior might be expected.

After the discovery of the apparent Parkfield cycle, large numbers of instruments and researchers were marshaled in what was called by the U.S. Geological Survey "the Parkfield earthquake prediction experiment." The cyclical pattern suggested that the next Parkfield earthquake was to have been expected in about 1988, with a statistical variation of about four years. Because an earthquake was confidently expected to strike Parkfield soon, the area was viewed as an ideal place to look for precursors. The limits of technology were stretched as seismologists installed a cluster of high-resolution monitoring devices to measure characteristics such as tiny variations in the pattern of small local earthquakes, ground deformation changes such as tilt, electromagnetic properties, and many more.

As this book was being completed in December 1992, the assigned window for a repetition of the 1966 Parkfield earthquake came to an end, and the predicted earthquake had not occurred. At the annual western meeting of the American Geophysical Union in San Francisco, a special postmortem session was held on the Parkfield experiment. It was conceded that the prediction had failed, perhaps because the hypothesized characteristic earthquake mechanism was untrue, perhaps because the other large recent earthquakes in central California had changed the pattern of repetition, perhaps be-

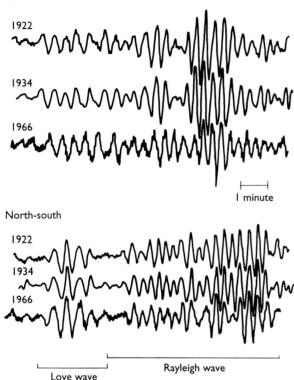

East-west

1922

1934

1966

|——| 1 minute

North-south

1922

1934

1966

|— Love wave —| |— Rayleigh wave —|

These surface waves from Parkfield earthquakes in 1922, 1934, and 1966 were recorded on the same seismograph in Debilt, The Netherlands. The nearly identical waveforms and amplitudes led W. Bakun and T. V. McEvilly in 1984 to propose repeated rupture of the same segment of the San Andreas fault as the mechanism of large characteristic Parkfield earthquakes.

geophysical monitoring instruments. The public alerts that had been issued, although false alarms, had advanced public knowledge and earthquake preparedness. As the Parkfield prediction experiment recedes into seismological history, we can be certain that large earthquakes will someday occur again at Parkfield. Strain along the San Andreas fault there, as elsewhere, continues to grow inexorably as the Pacific and North American plates follow their opposite trajectories.

THE CONSEQUENCES OF EARTHQUAKE PREDICTION

As seismological discovery continues, numerous earthquake warnings from credible sources will probably be issued in various countries. In Western societies, studies have been made on the unfavorable as well as the propitious consequences of prediction. For example, if the time of a large damaging earthquake in California were accurately predicted a year or so ahead of time and continuously updated, casualties and even property damage might be much reduced; but the communities in the region might suffer social disruption and economic decline, as investment dropped and people relocated their homes and businesses. Very short term predictions would allow immediate preparations to minimize seismic risk at home and at work; in addition, medical, police, firefighting, and other lifesaving services could be placed on continuous alert. If the alert continued for any length of time, however, there would inevitably be social distress from the rescheduling of public events, the cessation of work activity, the closing of schools, and so on.

cause the statistics used to calculate the odds were unsound.

On the positive side, speakers at the review session pointed to the experience gained in the design, installation, and field operation of special

The realistic approach at present is to accept that earthquake prediction in the strictest sense is not now feasible. Yet in some parts of the world, particularly along plate margins, the maximum size of a future earthquake can be estimated and some reasonable statement made about the probability of such an earthquake in the next few decades. So long as such statements are not allowed to foster misleading confidence in what remain very uncertain odds, they can be helpful in guiding public policy on the commitment of resources for reducing earthquake risk.

9

REDUCING
SEISMIC RISK

OF GEOLOGICAL HAZARDS such as avalanches, volcanoes, and floods, it is earthquakes that arouse the greatest concern for life and well-being. In 1976, within a single year, devastating earthquakes in Guatemala, Italy, and China alone killed more than 300,000 people. The potential for calamity is greater still. The official Chinese catalogue estimates that 830,000 people died from all causes in the earthquake that struck Shensi province on January 23, 1556.

Destruction of property can be almost as appalling as casualties. Earthquakes play havoc with the economy of many countries: the Mexican seismic disaster of 1985 produced a loss of more than $4 billion, and the moderately sized Loma Prieta earthquake that struck central California in 1989 caused about $6 billion in damage. The Armenian earthquake of

Buildings of unreinforced masonry, like these on a hillside
in Gibellina, Sicily, damaged in a 1968 earthquake, are
particularly vulnerable to strong shaking.

1988 destroyed large sections of several industrial cities and bankrupted the entire national economy. The economic losses from this one earthquake may reach $16 billion.

In the first major attempt to reduce the risk from natural hazards throughout the world, the General Assembly of the United Nations has designated the 1990s as the International Decade of Natural Disaster Reduction (IDNDR). United Nations commissions, national organizations, and professional engineering and geological associations are uniting to reduce the effects of natural hazards, including earthquakes and associated dangers such as tsunamis. Society is helpless to prevent the earthquake *hazard,* a term we use to designate an event with potential danger. But the United Nations program hopes to lower greatly the *risk* from earthquakes, the amount of damage to humankind and its works.

With the Tsunami Warning System explained in the box as a successful example, the nations participating in the IDNDR expect to accomplish much more working together than any country could working alone. To analyze the seiches behind a large dam, for instance, requires data on seismic motions at the points of contact between the dam and the canyon floor and walls. A single country instrumenting some of its dams might have to wait a long time before recording the desired information. By instrumenting dams in several seismically active countries, the IDNDR hopes to provide the information much sooner.

Among its many projects aimed at seismic disasters, the IDNDR program is developing short-term warning systems that would exploit the finite speed of P and S waves through the crust. When an earthquake strikes, its focus and origin time could be fixed by a computerized, dense local network of seismographs in, say, 4

TSUNAMIS AND SEICHES

Along the ocean margin, hazardous sea waves may rush up the coastline and devastate coastal properties, perhaps causing more death and destruction than the shaking itself. The sea waves are called tsunamis, to avoid the misleading popular term "tidal wave." Tsunamis can be generated by different types of disturbances, such as submerged landslides and the explosion of volcanic islands, but it is the earthquake fault source acting as a giant paddle at the bottom of the ocean that produces the most catastrophic of these very long wavelength water waves.

In the open sea, the speeds of tsunami waves exceed 700 km/h, and their lengths dwarf the usual ocean swells, as the distances between crests may exceed 100 km. But because the crest heights in the open sea are less than 1 m, the waves are undetectable to ships. As the tsunami reaches shallow water, its speed decreases sharply while the wave height increases many times, sometimes to as much as 25 m.

Spectacular tsunamis have affected countries with coasts on the Pacific Ocean, particularly Japan. In the United States, damaging tsunamis have battered shorelines in the Hilo region of Hawaii, along the northwest coast of North America, and dramatically in the 1964 Alaska earthquake.

Considerable relief from the tsunami hazard has been achieved around the Pacific coasts by the Tsunami Warning System developed through the cooperative efforts of a number of countries after the devastating Aleutian tsunami of April 6, 1946. When seismographs in the region detect and locate large earthquakes, seismologists notify the system headquarters in Hawaii, which sends out rapid warnings of possible tsunami generation. Not all earthquakes along the oceanic margins of the tectonic plates are accompanied by noteworthy tsunamis, however, because to produce this hazard the ocean floor must move vertically along the fault. This type of displacement is most common in subduction zones.

In lakes and reservoirs, the collapse of retaining walls or the plunging of large landslides into the water can pose serious risks for people living downstream and for their docks, dams, and sewage systems. When an earthquake of magnitude 7 shook Lituya Bay in Alaska on July 9, 1958, it triggered a massive landslide into the bay that produced a water surge 60 m high. Boats were carried over trees 25 m high, and water velocities were high enough to strip the vegetation from the shoreline.

Oscillations of the water surface called seiches may be set up by the shaking of the ground, like water sloshing in a dish as it is moved to and fro. Great earthquakes have been known to generate seiches at considerable distances. The Lisbon earthquake of 1755 created palpable oscillations in canals and lakes as far away as Holland, Switzerland, Scotland, and Sweden. About 2000 km from Lisbon, Angus MacDermot, an innkeeper in Scotland, saw Loch Lomond suddenly and "without the least gust of wind, rising and retiring against its banks, and five minutes later subsiding."

After a tsunami swept the Indonesian island of Flores, tuna fish littered a street in the town of Maumere. The tsunami was generated on December 12, 1992, by an earthquake source that was responsible for the deaths of more than 2000 people.

seconds, and a message could be telephoned or radioed almost instantaneously to places several hundred kilometers away. The damaging S waves would not arrive until about half a minute later—perhaps enough time to shut down earthquake-sensitive equipment. A similar earthquake warning system has been operated for 25 years by Japan Railways. The "bullet trains," or Shinkansen, which reach speeds of 240 km/h, are in danger from sudden damage to the track in an earthquake. Whenever seismographs near the track indicate that ground acceleration exceeds a given fraction of gravity by a specified amount, the electric power to the Shinkansen is shut off.

In another part of the IDNDR program, state-of-the-art intensity maps are being developed that will predict the levels of shaking, soil liquefaction, and other seismic effects. Such maps will assist engineers in selecting the techniques of building design and construction that will most effectively minimize the damage from an earthquake.

DEVASTATING A SMALL COUNTRY: THE 1988 ARMENIA EARTHQUAKE

In far too many seismically active parts of the Earth, modern industrialization carried out with little attention to seismic hazards has been the root of tragedy. An indelible example is the earthquake that struck northern Armenia on December 7, 1988, at 11:41 A.M. local time, destroying a great many buildings and factories in the cities of Spitak, Leninakan (now called Gumri), and Kirovakan. In the surrounding countryside, 58 villages were leveled and 100 significantly damaged. One government report, based on the recovery of bodies from the rubble, estimated that 25,000 people perished. Out of a local population of 700,000, the earthquake left at least 514,000 homeless and 30,000 injured.

Some of the strongest ground shaking occurred in highly industrialized areas containing large chemical and food processing plants. Many of the numerous large electrical substations and thermal power plants in the region were damaged. Although a nuclear power plant near Yerevan, about 75 km from the fault source, was not harmed, the plant was afterward closed permanently because of the earthquake risk, despite the great economic distress created by the dissolution of the Soviet Union and the cessation of oil supplies from Baku.

The source of the main shock was a fault rupture about 40 km south of the spine of the Caucasus Mountains. This magnificent range is a segment of the belt of high mountains running from the Alps across southern Europe to the Himalayas of Asia; these mountains are the result of pressure in the Earth's crust caused by the convergence of the Arabian and Eurasian tectonic plates. The whole belt is the site of continual seismic activity; major earthquakes occur frequently from the Aegean Sea, across Turkey, and into Iran and western Afghanistan and Tadzhikistan. While the frequency of earthquakes in Armenia does not match that in some other segments of this active belt, the crust is deforming with geological rapidity in that country's vicinity, and its deformation is marked by active thrust faults and volcanic activity. One of these volcanoes is the famous Biblical prominence Mount Ararat, 5165 m high, which is 100 km south of the epicenter of the 1988 earthquake.

The aftermath of the 1988 Armenia earthquake.

On December 7, seismic waves radiated from the rebound of a previously strained, but unnamed, fault at least 60 km in length. The rupture extended west-northwest from close to Spitak across the fields and mountainsides with a strike parallel to the Caucasus Range and a dip toward the north-northeast. The vertical component of slip along the main part of the surface rupture was 1.6 m near the southwest end and averaged 1 m along most of the scarp.

Why did the earthquake cause so much death and destruction? The few recordings available suggest that the shaking was not exceptional, although it was perhaps amplified in Gumri by a deep soil layer. Rather, Armenian and Russian engineers who studied the earthquake reported that the building code provisions were inadequate for the seismic hazard of Armenia. Yet even these provisions had been ignored: precast reinforced concrete structures had not

been well designed, and the quality of construction was often poor. The lurching or failure of the ground and the uneven ground settlement that so often damage structures could have been countered by applying an appropriate treatment to the site before construction, such as the excavation of weak soil, or by installing appropriate foundation systems, such as wooden or concrete piles that reach down to bedrock. In 1992 I was able to help initiate a major program of strong-motion instrumentation in Armenia. Many presently unanswered questions will someday be solved from the recordings.

ACCEPTABLE EARTHQUAKE RISK

The odds are high (from over 60 percent to 100 percent) that a damaging earthquake will strike when most people are at home. Unfortunately, in many places the housing is seismically hazardous. In Armenia, as well as in regions of the Mediterranean, Turkey, Iran, South and Central America, China, and elsewhere in Asia, the unreinforced stone and brick materials and heavy roofs almost guarantee high death tolls during even moderate shaking.

In contrast, the single- and two-story wood-frame houses typical of the United States and New Zealand and the light wooden buildings of Japan are among the safest kinds of places to be in an earthquake. These buildings can suffer damage, but they are unlikely to collapse because the strength of the strongly jointed timber frame can easily support the light loads of the roof and upper stories under even strong vertical and horizontal ground acceleration.

One of the major lessons of recent earthquakes in California is the importance of bolting timber-framed homes to their foundations to prevent separation. Surveys show that about 15 percent of one-story wood-frame houses are damaged because they fall off their foundations, mostly those more than twenty years old and often those with no lateral bracing.

Reducing seismic risk, by strengthening or relocating structures, is expensive. In allocating money, planners must balance the threat to life and property posed by earthquake hazards with the cost of reducing risk. The first step is to evaluate the potential hazard. In the United States, maps of ground-shaking hazard have been prepared for specific regions and for the country as a whole. These maps give the expectation that

Soil failure led to the tilt of these wood-frame houses in the 1906 San Francisco earthquake.

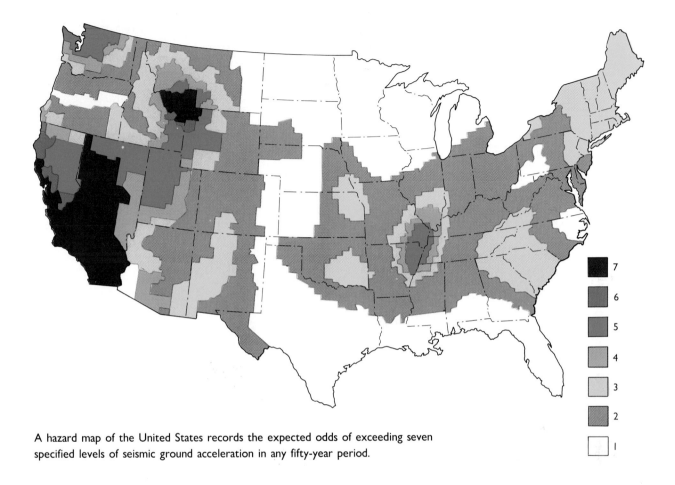

A hazard map of the United States records the expected odds of exceeding seven specified levels of seismic ground acceleration in any fifty-year period.

seismic intensity parameters (such as acceleration) will be exceeded in a given time, say fifty years. In creating these maps, the older concept of discrete hazard zones, drawn mainly on the basis of the historical seismicity and intensity maps, has been abandoned; instead, the maps show the frequency of earthquakes of various magnitudes weighted by geological evidence of active fault systems. Such maps have now been incorporated in many building codes, with the explicit understanding that in planning a structure builders

must balance the risk of stronger shaking against the high cost of overdesign.

Older structures present the greatest overall risk. The trade-off between saving lives and lowering reconstruction costs is well illustrated by recent studies of the seismic resistance of state-owned buildings in California. Much of the more than $20 billion worth of state properties is vulnerable to damage in an earthquake. A review board conducting one of the first quantitative studies of this problem, begun at the University

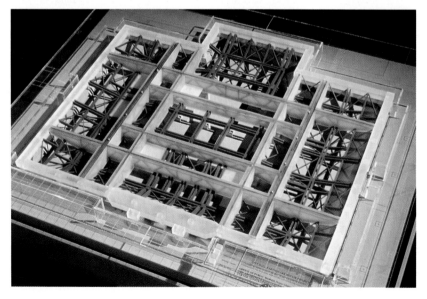

The 18-story Oakland City Hall, an architecturally notable building completed in 1914, was damaged in the 1989 Loma Prieta earthquake and subsequently closed down. Architects have built models showing the proposed seismic strengthening of the structure: A steel framework within the walls will tie together the main structural elements (*top right*). The elastic flexibility of the building will be further increased by introducing additional interior steel bracing into the upper stories and towers (*bottom left*).

of California, Berkeley, in 1974, chose the preservation of life as its highest priority. There was agreement that, when strengthening or reconstructing buildings, the builders should comply with the code requirements aimed at preventing loss of life.

Subsequently, the California Seismic Safety Commission recommended that all state-owned structures be assigned priorities to determine the order of upgrading. These priorities were based on a benefit-cost ratio (BCR), defined as the number of lives saved per reconstruction dollar. The immense task of ranking many thousands of buildings is now well under way.

Certain classes of construction perform poorly in earthquakes, whereas other classes resist the shaking. A life safety ratio (LSR) predicts the expected number of fatalities per 10,000 occupants before reconstruction, given the class of the structure and the predicted intensity of shaking for the seismic zone. Thus, from experience, unreinforced masonry buildings have been allocated a particular LSR value and reinforced concrete structures another.

The computational equation is

$$BCR = \frac{(LSR)(ECO)(SCF) - (LSRG)(ECO^*)}{10,000\ (RC)}$$

where ECO (equivalent continuous occupancy) is the average number of persons occupying the building each 24-hour day of the year, SCF (seismicity correction factor) depends on the earthquake occurrence rate in the zone, and RC (reconstruction cost) is the cost to rehabilitate this class of structure in order to reduce the risk to a specified life safety ratio goal (LSRG). The single

asterisk denotes the value after reconstruction. In California, BCR ratings have been used to allocate funds for more detailed engineering studies and, when combined with additional engineering evaluation, to set priorities for reconstruction.

Unquestionably, there is strong pressure in earthquake-prone countries to maximize the preservation of life rather than to prevent economic loss. Yet when minimal building standards apply, damage to structures can be significant even though loss of life is low. The practical problem, of course, is how to preserve both life and property.

Recent experience suggests that the exclusive emphasis on life safety deserves reexamination. One of the lessons of the 1989 Loma Prieta earthquake was the seismic fragility of many of modern society's "lifelines"—electrical power, water, sewage, communications, and transportation. The severance of the San Francisco Bay Bridge on October 17, 1989, and a widespread power failure in San Francisco, 70 km from the seismic source, proved this point. The same problem has long concerned authorities in Japan. The soaring real estate values in Tokyo continue to encourage the filling of coastal land tracts, and these have become heavily populated industrial and commercial zones. It is estimated that the liquefaction produced by a magnitude 7.9 earthquake, similar to the great earthquake that devastated Tokyo in 1923, could disrupt lifelines throughout 69 sq km of reclaimed land along the city's major waterways.

Can the promise of an era of minimal risk be delivered during the International Decade of Natural Disaster Reduction? There has been an undoubted improvement in construction codes in recent decades, as engineers have learned about

Water-saturated sandy deposits liquefied in the June 16, 1964, earthquake at Niigata, Japan. Although not damaged in the shaking, the apartment buildings tilted precariously after the foundation soils failed.

the relative effectiveness of various types of structures in strong shaking. New design techniques for limiting shaking have been introduced, such as the partial isolation from the ground of buildings at their foundations. Yet grave doubts have arisen about the promise of the IDNDR because financial support has declined as costs have risen. The most difficult problem is finding the capital, against competing economic demands, for reconstructing vulnerable buildings and lifelines. In addition, earthquake engineers and earth scientists around the world have complained of a reduction in research funds since 1985. One casualty will be seismic risk maps, which differ from the seismic hazard maps referred to earlier in that they consider the types of structure in the area. It is known that the effects of ground shaking vary dramatically from one earthquake or region to another, but seismic risk maps with adequate detail are available for only a few regions in the world. Thus, the full benefit of quantitative mapping will not be obtained until subsurface properties have been measured in all regions at risk, at substantial one-time costs.

Paradoxically, the practical aspects of earthquake risk reduction both contribute to and inhibit the mustering of broad political support for achieving safety goals. Although the benefits of research and application would appear to be obvious, in fact both are subject to deadlines, feasibility questions, and conflicts of interest that dampen enthusiasm and public support. It might be expected that the risk posed to the national welfare by earthquakes would give special force

The response of multistoried elastic structures to shaking is tested by vibrating the table at their bases. The particular wave frequency is causing the high rise to vibrate much more than the shorter models.

to the claims on funds and resources by earth scientists, engineers, planners, and others working to enhance seismic safety, but history tells otherwise. Damaging earthquakes spur bursts of activity and political support for risk reduction, but in a year or so public effort recedes.

It is clear that major earthquakes near metropolitan areas will have serious economic consequences, not only regionally but nationally. Industries and institutions will be unable to operate effectively for a considerable time afterward, reducing the living standards of the whole country. One or more megacities of the world such as Tokyo, Los Angeles, Mexico City, or Manila is likely to experience strong ground shaking in the next ten or twenty years. Despite the difficulties of predicting earthquakes and the technical gaps in engineering, there are no insurmountable reasons that earthquake risks cannot be reduced to acceptable levels during the next decade. One essential element continues to be the application of geological knowledge of the structure and dynamics of the Earth. The more we can discover about the generation of earthquakes, the closer we will come to removing seismic hazards from their present pride of place in the hierarchy of natural disasters.

ABRIDGED MODIFIED MERCALLI INTENSITY SCALE

Note: The mean maximum acceleration and velocity values for the wave motion are for firm ground but vary greatly depending on the type of earthquake source.

Average peak velocity (cm/s)	Intensity value and description	Average peak acceleration (g is gravity = 980 cm/s²)
	I. Not felt except by a very few under especially favorable circumstances. (I Rossi-Forel scale)	
	II. Felt only by a few persons at rest, especially on upper floors of buildings. Delicately suspended objects may swing. (I to II Rossi-Forel scale)	
	III. Felt quite noticeably indoors, especially on upper floors of buildings, but many people do not recognize it as an earthquake. Standing automobiles may rock slightly. Vibration like passing of truck. Duration estimated. (III Rossi-Forel scale)	
1–2	IV. During the day felt indoors by many, outdoors by few. At night some awakened. Dishes, windows, doors disturbed; walls make creaking sound. Sensation like heavy truck striking building. Standing automobiles rocked noticeably. (IV to V Rossi-Forel scale)	0.015g–0.02g
2–5	V. Felt by nearly everyone, many awakened. Some dishes, windows, and so on broken; cracked plaster in a few places; un-	0.03g–0.04g

Average peak velocity (cm/s)	Intensity value and description	Average peak acceleration (g is gravity = 980 cm/s²)
	stable objects overturned. Disturbances of trees, poles, and other tall objects sometimes noticed. Pendulum clocks may stop. (V to VI Rossi-Forel scale)	
5–8	VI. Felt by all, many frightened and run outdoors. Some heavy furniture moved; a few instances of fallen plaster and damaged chimneys. Damage slight. (VI to VII Rossi-Forel scale)	0.06g–0.07g
8–12	VII. Everybody runs outdoors. Damage negligible in buildings of good design and construction; slight to moderate in well-built ordinary structures; considerable in poorly built or badly designed structures; some chimneys broken. Noticed by persons driving cars. (VIII Rossi-Forel scale)	0.10g–0.15g
20–30	VIII. Damage slight in specially designed structures; considerable in ordinary substantial buildings, with partial collapse; great in poorly built structures. Panel walls thrown out of frame structures. Fall of chimneys, factory stacks, columns, monuments, walls. Heavy furniture overturned. Sand and mud ejected in small amounts. Changes in well water. Persons driving cars disturbed. (VIII+ to IX Rossi-Forel scale)	0.25g–0.30g
45–55	IX. Damage considerable in specially designed structures; well-designed frame structures thrown out of plumb; great in substantial buildings, with partial collapse. Buildings shifted off foundations. Ground cracked conspicuously. Underground pipes broken. (IX+ Rossi-Forel scale)	0.50g–0.55g
More than 60	X. Some well-built wooden structures destroyed; most masonry and frame structures destroyed with foundations; ground badly cracked. Rails bent. Landslides considerable from river banks and steep slopes. Shifted sand and mud. Water splashed, slopped over banks. (X Rossi-Forel scale)	More than 0.60g
	XI. Few, if any (masonry) structures remain standing. Bridges destroyed. Broad fissures in ground. Underground pipelines completely out of service. Earth slumps and land slips in soft ground. Rails bent greatly.	
	XII. Damage total. Waves seen on ground surface. Lines of sight and level distorted. Objects thrown into the air.	

FURTHER READINGS

Bolt, Bruce A. 1993. *Earthquakes,* 3d ed. New York: W. H. Freeman.
A concise, easy-to-grasp account of the science of seismology, including the origin, impact, and aftermath of some of history's most devastating earthquakes.

Bolt, Bruce A. 1982. *Inside the Earth.* San Francisco: W. H. Freeman. Reprinted by Tech Books, Fairfax, Virginia, 1992.
An explanation of the way earthquake recordings are used to map the three-dimensional structure of the Earth's interior.

Ferrari, Graziono (ed.). 1992. *Two Hundred Years of Seismic Instruments in Italy 1731–1940.* Bologna: SGA.
A beautifully illustrated book with color photographs and references on early seismographs.

Fowler, C. M. R. 1990. *The Solid Earth: An Introduction to Global Geophysics.* Cambridge, England: Cambridge University Press.

Herbert-Gustav, A. L., and P. Mott. 1980. *John Milne: Father of Modern Seismology.* Tentenden, England: Paul Morburg.
A fascinating account of the contribution of one of the central pioneers in earthquake studies.

Kulhanek, O. 1990. *Anatomy of Seismograms.* Amsterdam: Elsevier.
An attractive and clearly presented manual of characteristic earthquake records and clues to their interpretation.

Litehiser, J. J. (ed.). 1989. *Observatory Seismology.* Berkeley: University of California Press.
The history and development of earthquake observatories described in a collection of papers by well-known seismologists.

Loma Prieta's Call to Action. 1991. Sacramento: California Seismic Safety Commission.

Property Owner's Guide to Earthquake Safety. 1992. Sacramento: California Seismic Safety Commission.

Shultz, Christopher H. 1990. *The Mechanics of Earthquakes and Faulting.* New York: Cambridge University Press.
A thorough, advanced description of the generation of earthquakes by movement along faults.

Walker, G. 1982. *Earthquake.* Alexandria, Virginia: Time-Life Books.
A well-illustrated popular account of earthquakes and seismic hazards around the world.

Wallace, R. E. 1990. *The San Andreas Fault System, California.* U.S. Geological Survey Professional Paper 1515. Washington: U.S. Government Printing Office.

Yanev, P. 1990. *Peace of Mind in Earthquake Country.* San Francisco: Chronicle Books.
An elementary presentation of earthquakes writ-ten from the viewpoint of architects and engineers.

Ziony, J. J. (ed.). 1985. *Evaluating Earthquake Hazards in the Los Angeles Region: An Earth-Science Perspective.* U.S. Geological Survey Professional Paper 1360. Washington: U.S. Government Printing Office.

SOURCES OF ILLUSTRATIONS

All line illustrations are by Fine Line Illustrations, Inc. Illustrations on pages 3, 15, 19, 35, 53, 55, 99, 101, 108, 120, 155, 169, 170, 173, 185, 189, 196, 203, and 213 are by Joe LeMonnier. Illustrations on pages 33, 70, 76, 81, 86, 107, 113, 127, 140, and 147 are by Tasa Graphic Arts, Inc.

Frontispiece: Collection of Bruce Bolt.

CHAPTER 1 *Facing p. 1:* Mechanics Institute, San Francisco. *p. 4:* A. Kircher, Mundus subterraneus, 3d ed. 2 vol, Amsterdam, 1678. *p. 5:* Dept. of Prints and Drawings, Zentralbibliothek, Zurich. *p. 7:* T. C. Lotters geographischem Atlas, Augsburg, nach 1755 (Jan Kozak, Prague). *p. 10:* The Royal Society, London. *p. 12:* State Historical Society of Missouri, Columbia. *p. 16:* (top) The Fine Arts Museums of San Francisco, Achenbach Foundation for Graphic Art. (bottom) San Francisco Archives, Public Library. *p. 21:* The Frank Lloyd Wright Foundation, © 1962.

CHAPTER 2 *p. 24:* James H. Karales/Peter Arnold, Inc. *pp. 28, 29:* J. Pierce and M. Noll, *Signals: The Science of Telecommunications,* New York, W. H. Freeman, 1990. *p. 32:* Fred Padula. *p. 34:* Luana George/Black Star. *p. 35:* USGS. *p. 39:* O. Kulhanek, *Anatomy of Seismograms,* Amsterdam, Elsevier, 1990. *p. 40:* Collection of Bruce Bolt.

CHAPTER 3 *p. 42:* Charles O'Rear/West Light. *p. 44:* James Stanfield, © 1986 National Geographic Society. *p. 45:* Museo dell' Osservatorio Vesuviano/ Storia Geofisica Ambiente Srl. *p. 46:* Mary Lea Shane Archives of the Lick Observatory. *p. 51:* Kinemetrics, Inc. *p. 57:* California Institute of Technology Archives. *p. 59:* A. Feuerbacher. *p. 62:* (left) Collection of Bruce Bolt. *p. 64:* David Graham/ Woodfin Camp & Assoc.

CHAPTER 4 *p. 66:* Armando Cisternas Institut de Physique du Globe de Strasbourg. *p. 69:* Tom Bean. *p. 72:* (top) T. J. Chinn, Geological and Nuclear Sciences, N.Z. (bottom) New Zealand Seismological Observatory. *p. 74:* James Stanfield, © 1986 National Geographic Society. *p. 76:* G. K. Gilbert, USGS. *p. 78:* NASA/JPL. *p. 79:* John Livzey/DOT. *p. 80:* From R. S. Stein, G. C. P. King, and J. Lin, *Science* 258(1992): 1328–1331. *p. 82:* Paul Link. *p. 86:* C. Frohlich, Deep earthquakes, *Scientific American,* January 1989. *p. 90:* Los Alamos National Laboratory. *p. 92:* H. J. Pahon and W. R. Waller, Regional moment-magnitude relations for earthquakes and explosions, *Geophys. Res. Letters,* 1992.

CHAPTER 5 *p. 94:* James Balog/Black Star. *p. 97:* T. H. Jordon, The deep structure of the continents, *Scientific American,* January 1979. *p. 98:* Zvjezdarnica

Hrvatskoga Prirodoslovnog Drusta, Zagreb. *p. 105:* Anthony Lomax. *p. 106:* Collection of Bruce Bolt. *p. 109:* USGS. *p. 110:* Painting by Heinrich Berann, Bruce Hee Heezen and Marie Tharp, World Ocean Floor, 1977, © Marie Tharp. *p. 111:* Geologic Survey of Israel. *p. 113:* British Museum. *p. 114:* Gudmundur Sigvaldson/Norduc Volcanological Institute. *p. 116:* Peter Yanev/EQE International. *p. 121:* USGS. *p. 123:* Lloyd Cluff.

CHAPTER 6 *p. 124:* J. P. Montagner and G. Roult, Laboratorie de Sismologie, Paris. *p. 132:* B. Bolt, The deep structure of the Earth's interior, *Scientific American,* March 1979. *p. 135:* National Portrait Gallery, London. *p. 137:* Royal Danish Geodetic Institute, Copenhagen. *pp. 140 (left), 141, 142:* B. Bolt, The deep structure of the Earth's interior, *Scientific American,* March 1979. *p. 150:* Toshiro Tanimoto.

CHAPTER 7 *p. 152:* Herman KoKojan/Black Star. *p. 160.* Kinemetrics, Inc. *p. 165:* National Park Service. *p. 167:* James Sugar/Black Star. *p. 172:* Charles O'Rear/West Light.

CHAPTER 8 *p. 180:* James Balog/Black Star. *pp. 186, 187:* Yang Zhe. *pp. 192, 193:* G. C. Jacoby and P. Sheppard, Lamont-Doherty Geological Observatory. *p. 194:* USGS. *p. 195:* Bruce Bolt. *p. 197:* Gary Carver. *p. 198:* Atwater/USGS, Seattle. *p. 200:* Gary Carver. *p. 203:* USGS.

CHAPTER 9 *p. 206:* Picturepoint, London. *p. 209:* Reuters/Bettmann. *p. 211:* Peter Turnley/Black Star. *p. 212:* Bancroft Library, Berkeley. © Regents, University of California. *p. 214:* (top right and bottom) VBN Architects, Executive Architects; Michael Willis & Assoc., Associate Architects; Carey & Co. Architecture, Preservation Architects; Forell/ Elsesser Engineers, Structural Engineers; model photography by Douglas Symes. *p. 214:* (top left) Oakland Public Library. *p. 216:* H. Bolton Seed. *p. 217:* James Sugar/Black Star.

INDEX

OTHER BOOKS IN THE SCIENTIFIC AMERICAN LIBRARY SERIES

POWERS OF TEN
by Philip and Phylis Morrison and the Office of Charles
and Ray Eames

HUMAN DIVERSITY
by Richard Lewontin

THE DISCOVERY OF SUBATOMIC PARTICLES
by Steven Weinberg

FOSSILS AND THE HISTORY OF LIFE
by George Gaylord Simpson

ON SIZE AND LIFE
by Thomas A. McMahon and John Tyler Bonner

FIRE
by John W. Lyons

SUN AND EARTH
by Herbert Friedman

ISLANDS
by H. William Menard

DRUGS AND THE BRAIN
by Solomon H. Snyder

THE TIMING OF BIOLOGICAL CLOCKS
by Arthur T. Winfree

EXTINCTION
by Steven M. Stanley

EYE, BRAIN, AND VISION
by David H. Hubel

THE SCIENCE OF STRUCTURES AND MATERIALS
by J. E. Gordon

SAND
by Raymond Siever

THE HONEY BEE
by James L. Gould and Carol Grant Gould

ANIMAL NAVIGATION
by Talbot H. Waterman

SLEEP
by J. Allan Hobson

FROM QUARKS TO THE COSMOS
by Leon M. Lederman and David N. Schramm

SEXUAL SELECTION
by James L. Gould and Carl Grant Gould

THE NEW ARCHAEOLOGY AND
THE ANCIENT MAYA
by Jeremy A. Sabloff

A JOURNEY INTO GRAVITY AND SPACETIME
by John Archibald Wheeler

SIGNALS
by John R. Pierce and A. Michael Noll

BEYOND THE THIRD DIMENSION
by Thomas F. Banchoff

DISCOVERING ENZYMES
by David Dressler and Huntington Potter

THE SCIENCE OF WORDS
by George A. Miller

ATOMS, ELECTRONS, AND CHANGE
by P. W. Atkins

VIRUSES
by Arnold J. Levine

DIVERSITY AND THE TROPICAL RAIN FOREST
by John Terborgh

STARS
by James B. Kaler

EXPLORING BIOMECHANICS
by R. McNeill Alexander

CHEMICAL COMMUNICATION
by William C. Agosta

GENES AND THE BIOLOGY OF CANCER
by Harold Varmus and Robert A. Weinberg

SUPERCOMPUTING AND THE
TRANSFORMATION OF SCIENCE
by William J. Kaufmann III and Larry L. Smarr

MOLECULES AND MENTAL ILLNESS
by Samuel H. Barondes

EXPLORING PLANETARY WORLDS
by David Morrison